Meetings with Poets

OTHER WORKS BY JACK LINDSAY

Historical

SONG OF A FALLING WORLD
BYZANTIUM INTO EUROPE
CIVIL WAR IN ENGLAND
THE ROMANS WERE HERE
ARTHUR AND HIS TIMES
1764
THE WRITING ON THE WALL
DAILY LIFE IN ROMAN EGYPT
LEISURE AND PLEASURE IN
ROMAN EGYPT

Biographical

MARC ANTONY
JOHN BUNYAN
CHARLES DICKENS
GEORGE MEREDITH

Autobiography

LIFE RARELY TELLS
THE ROARING TWENTIES
FANFROLICO AND AFTER

General

ANATOMY OF SPIRIT
A SHORT HISTORY OF CULTURE
HANDBOOK OF FREEDOM

HISTORICAL NOVELS

Ancient World

WANDERINGS OF WENAMEN
COME HOME AT LAST
(Short stories)
HANNIBAL TAKES A HAND
ROME FOR SALE
CAESAR IS DEAD
LAST DAYS WITH CLEOPATRA
STORM AT SEA
(Golden Cockerel Press)
DESPOILING VENUS
BRIEF LIGHT
THE BARRIERS ARE DOWN
THUNDER UNDERGROUND

English History

THE GREAT OAK
FIRE IN SMITHFIELD
THE STORMY BARRIER
SUE VERNEY
1649
LOST BIRTHRIGHT
THE PASSIONATE PASTORIAL
LIGHT IN ITALY
MEN OF FORTY-EIGHT
ADAM OF A NEW WORLD
(Italy)

CONTEMPORARY NOVELS OF THE BRITISH WAY

END OF CORNWALL
WE SHALL RETURN
BEYOND TERROR
HULLO STRANGER
TIME TO LIVE
ALL ON THE NEVER-NEVER
CHOICE OF TIMES

BETRAYED SPRING
RISING TIDE
THE MOMENT OF CHOICE
LOCAL HABITATION
REVOLT OF THE SONS
THE WAY THE BALL BOUNCES
MASKS AND FACES

Translations of Theocritus, Aristophanes, Catullus, Longus, Apuleius,
Medieval Latin Poets, etc.

JACK LINDSAY

Meetings with Poets

Memories of: Dylan Thomas
Edith Sitwell
Louis Aragon
Paul Eluard
Tristan Tzara

FREDERICK UNGAR PUBLISHING CO.
NEW YORK

First American edition 1969

Copyright © 1968 by Jack Lindsay

Library of Congress Catalog Card Number 73-81572

Standard Book Number 8044-2526-4

Printed in Great Britain

Contents

	page
Author's Note	vii
Dylan Thomas	3
Last Words with Dylan	45
Edith Sitwell	51
Edith Sitwell in London	160
Aragon, Eluard, Tzara	167
The Starfish Road	227
Last Words	233
Index	239

27715

Author's Note

THIS book began as a number of poems addressed to poets whom I had known. Then, after getting several queries from the USA about Dylan Thomas, I decided to write a comprehensive account of my memories of him rather than a set of scattered answers to various questions. I wrote the essay on Dylan in late 1964, and then felt that I should add a companion-piece on Edith Sitwell. However, I did nothing till her death. Then the bad conscience I describe in my essay about *The Starfish Road* was acutely revived, and I knew I could not delay in making a fresh effort to express what I felt of her and her work. In writing about her I found my memories of Eluard and Tzara sharpened, for reasons that will be clear from my account of *The Starfish Road*. And once I began on these poets I found I could not exclude Aragon and the whole question of Resistance poetry. Thus the book took the form in which it is here presented.

Each of the three sections has its own method, determined by my relations to the poet concerned. Thus, while I felt closely drawn to Dylan, I cannot claim to have affected his poetry in any way. Hence the essay on him is more descriptively detached, despite the many points of strong emotional implication. With Edith Sitwell the situation was quite different. I was long involved with her in discussions on poetry, and can claim, on the strength of her own statements, to have had a considerable effect on her mind in the years in question. So, while I attempt a portrait of her in the round as with Dylan, I have also to add a fairly detailed account of our intellectual exchanges. I am therefore myself much more in the picture than in the Dylan essay. When I come to the three French poets, I am dealing with persons with whom I was never in such a close relationship as with Dylan and Edith, and the picture is consequently more objective in style.

Yet I think the book is a unity, since each part needs the others if it is to be fully understood in all its implications. I have tried, perhaps too briefly and sharply, to bring out some of those implications in "Last Words." But the book was already of fair length, and I felt, that while some such finale was needed, it need not do more than provide a few signposts as to the general conclusions which I felt emerged from the lives and works of these poets.

The approach is essentially personal and biographical, but critical questions naturally assert themselves; and in the end I hope that something of a poetic worldview, shared in different ways by my poets, begins to come through.

The Dylan essay has appeared in *Meanjin* (Melbourne, Australia) Autumn 1966 in its first version. There are only a few changes in the version given here; for instance I have added some comments on Dylan's childhood after reading Constantine Fitzgibbon's biography. All the translations in the third section are by myself.

JACK LINDSAY

Dylan Thomas

I FIRST MET Dylan in 1943. I was passing through London on leave and went to see my brother Philip, who took me along to a pub in Kings Road, Chelsea, where he was meeting Dylan. If Dylan liked you, it didn't take long to get inside his world, or at least certain sections of it, and you left him with the conviction that you had known him for years, had always known him. The word poet was not mentioned; what the evening brought out was mainly the delightful way in which Dylan and Phil companioned one another in quip, argument, anecdote, and other ways of expressing an unquenchable delight in life. Then, as always, their conversation together constituted an easy flow of shrewd laughter, with an effect of steady crescendo which was without strain, a spontaneous and chuckling tribute to everything that lived. I departed next morning with the feeling that I must reread Dylan's poems, that there was something in him much bigger than I had expected, and that under the intense but narrow world of the poems was a broad base, a power of enjoyment which could encompass anything human.

Later in the summer I was given a fortnight's compassionate leave as someone, whose name I will not mention, had written in to the colonel that Philip was suffering from DTs and needed my presence. When the officer in charge called me out of bed to say I was to go off first thing in the morning, I told him that I didn't believe the story. But he replied that the leave had been granted and I was to take it. I won't go into this story further here, except to mention that Philip had nothing to do with the application. However, the leave meant that I spent a fortnight with Philip and Dylan in Chelsea. Later that year, by a set of odd chances, I was transferred to the Education Department of the War Office, under the ABCA division, as a script-writer for the Army Theatre that was being set up. The Army Council in its section dealing with Establishments had agreed that groups of soldiers and ATS should be collected as actors by Michael MacOwan (then Captain, soon afterwards Major), but had refused to allow the inclusion of a script-writer—though the whole point of the scheme was that the groups should perform a new sort of play, topical and instructive. This typical bit of army crassness was overcome by taking me on as an actor, while in fact I sat in the War Office and did what was at least a captain's work. On paper I was still a mere signalman, but I had a most interesting job, at which I remained for the rest of the war. Most of the time I was in London, at the offices in Eaton Square, with lodgings in Pimlico. I was thus close to Dylan in Chelsea (Phil had married and lived at Earls Court), and we spent much time together till Dylan decided to evacuate himself and family from a London under the attack of flying-bombs. In the postwar years I saw less of him, especially after I retired to a Kentish forest in 1949. Still we met now and then even in those last three years and continued to be good friends.

I thus came to know Dylan fairly well, at a time before the curse of booze had come down upon him. I was never, however, so close a friend of his as Phil was. There was a strong bond between those two. In the years before the war Phil had lived with Dylan, in the same room, and for long they worked together in documentary films, Dylan's main source of funds and patronage before he turned to the BBC and then to the tours in the USA. Despite some sharp differences in character, there was much akin in Dylan and Phil, in their way of life and in their values. Both had the capacity for something like a total surrender to life, to what was felt to be its fundamental impulses and needs; both at the same time had certain unbreakable powers of resistance, a determination to be true to their essential positions at whatever cost to themselves and everyone else. They reserved the right to make a clear and downright judgement of persons and things after having renounced all right or desire to judge. Both were imperturbably amiable and yet capable of violent repudiations and plain rudeness, once they felt their scheme of values to be

4

threatened. But though Dylan had his own kind of honesty, which I shall try later to define, Phil was by far simpler and more direct in his reactions, his refusal to make the least compromise. Both had profoundly anarchist attitudes, but after 1939 Phil's views tended to be exasperatingly rigid, even childishly so. Dylan's ironic sense went much deeper, taking in his own views of himself and his ideas, so that his anarchism was far suppler and more devious, capable of rounding on itself and even turning into its opposite. This means that despite the emotional similarities with Phil's careless and tangential way of crashing through whatever scene entangled him—an unconcern which however included a fine casual courtesy and a capacity to reassert sympathy in the most unlikely ways—Dylan's views had underneath a strong intellectual system which it was easy to miss and which only a prolonged knowledge of both the man and his poetry made one able to recognise. Dylan felt in Phil his own lighter-weight brother, himself freed from the burden of poetry and encountering life with a genuine freshness at each new pub-counter, as if nothing had been learnt till that moment and as if everything was now being learnt in a burst of comprehensive joy and irresponsible love. It would be too simple to say that Phil expressed in fact the spiritual state that Dylan coveted and slyly enacted, but there is something in the comment. Dylan was an intellectual who aspired to shed every atom of the intellectual's pride in isolation, in superior knowledge, in abstraction of idea. For him the idea was life, the idea was poetry; any other moment of its existence was anathema. Phil was able to incarnate this attitude without self-consciousness. That was what endeared him to Dylan, in whom however it was highly self-conscious. For Dylan the detached idea, which could be developed in an intellectual argument and which could consequently be set against life, making demands upon him and insisting that action be taken on its behalf, was something that had to be fought and evicted. Not that the fighting was done by any prolonged inner argument. The conflict was emotional, however many intellectual factors it brought into play; the evictors were a set of fears and anxieties that had been built up in Dylan's adolescent years as he first struggled to achieve poetry.

I feel sure that I am correct in saying that in all their long friendship no strain or conflict of any kind ever showed itself between Phil and Dylan. In each of them the anti-intellectual anarchism went too deep for the compact to wear thin and reveal elements of chafed falsity, irritated boredom: the sort of thing which seems a recoil from someone else, but is in fact a recoil from one's own unresolved conflicts uncomfortably bared in the other's inadequate or overpitched behaviour. *Par nobile fratrum.* In all this I recognise a greater closeness of Phil to Dylan than to myself. Dylan once told me, "I love Phil as I love no one else, but I can't read his books." The pure spontaneous element in Phil which created his charm had a marring effect on his work. Phil himself admired Dylan's poems whole-heartedly and had long considered him a great poet; he saw in them his own impulses and attitudes given definitive form.

During my Chelsea leave I came up against the deep inner conflict in Dylan, that found its outer expression in his relations with Caitlin. One morning I drifted into their rambling apartment. Dylan lay sore-headed abed, making a few gruff remarks as he smoked. Caitlin said that late at night, after we others had gone, he had torn up his poems in disgust and thrown them into the rubbish-tin.

"You rescued them," I said. "That's the job of the poet's wife. To rescue his poems from the rubbish-tin when life gets too much for him."

She shrugged, and her handsome face with its faint golden glow sharpened in a shrewish way. "No, you're quite wrong. It's the last thing I'd do. Dylan's corrupt. Corrupt right through and through. It's not for me to save him from himself. If he can't do it himself, let him rot."

I was startled, shocked. My too-simple picture of Dylan as the pure lyric poet crumpled up, and I realised that I knew nothing of him or of his poetry. My only course was to start from the beginning all over again and look at the real poet, not my fantasy of him. I was also hurt on Dylan's behalf, wanted to say something that would ease the situation for him without annoying Caitlin, who had spoken with a quiet but deadly intensity. I couldn't think of anything to say, and stole a side-glance at

Dylan. He went on smoking grumpily as if he hadn't heard his wife's words or as if they were not worth comment. Finally, he spat, coughed, and asked about Phil.

I gathered that he had had to undergo the shame of rescuing the torn manuscript himself, under Caitlin's scornful eyes. She had known he wouldn't sacrifice the poem, and he had to admit that she was right and that the tearing had been only a romantic gesture, an act of self-demolition that he couldn't sustain. I am not sure, but think that the torn poem was the *Ballad of the Long-Legged Bait*. He was working at that poem at the time and had almost completed it, though he was still worried about a few small points. Some nights later, when he had retired to bed with a wambly stomach, he read it out to Phil and myself as well as several others of his poems. This was the first time I heard him read poetry, and I was deeply impressed. A mixture of sonority and deep though controlled feeling gave a fresh dimension to the words and revived my feeling of him as a poet whose work had a peculiar organic unity and implicated the whole universe in each statement, each image. But now I felt that he was also acting the part of the complete poet and that sometimes he didn't know the reality from the role. Against my will Caitlin by the force of contempt and suffering in her voice had convinced me that he was charlatan as well as marvellous boy, unscrupulous entrepreneur as well as dedicated poet. My confusion and my divided mind about his work were increased by the fact that though I was carried away by the *Ballad* in his splendid rendering I was repelled by the sadistic image of the girl bloodily hooked. I knew how it could be symbolically explained away, but under all the meanings I felt the plain fact of a ferocious conflict between him and Caitlin. And I felt that in this relationship of love and hate, which I was only beginning hazily to apprehend, she was as interesting as he was. (*Into her Lying-down Head* was written not long after, I think, though I did not hear him read it for some months.)

A few days after Caitlin's outburst I had a chance to talk to her alone for two or three hours in one of the Chelsea pubs while Dylan and Phil were busy on some film-script. I tried to find out just what she had meant by calling Dylan corrupt. But she was one of the most difficult persons I have ever tried to pin down to a definite meaning. She was voluble, despite painful silences, but desperately unable to find in the dictionary of common associations the words that would express her precise point—and nothing less than those words would suffice. Any falling-back on cliché and conventional terms would dishonour both herself and Dylan. For it was at once clear that in condemning Dylan she was simultaneously cutting herself off from him and uniting with him in a fiercely protecting love. Both the separation and the union made her feel intensely proud. In one sense, she felt herself so much a part of Dylan that in denouncing him she was also proving his integrity, proving that he was aware of the worst that could be said of him, and getting in first with the admission so as to deny the world the right to repeat her words. Both the union and the separation made her suffer; and when she suffered it was with every fibre of her being. She knew well enough what she meant. She was able to express herself strongly, as in the attack on Dylan I have quoted, and her unusual angles of approach gave her words a remarkable directness and originality. But the words themselves could not be considered apart from the totality of the situation. What she said was complicated, wavering, full of obvious contradictions, edged with laconic subtleties. Written flatly down, it would have seemed erratic and uncertain; but taken in its total set of dovetailing and intricate implications, it had its own logical coherence. A coherence that was further composed of the varying inflections, the deep silences into which she gazed, the changes of the pupils of her eyes and the muscular tensions about her lips, the particular tilt or tensity of her body on the bar-stool.

A conversation of that sort can be infinitely exciting and satisfying at each moment of its rich modulations, but the moments tend to cancel one another out when at the end one asks: What exactly was said, decided, summed up? All the same, I think I gained a clear and indelible comprehension of the peculiar tension between her and Dylan, its destroying and its creative quality. What I could not grasp or bring our of her was what she considered the alternative, the non-corrupt way, which she wanted Dylan to follow. She was as far as Dylan himself from any wish to see his poetry linked with a guiding idea, a cause of

8

any kind. I was hoping that she would show some signs of this sort of wish, and did my best to push her in its direction. But she shied off any such interpretation. I wanted to say that while I agreed about the essential concreteness of poetry, that concreteness developed most fully and valuably in its conflict with ideas, in the acceptance of the human universal as a cause that must be striven for—which involved the organic being of the poet with an historical situation. And so on. I wanted to say that the purity she wanted would become a negation—stirring her bitter rejection—unless it accepted the sort of struggle I had in mind. But I was not sure enough that I understood her, and above all I wanted to see into her mind, see what lay at the bottom of those pools of silence into which she stared. I feared to muddy the waters by intelligent and irrelevant comment. I felt a very strong sympathy for her, a sort of love, but not a love that could be abstracted from the warmth I felt for the pair of them, Caitlin and Dylan in the bed of his poetry, tormented with all the fleas of a rivalry and a jealousy I had begun to understand. Waspish as she could be, I somehow always saw her as a distracted small girl who smacked the world in the eye to save herself from bursting into tears.

My rindy fruit of bitterness, already installed since childhood, though I can trace no evidence of suppression—it might have been more salutary had I been suppressed earlier and more thoroughly—swells to top-heavy proportions; dwarfs the happy landscape, colours with venom the smiling peasant. It even darkens the sun, pressing a ferocious torpor down behind my eyepit sinews. My bitterness is not an abstract substance, it is as solid as a Christmas cake; I can cut it in slices and hand it round and there is still plenty left, for to-morrow.

In such passages from *Leftover Life to Kill* she catches an essential characteristic of herself, with the deliberately embarrassing note which was inseparable from her self-assertions. The whole book is a remarkably sustained piece of self-exposure, in which the lacerating comprehension of her thorny self is merged with a total inability to do anything about it all. Here self-knowledge is immediately inverted into a bitter resentment; it

9

appears as an act of revenge which is impotent except to rub salt in wounds. Anger has so long been convinced of its ineffectiveness that Caitlin can only conceive the revelation of pain as a wild accusation aimed at Dylan, her parents, the world, nobody, herself; a circular rage returning to the dead centre, exultant in its proof of a pointless crucifixion, a deaf universe. Love and hate have lost their Catullan contradictions; they merge in a numbed distraction where nobody and everybody is the enemy, and the lover has dwindled to a nagging ghost of self-torment.

Another ten years were needed to bring Caitlin to this state, which was however the logical conclusion of the attitudes to which she had irrevocably assigned herself. Not that the attitudes can be understood apart from Dylan, from the demands he made on her and the role he allotted her. A hopeless contradiction ruled at the heart of the relationship between them. She wanted the pure poet who transformed the impulses of his life into crystalline form; he wanted the pure mistress who reflected in her caprice the unpredictable movements of his poetry. But the poet's impulse, in her conception, needed to be the harmonious reflection of her caprice; and the mistress's caprice, in his conception, needed to be the delighted reflection of his liberated senses. In fact such an ideal could only work out in a series of deepening discords. Caprice and impulse collided in all sorts of ways, and what should have been their harmony appeared as a ceaseless conflict of egoist demands. The mistress wanted the lark of the song caged in her hand or at least nested in, and soaring over, her private piece of wild nature; the poet wanted a self-effacing wife who didn't need to be dragooned into wearing the correct dress for a Carmarthen marketday. Dylan wandered off on his loose tangents of seduction and booze; Caitlin accumulated bile in her corner of frustration, a witch whose spells evaporated in an atmosphere of frying chips and boiling napkins. The sacrifice of her ambitions as dancer and poet was not considered important enough to deserve even a patronising pat of thanks.

I did not at first realise that Dylan's love of life had to struggle every moment of the day and night in order to keep ahead or even abreast of his pursuing fear of death. There lay the cardinal weakness of his character and his poetry, a weakness which however provided in turn the dynamic force of his virtues, his consuming need to find the image that would be large enough, and crafty enough, to bar the way of the pursuing fear. His fear expressed itself in the compulsive need to touch a woman; and because one touch led to another, led the way through the labyrinth of the senses to the centrique part, his need was to pierce through all defences into the helpless womb, the continuous present of salvation, the eternal moment outside time. Later, drink became a compulsive need, but that was a derivation from the primary compulsion to achieve an absolute contact without the need of communication. His power of seduction lay in his power to present himself as requiring solace and sustenance as simply and unquestioningly as a newborn baby placed for the first time at the mother's breasts. But he needed booze in order to set free this hypnotic quality in his eyes and hands. And if the appeal didn't work with full effect, it didn't work at all. I have known women who found Dylan at any stage of his booze-release as something quite disgusting and repulsive.

The day before Dylan read us the *Ballad* he had been commenting on a tall girl with whom he had had a few drinks. A tall lank girl with a bell of strawgold drowned hair and cold lost grey-green eyes, the mistress of a film-producer, who lived in Chelsea. As we left her, Dylan murmured to me, "Did you see that she had leg-irons? Last week when I lay between her legs, I got a shock as the iron scraped against me. I'd forgotten it." When he read the *Ballad,* I myself suddenly felt the shock of iron chafing against the flesh at its moment of supreme surrender. The tall lean girl plunging on the bed and pinned down brutally, slithering outside time and mortally hooked, unable to escape. I saw the long slow curve of her unresisting body as she sat with a cigarette in her slender fingers opposite Dylan; and Dylan, plump and taut inside his plumpness as a gamesome dolphin, sporting on the edge of her distrait vision. And then, in a succession of confused images, all the many girls into whom Dylan fled and from whom he fled, afraid of claims and responsibilities, and Caitlin at the heart of the swirl of transformations, the wife from whom he fled into the masquerade, and to whom he fled back in order to escape claims and responsibilities. Caitlin, aware of all this shapeshifting, its

Circean mistress and yet its dupe, forcing Dylan into it and yet angrily demanding a totally different way of life. Dylan, unable to keep his fingers from the palm, the breast, the inner thigh, but struggling all the while to delay the moment of triumph, which was also the moment of absorption by the woman, the moment of his disarming. The moment of impotence that follows the arrogant orgasm; the mockery of death that echoes the cock-crowing exuberant life. Dylan, resentful because Caitlin couldn't beat him into fidelity as a release from the widening circle of seductions which kept on worsening the fear of death by setting his small mortal mechanism of responses against an infinity of hungry challenging wombs. Each infidelity, by proving the fallibility of women, made more plausible the fear that Caitlin too had found her lover, was finding him, was at that very moment by the necessary irony of things plunging and pierced in the bed of the faceless enemy; was betraying Dylan to the loss and the void which was death. Dylan had no consolation that didn't double-cross him and intensify the fear it was meant to dissipate.

Yet Dylan need not have feared at least the falling-away of Caitlin; for if his ideal was the sure home-centre that gave him freedom for all peripheral backslidings, hers was the sure home-centre that salved the wounds of man and wife by merging them, by enforcing an identity of crucifixions and thus achieving a simultaneous resurrection in which he and she were lost in a common joy and fear. They thus both needed the sure home-centre for opposite reasons. In her bitter strivings with Dylan, Caitlin must often have been tempted to sheath her forbidding rancours, assume her face of lyrical charm, and whistle up a string of lovers. But her stubborn hopeless integrity, her once-for-all-times-taken stand, prevented her from such an obvious retaliation. She continued to fight things out on her doomed ground, jealously cherishing that ground all the more for its untenability. Both he and she had the strength and the weakness of conducting a fated conflict, to the tragic and ridiculous terms of which they had to cling as the sole pledge of personal value.

Always Caitlin fascinated me by her precarious perch, from which nothing could dislodge her. I happen to have kept, out of many scribbled notes and sketches for poems, a few lines that I wrote down the evening when Dylan was reading the *Ballad*. I cite them here as at least showing how my attention was concentrated on her, seeking to read the critical light in her eyes. She was one of those persons who own a naked face, a face that lacks some of the normal layers of disguise, reserve, falsity. For this reason it was often hard to interpret as it shone in its sharp separateness, its pallor of tense surfaces, its locked conflicts. We are more used to faces in which we seek to catch the reluctant momentary exposure. What my lines sought to express was Caitlin's element of glittering separateness, which, coupled with the need to achieve a total judgement of the scene, involved also a cold but passionate impact on us others—though what interested her was not the others but Dylan alone, in whom everything was summed up. On the other hand, Dylan, whose companionable warmth included us all in every intonation of his voice, every movement of his jovial body, seemed perfectly unaware of her presence and its questioning silence, its flawless resistance to everything he did or said.

> The bush of light I saw
> in a hush of warm awe
> had strawgold plaited in it,
> limelight of the mad minute,
> o flaxen flash, o doll
> birdkeen watching us all
>
> because the flash was stillness
> small but still with fullness
> preening the clear face
> awareness poised as grace
> wildbird what made you linger
> on my stiff pedantic finger

I wanted to define something of her strange immediacy as a radiant presence and an effaced ghost.

If Dylan's inner conflict could be defined at one level as an effort to oppose and reconcile the sure home-centre (poetry as union) with the peripheral submissions to impulse (poetry as freedom), the insuperable contradictions of his position appeared in his relation with the money-world. Life (poetry and copulation)

13

was felt to exist in a world where money had not yet been born—just as love is too young to know what conscience is. If life were reduced to its primary elements, to the moment of birth as the rhythmic moment of in-and-out, advance-and-retreat, light-and-darkness, then it was purely a matter that concerned only the poet and his immediate otherself (the mother, the organic universe, the lover). No one else could intrude; no responsibility existed except the need to realise the moment in its fullness, to inhabit the continuous present. Here was given the pure pattern of experience, and anything that attempted to distort or confuse it was the enemy, was the arresting abstraction which upset the eternal rhythm of immediate apprehension and gave power to the one-sided approach of death. Money was therefore the great enemy, the supreme abstraction, the pure enbodiment of death.

Hence the unnerving terror that overcame Dylan whenever he moved from the birth-moment as the primal moment of union-separation, and confronted the world of adult responsibilities. Money was the castrating sword that flashed in his eyes and drove him back into the garden of Eden. A garden of Eden cursed with the omnipresent sense of sin; childhood become precious because it was not adult life, and realised as the eternal moment because of the dire and unceasing pressure of abstraction in the adult consciousness. The garden became a prison, yet had to be realised as freedom. Only poetry could so realise it, and therefore poetry was racked by a diabolic paradox. The sense of sin, of death's dominion, had to be intensified by an infinite titillation so that the poet might be driven with all possible passion and anguish back into the garden, into the pure moment of contact with otherness, obliterating the very passion and anguish which he needed for the return-journey.

Money therefore became the crucial thing, indistinguishable in the last resort from the intellectual abstraction that alienated men from the real world, the flowing and irreversible world, the world that remained entire and seamless despite its judicial and murderous rending at every moment of the busy day. To settle to any means of earning money was thoroughly repugnant to Dylan, and became more so, all the while. His fear of death and

impotence was reflected in a fear of being unable to earn the sub-
sistence of himself and his family; and this fear went far too deep
for any rational control or resolution. If you are sufficiently
afraid of poverty and starvation, you do not hoard and count
every penny; you throw it away as soon as you get it. You do the
very thing you are most afraid of, in order to find out if the fear is
real and if it is owns the complex consequences that you have
attributed to it. The more money Dylan earned, the less he was
capable of mastering it. Who wants to keep a murderer in the
household?

There was more satisfaction in being kept than in earning one's
keep, in stealing a thing than in buying it. For money that came
from a theft or from patronage was not the abstract money of the
exchange-market; it had become personalised by its passage
through the hands of someone who was not striking a bargain
with the poet, it had lost its exchange-value, its equation of men
with things. Dylan was far too shrewd and sensible to become a
thief in any ordinary sense, though his attitudes, if the sense of
poetic vocation had been lacking, could easily have led into any
delinquency. What he did enjoy was the taking of things like
shirts from his patrons. He early put such mild pilferings into
practice, carrying off shirts or pyjamas from the directors who
helped him to find his footing in documentary films; and he was
still liable to purloin such articles in the days of his American
tours, when he was incomparably better-off. He would never
have dreamed of stealing a pin from one of his friends; it was the
theft from a patron that he enjoyed and considered a just act. He
needed patrons and used all his great charm to collect them, but at
the same time he despised and resented them. Through his thefts,
which were prudently of the kind that could be explained away as
absent-minded borrowings, he got rid of his sense of inferiority
by a demonstration that he looked on a patron as a mere instru-
ment for his own convenience. Oddly, no one ever seemed to
resent such actions.

What then had Caitlin meant when she said that Dylan was
corrupt through and through? I still find it hard to say in a few
words what I decided that she meant. The fierce independence of
her spirit was in many ways the direct opposite of Dylan's

assertion of superiority, or at least of the poet's right to use subservience as a way of cheating the cheaters, of removing the snake-sting from money by treating it as something utterly unimportant, something so evil by its very nature that any trick with it was excusable. I cannot imagine her in the slightest of underhand manoeuvres. Her pride lay in extenuating nothing about herself—or about Dylan. It had a simple nobility about it, a puzzled and pained nobility, which was very different from the poet's extrication of his dignity by assuming that he has none, by acting the part of a buffoon so as to hide the deepmost buffoonery of all, the inability to believe that any action at all possesses value except in so far as it leads back into the formation of an image which seems dynamically self-sufficient.

I take Caitlin to have been referring to the whole body of Dylan's compulsions, his sly submissions to booze, sex, and money in the name of a poetry which excluded her. Excluded her at that level, anyway. I do not mean that she was standing apart and judging some peccadillo, but that she was standing in his centre and judging the peccadilloes as the expression of a total personality. And yet, in saying all that, one is saying no more than half the situation. She considered Dylan to be corrupt, but she loved him; she had married him as the pure poet and she continued to find that poet in the stye of corruption, miraculously reborn out of the muddy deaths. She criticised him in terms of her own callow and splendid certainties, but she criticised him also in the terms laid down by his poetry. The conflict was in the poetry as well as in her, though more hidden and doggedly slow in its working-out. Dylan was not only corrupt, or his poetry would have been of little value; the ultimate values lay in Caitlin's love for Dylan (and his for her) and in his poetry. And this was what held them together despite all the long chafings and the sudden flares; what gave the poetry its validity and its obdurately fought-out quality. In the last resort the love and the poetry alone mattered, a poetry into which he refused to admit a word, a single chime of sound, until he had tested and retested it for its truth, its human and poetic truth, to the utmost of his ability and the scope of his vision. But, in his devious system, the cost of that uncompromising truth was a perpetually compromising evasion in everyday life, the cost of the love was a perpetual flight from its steadfast presence.

> He was never his proper self till there was something wrong with him; and if ever there was a danger of him becoming "whole," which was very remote, he would crack another of his chicken bones, without delay, and wander happily round in his sling, piling up plates with cucumber, pickled onions, tins of cod's roe, boiled sweets; to push into his mouth with an unseeing hand, as they came, while he went on stolidly reading his trash. His passion for lies was congenital: more a practice in invention than a lie. He would tell quite unnecessary ones, which did not in any way improve his situation: such as, when he had been to one cinema, saying it was another, and making up the film that was on: and the obvious ones, that only his mother pretended not to see through, like being carted off the bus into his home, and saying he had been having coffee, in a café, with a friend.

So Caitlin records, with domestic verisimilitude. Much of their marriage was a duel of jealousies. If Dylan was tormented by the thought

> The second comers, the severers, the enemies from the deep
> Forgotten dark, rest their pulse and bury their dead in her
>   faithless sleep,

she was tormented by her jealousy of his masculine freedoms (in booze and love-making, in desertion of the home) and of his poetic achievement. Carelessly and ruthlessly he brushed aside her own aspirations to self-expression in verse or dance. She could have accepted all that if she had seen it as part of the expression of a non-corrupt poet; but as things were, she could not accept it. She could carry on only if she resisted and denounced every symptom of corruption; and those symptoms she found in any manifestation of praise or patronage of Dylan, any response on his part to the flattering world. So, if Dylan's way of meeting patronage was by sly unscrupulous exploitation of it, with caustic debunking asides to his friends, her way was by frank and violent repudiation. Hence the deliberately uncouth and unconciliating behaviour at any parties or gatherings where she considered that Dylan was being lionised. Unless she smashed up some of the

17

furniture and heavily embarrassed Dylan, she felt that she had been defeated and made an accomplice of the corrupting thing. Any attempts to draw her in and placate her, she took as an insult. She noted her "chronic fear of friendship," and the fact that, "like all prodigiously vain people, packed with false pride, I wanted to be loved for myself alone." After Dylan's rise to fame, she found it impossible to believe that she was being loved or courted for herself alone.

It is easier to analyse the points of dissension between her and Dylan than to express the quiet centre at which despite everything they did meet in happiness and concord. But without the latter the dissension would have been meaningless and the marriage would have broken up at an early stage in futile recriminations. Caitlin called Dylan corrupt because she knew that in an essential place he was untouched by corruption; she showed her bleak faces of discontent because she was sure of the love she shared with him; she was jealous of him because she was also proud of him. She resented the abandonment of her own ambitions, and yet at the innermost core she acquiesced and was happy, because she suckled the poems as well as the children. Dylan grumbled or took a blank or bland attitude of disregard for her irrationalities. Though he disliked her wrecking activities at parties, he gained a certain satisfaction from them. They were like some of his own daydreams being put into practice—though they had aspects of nightmare. For in them he was caught in a cleft stick, between his ideals of domestic decorum and respectability, and his own feckless bohemian behaviour. The actual moments of violence were embarrassing and disturbing, because they thrust on him the need to do something, to accept some sort of responsibility; but in retrospect they became the source of a savage comoedic glee.

I should like to round off this account of Caitlin by a few words on our last significant meeting. I had gone to Oxford where a group was putting on a play of mine about Robin Hood, and called down to see the Thomases at the cottage they rented from A. J. P. Taylor and his wife in a rather swampy place not far from the walls of Magdalen College. Dylan was away, but Caitlin emerged from a littered kitchen that was dominated by a huge calf's-head on a dish. "It's beginning to stink," she observed, as if remarking on a fact of nature about which nothing could be done. With her sleeves rolled-up she looked like a captive princess in some folktale servitude, puzzled and still hopeful. Indeed, set amid gurgling water and mud, weeping trees and discreet bird-gossip, the cottage was an odd sort of place. As I gazed, I saw that the kitchen was more or less the whole place, variously modified and hung about—as if its family was one of refugees who had just moved in on a night of panic and had not yet had time to sort out their random belongings. The total effect was somewhat that of a multiple stage-set in some rehearsal confusion; there was only one room in a kind of circular log cabin and I expected the unreal thing to start revolving and turn into something else, a pantomime transformation with Caitlin-Cinderella suddenly assuming the dancing-robes of her glistening otherself. But instead a three-year-old Aeronwy wailed and Caitlin was simply a lovely slattern. Perhaps we had arrived on her washing-day; but however hard one looked, the oddity of her cramped circular logbog-fantasia remained. "I suppose I ought to throw it away," she said with a venomous glance at the calf's-head, as if it were the cause of all her troubles, the spell-object chaining her to the boggery, "but Dylan would be annoyed."

She met us later for some drinks; and as usual I felt happy in her company, convinced (perhaps delusively) that we understood one another. We ran and rambled through the streets in an obscure game of hide-and-seek, ending in a don's room in Balliol. There we danced, shaking the shelves of books, a sort of dance-mime in dim light peopled with shadows. More than ever I felt that we understood one another, beyond words, in a turmoil of shuffling shadows. Shadows that scraped and bowed in a swinging cage about us, outside the world. In her concentrated grace I felt there was sufficiently expressed all that she meant of poetry and its corruption, a harsh harmony of exchanges, a benediction flowering from a pure centre. And at the same time a mockery, a deft parody, a tenaciously virginal image of the self, an animal cry of *noli-me-tangere* with bared teeth.

However, on the way back, sliding along the slippery tracks that wound among the clump of trees by the waterside near her cottage, I bashed myself against a treetrunk and made my nose copiously bleed. Waking next morning with a sore and bloodied face, I felt that the night's conclusion had perhaps been correct, a salutary reminder that the sort of journey I had been making into Caitlin's spirit meant in the end a collision with a brickwall or some other insuperable maze-obstacle. So I finish off my Caitlin quest with this slap in the face, a slap which I myself, and not she, gave me.

[2]

Back then to Dylan. His drinking habits had begun to worsen in the years I first knew him, though my impression is that he had been a fairly steady beer-drinker before the war, but in no way an obsessional boozer as he later became. Probably the strain of the early war-years first drove him into serious drinking. In 1943 he could imbibe large quantities of drink, but in the periods when he, Phil and I were much together, he seemed to suffer from pro-longed after-effects much worse than we did. One story will illustrate his capacities. I had wandered off from the War Office one lunch-hour to the pub we called the Burglar's Arms near Charlotte Street. I found Dylan leaning on the bar there in a soaked condition, with a dab of a cigarette in a corner of his sagging mouth and a dull glaze over his eyes. While in his sober periods he still had something of his chubby cherubic youth, in drink he rapidly grew his piggish mask, heavy-lipped and snouted, with his big white hands floundering, his big brown eyes growing more protuberant. Now, seeing his sozzled state, I felt that I could not leave him to a gutter-fate. Secure in the knowledge that no one would miss me in Eaton Square, I told him that I'd see him home. He responded with a belch and a grunt, and despite my remonstrances managed to wheedle two more pints out of the barmaid. "When the pub shuts," he muttered. "Not before. Gainst my principles." So we stayed on drinking. Just one more pint. And another. Then the pub shut and we moved out into Soho. Dylan insisted he had to see someone in a club. We found the club, but the only person Dylan wanted to see was the barman. After a few hours we moved on to another club. I had given up suggesting that we should find a taxi. As I grew drunker, Dylan grew soberer, or so it seemed. The pubs had opened and we spent most of our remaining cash. Then Dylan managed to cajole his way into another club, an expensive one, where we went round the tables of various acquaintances of his, who bought us drinks. I said nothing, but was tolerated as a hanger-on of Dylan's, who was in army-uniform. About one o'clock we left and found a taxi. In my memory, Dylan now seemed quite sober, having gained a second or third wind; but no doubt I was no longer capable of an objective judgement. I just had enough sense to stop the taxi as it was passing Victoria station, hand the driver the few pennies and sixpences I had left, and tell him to drive on to Dylan's address. A volubly-protesting Dylan was thus planted with the problem of somehow settling accounts with the driver. I chuckled vaguely as I staggered to my lodgings.

Towards the end of the war the first full nemesis came on Dylan for his way of life, a nemesis that he always referred to as cirrhosis of the liver, no doubt with romantic simplification. I forget the exact date when he was taken off to hospital. I was not present at his emergence; but the Irish couple who went to welcome him back into the noisy world declared that his first words as he looked dazedly round were, "Where's the nearest pub?" He had been warned that he must stop drinking. A few days later I remember drinking with him and the couple to the accompaniment of records of James Joyce reading *Anna Livia Plurabelle*.[1]

But though Dylan was carried on a wave of terror and fascinated submission to the death which he made into a fated one, it is not true that he contemplated the certain end with any stoic calm or settled acceptance. He even made an effort at this time to cure himself of his drinking habits. A Danish woman whom I knew and who was married to a doctor was then doing some psychiatric work at one of the large London hospitals. She told me years later that Dylan called in, described himself as a poet, and asked to be cured of drinking obsessions. The psychiatrist treated him as something of a joke and bantered him about being a poet; he had never heard of Dylan and was mildly irritated by a

[1] Constantine Fitzgibbon says he had been in a state of nervous hypertension and collapsed with alcoholic gastritis.

patient portentously announcing himself in such terms. Dylan didn't take the raillery at all well and failed to turn up for the appointment that was made. One wonders what might have happened if he had encountered an intelligent and sympathetic psychiatrist. Probably nothing.

The ignorance of the psychiatrist about Dylan brings up the role of mass-media in forming reputations. From the time of his competition-successes in the *Sunday Referee,* and then after Edith Sitwell's review in 1936, Dylan had a certain reputation among highbrows; he came also to be wellknown in the documentary-film world as well as the literary pubs. But, though *Deaths and Entrances* sold well and established his position, it was not till the documentary-film market began to dry up after the war and he turned to the BBC as a reader of poetry, that he reached a large-scale public. I recall noting the very moment of his reputation's expansion. He was one of several of us who read verse at the Ethical Society's rooms in Bayswater; his extremely fine and con-trolled reading of *Into her Lying-down Head* remains clear in my memory. There was only the usual small audience. Then, a few months later, with his first important BBC renderings having intervened, he gave a reading (somewhere in Kensington, I think) at which there was an overflowing and rapturous audience of young people.

I should like to stress the considerable difference between his early readings, at home or to small groups, and those given on radio and then to meetings in the USA. His early style was richly eloquent, but with no paraded effects; in particular his readings of D. H. Lawrence's poems on flowers and animals had a fine subtlety of sustained rhythm. On the radio, generally after encouraging himself with much booze, he fell back on the stunning power and volume of his palpitatingly Welsh flow-of-sound, pulling out all the stops of what was described as his mighty Wurlitzer. He had recourse to increasingly ham-effects; and though the resulting Wagnerian effusion had its grandeurs, it quite lacked the intimate sensitivity of the days when he read solely for his own delight.

At some time in his life—presumably before he first left Wales—Dylan had read well and widely. Phil speaks of him as the condemner of practically all his contemporaries, who yet had genuine humility—though he rarely spoke of his writings, save mockingly—when he was at work. He wrote in school exercise-books in a laboured, childlike hand; and I have seen him bent for hours over those books, often beside him a glass of beer or his children's sweet-rations, while carefully he wrote and then crossed out what he had written, hours—indeed, days—being spent pondering on one word. Those who saw him only as the truculent braggart in pubs, a cigarette forever dangling from his bottom-lip, or laughed with him when his fat little body quivered with laughter (for I cannot ever remember him laughing loudly) or watched him tense over the shove-ha'penny board, ready to lose his temper should he be beaten—he was an excellent player—knew only one side, the Panurge-side, of the man. They did not know those hours of torment over his childish exercise-books scrawled with his childish writing.

Only once did I catch Dylan reading a good book, and that was *Dombey and Son,* for he had a natural love of Dickens, one of whose characters he might well have been. Otherwise he read only detective-fiction, and usually while he lay in bed. At one time, however, he must have read deeply, his knowledge of poetry being no slight one, and when with friends we used sometimes to play a game in which each wrote a parody of some poet—Shelley, Byron, Browning, and so on—Dylan's effort not only showed that he knew the man's work well but it was often an excellent poem in its own right. Deeply do I regret having lost a parcel of these taken from him one night in a pub.

In 1943 he was much taken up with a periodical that dealt with various perversities, in particular those connected with rubber. He read passages out with much gusto. I found the accounts of naked lovers tied up or variously garbed in rubber rather mysterious, funny but unexciting. However, the imagery remained with Dylan (though not affecting his poetry, I think), as is to be seen in his retorts to persons who asked him why he had come to America: "To continue my lifelong search for naked women in wet mackintoshes."

One may say that, roughly, there were three Dylans. First there was the quiet well-mannered unobtrusive Dylan of his quite sober moments. (Phil mentions meeting Dylan soon after his first arrival in London, at the Angel and Crown in St. Martin's Lane, and finding him then "shy, almost timid," with little to say.) The time when I saw him most invincibly reserved and modest in demeanour was during a visit of his parents to London. In his father's presence he was quiet, waiting to be spoken to, without the least fraction of his pub-swagger. Of his parents I recall only their typically Welsh lower-middleclass appearance, gentle and assured. His father gave rather the effect of a capable but mild-mannered schoolmaster, very proud of his favourite pupil but careful to say or do nothing to make him conceited; benevolent and yet aware of being a little out of his normal habitat. (I did not then know that he had been a schoolmaster; he might equally have been the village chemist with devout and secret hopes of becoming the chosen bard at the Eisteddfod.) The mother showed her admiration more plainly, as also her uncertainty in that London setting. She spoke more than her husband, but not with the garrulity of which I understand she was capable. Dylan, as he deferentially watched them, echoed in his own behaviour their sterling and unemphatic qualities, with no sign whatever of rebellion or double-meaning. There was something touching about the reunion, a sense of extreme closeness between the three of them, but at the same time an uncomfortable admission of the distance which had grown up between Dylan and his parents and which nothing could even begin to bridge. As though they were playing a game which they knew was unreal and which yet implicated deep elements in each of them. Caitlin I can hardly recall in the scene at all, so effectively had she effaced herself, recognising the moment as that of the Thomases.[1]

Secondly, there was the halfdrunk Dylan, charming and overflowing with bonhomie and his particular kind of wit and humour. Thirdly, there was the drunkenly-snouted Dylan, capable of behaving in the grossest and most provoking way. The halfdrunk Dylan was the boon companion, who at his best

[1] I can recall only one occasion when Dylan and Caitlin attempted a formal gathering: an afternoon tea-party in the basement at Markham Square, Chelsea, a small flat taken over from Caitlin's sister Nicolette who occupied the rest of the house with her husband the portrait-painter A. Devas. Perhaps because it was a gloomy December day, or because Dylan didn't like Devas and felt peevishly unwanted in the place, or because he disliked such occasions and was dead-sober, the couple of hours there were the only dull ones I ever spent with him.

wove round himself delightful flights of fancy and liked to reveal his remarkable powers as a mime, a parodist, a pricker of all pomposities and falsities. I recall especially one evening spent at the pub at the end of Cheyne Walk, when he had Constantine Fitzgibbon in US uniform with him. Dylan went on improvising all sorts of bizarre characters, with Fitzgibbon giving him a grave-mannered support. By reading his lighter stories and *Under Milk Wood* one can get some idea of what his improvised characterisa-tions and his humorous inventions were like on such occasions. (A strong influence, by the way, which no one seems to have spotted in *Under Milk Wood* was that of T. F. Powys. To check up, I asked Phil and he told me that Dylan was a keen admirer of T.F.)

Once I showed Dylan some photos of paintings by my father, in which the nudes were particularly capacious and spacious. Dylan turned them over slowly with glistening eyes and then said in a whisper of hushed awe, of sheer incredulity, "And to think that there are fairies!" His dislike of homosexuals in general arose perhaps from this sort of astounded conviction that anyone who scorned the devious luxuries of female flesh was too perverse to deserve the status of human being. But it was also nourished by the prominence of homosexuals in most of the cultural fields today, especially in literature, and by their clannish tendency to help and praise one another. He heartily applauded a remark of mine, "To succeed as a writer in England one needs to be a homo, a Catholic, or a Trotskyist; and if one is all three together, one is made before one starts." (I apologise to the shade of Trotsky for using his name in a term that conveniently expresses the ex-leftist who remains idiosyncratically sectarian or who gains a quick reputation by attacking the Left.) Homosexuals he also equated with the upper-class: "snug as a bugger at Rugby."

Dylan liked Edith Sitwell and knew that he owed much to her. But while she was always devotedly tolerant of his waywardness and acquiesced in any violence or rudeness from Caitlin, he found in her kindness something of the patronage which he could never forgive. Her aristocratic presence, further, was the sort of thing that stimulated the irreverent mixture of smallboy and rebel in his make-up. At times he spoke of her as if she were an eccentric and troublesome aunt who had to be borne with; at times he was more

25

generous; but I never heard him give any unqualified praise of her work. Despite certain deep kinships with his own poetry, it put him off with what he felt its uncurbed magnanimity. He liked a firm hand controlling the protean substance of the poetic image rather than a gush of outswirling energies—though he was happily at home among Lawrence's *Beasts and Birds*. I think perhaps he felt the need to guard himself against Edith's work precisely because of the elements of kinship. I met him outside the theatre after the performance of *The Shadow of Cain,* with music by Humphrey Searle, in which he took part. He was in an unusually grumbling irritated mood and kept on making hostile comments about the performance. Perhaps because I myself had enjoyed it and felt exhilarated—though also because I had to catch a train—I refused his repeated invitation to go round the corner to a wine-bar; and so I left him, unclear whether he had been annoyed by frayed tempers behind the scenes—tempers had been frayed, I learned from Edith—or whether he really was reacting against the poem.

Of his second American tour, with Caitlin, Edith wrote to me, "I hear our dearest Dylan has been painting New York (literally) red. The centre of his activities being the Literary Salon of Mrs Murray Crane, the watchwords of the Salon being Decorum, Bonne Tenue, and the milder and more restrained forms of Evening Dress. At one of the interminable evenings of culture to which one is doomed there, Dylan suddenly sprang at Caitlin and (according to my informant) 'kicked, punched, and bloodily beat her.' Mrs Murray Crane shrieked and fainted—being revived with difficulty. There is then a gap in the narrative. I *think* Dylan was sent home, but do not know what happened to Caitlin. However Dylan soon reappeared, and demanded money for his taxi. My informant wrote, gloomily, 'I don't suppose he will be asked again.'!!" While theoretically Edith disapproved of all such indecorums and would have considered them mere loutishness in most other people, she in fact enjoyed Dylan's wildnesses, though I had the feeling that she never really faced up to the extent of his infidelities and clung to what Dylan had told her of his love for Caitlin—words that were true enough, but interpreted by Edith in too simple a sense.

His death was a heavy blow to her. In later 1953, when I was myself confronted with my wife Ann's mortal illness, though I was still trying to hope against hope, Edith wrote in apology for some slight delay that she had "been involved in every kind of fresh distress and worry incident on Dylan's death. It isn't only the *grief* of that, it was the terrible circumstances surrounding it, and the fact that everybody threw the wildest charges at each other, and, the moment I landed, tried to involve me in their rows and accusations. How deeply I felt what you said in your letter about the terrible character of hope. I wrote, once, about 'soft despair.' And I think I shall write again in the same vein." She was suffering physically and had been badly upset by a play which she took to be a gross attack on herself and Osbert. It represented them, she said, as a pair of sex maniacs. Writing in January 1954, she told me that she had been brought to a state of collapse by the play and by the shock of Dylan's death "in such frightful circumstances, far worse than anyone in England knows." Later, speaking of my *Elegy on Dylan,* she said that she thought it had a lovely passage (the middle section), but she did not understand it all or agree with it always; and she added, truly enough, "in some ways Dylan was 'all things to all men.' "[1]

[3]

I have stressed Dylan's fear and dislike of intellectualism. His effort to start poetry off from the simplest organic basis of experience, the birth-moment, implied a rejection of all imposed ideas or guiding lines. Not that Dylan of all people was so naive as not to recognise that in any concatenation of words there must necessarily cohere meanings applicable at all levels, social as well as personal, political as well as aesthetic. But this fact did not make the effort of reduction seem any the less significant or worthwhile in his eyes. It merely meant that the expanded meanings and complex associations should emerge from, and find their verification in, the organic image at its highest point of concentration—

[1] At the time I heard several detailed and circumstantial tales about Dylan's death, which made it a far more sordid thing than the story as now told. But the panic among those connected with it, which appeared in these tales, must have had its element of truth, as Edith's remarks corroborate it.

not from any intellectual line of argument or any external wish to be on the side of the angels. Thus Dylan was constantly aware of the wider relations of his images. Only the slightest oscillations of their particular point of balance was indeed needed to bring out a plain social application, as occurs, for instance, in an early poem *Our Eunuch Dreams*. Here his reaction to the world of the cinema, which meant so much to him, is so sharp that he is caught at the moment of the direct blow, a moment that he usually let pass before he mustered his poetic energies. He demands that the existing situation be reversed and that its false art, the anti-art of alienation, give way to the positive art of truth in which the liberated powers of men may be realised:

> The dream that kicks the buried from their sack
> And lets the trash be honoured as the quick.
> This is the world. Have faith.
>
> For we shall be a shouter like the cock,
> Blowing the old dead back; our shots shall smack
> The image from the plates;
> And we shall be fit fellows for a life,
> And who remain shall flower as they love,
> Praise to our faring hearts.

At the outset (in *New Verse* in 1934) Dylan had defined his creed: "I take my stand with any revolutionary body that asserts it to be the right of all men to share, equally and impartially, every production of man from man from the sources of production at man's disposal, for only through such an essentially revolutionary body can there be the possibility of a communal art." Treese has stated, "By 1938, when I was discussing this statement with him, Thomas felt that he should withdraw it, and that it no longer applied." I should like to know in more detail how that conversation with Dylan went. Certainly by 1938 he would have felt that the wording was too naive and absolute, too little related to actual politics; and perhaps at that moment he was at the height of his struggle to concentrate on the birth-death image. In any event the 1934 announcement remained in all essentials his creed, though in later years he understood something of the complexity of the issues that it raised. What had changed and developed were both his ideas of poetry and his ideas of revolution. Or, rather, what had changed was the perspective in which he viewed his original ideas, the range of possibilities that he now intuited. In Prague, in 1949, he is reported to have cried, "I am a Communist, but am I also a bloody fool?"

Augustus John has written, "At one time Dylan told me that he joined the CP, but, quite rightly, detached himself on finding that henceforth he would be expected to make his work a medium for propaganda. He was not a student of sociology, but, I think, like so many of his generation, discovered in himself a feeling for the underdog." I fear that John has confused some story that Dylan told him: perhaps that he had thought of joining the CP at one time, but was put off by the fear of pressures to turn him into a propagandist. It is barely possible, though not likely, that he had joined in Wales before coming to London, at the time when he had ideas like that cited above. If so, he may well have been pushed around by some jealous branch-secretary. During the period of the Spanish Civil War, though he was against Franco, he was too obsessed by the problems of hammering out the primary bases of his poetry to think much about politics; and if in the early years of the war he had joined the CP in a momentary wave of antifascist enthusiasm, Phil would certainly have known. (In 1934 we find him writing to the *Swansea and West Wales Guardian,* asking the editor to go as far as was possible in making readers aware "of the immoral restrictions placed upon them, of the humbug and smug respectability that works upon them all their handcuffed days." He said that "at the roots of being lies not the greed for property or money, but the desire, large as the universe, to express ourselves freely and to the utmost limits of our individual capabilities." He went on to denounce the fascist-minded.)

I have asked various persons who were in a position to know if Dylan ever joined the CP in London: A. L. Morton (who helped Neuberg on the *Sunday Referee* and recalled the arrival of Dylan's first poem), Randall Swingler, and Edgell Rickword. None of them had ever heard of Dylan as a Communist. Further, Dylan said to me more than once, around 1949–50, "If all the party-members were like you and John Sommerfield, I'd join on the spot." He never suggested that he had already joined and been driven out by sectarianism. He wrote to his socialist friend Bert Trick a scathing letter on well-to-do middleclass intellectuals who became Communists "with no idea at all of what they priggishly call the 'class-struggle.' " The individual and the mass can be made poetically important "only when the status and position of both are considered by that part of the consciousness which is outside both. . . . Historically poetry is the social and economic creed that endures."[1]

The essential point, however, is that, despite his deepgoing anarchism, he was never hostile to any part of the Left and that he remained all his life, as John says, a champion of the under-dog. I think his experiences of the early years of the war had much to do with the rebirth of his early political attitudes in a new form. Certainly those years did much to widen his experience and his sympathies. In his need to keep to traditional terms he expressed this new breadth mainly through religious imagery and idioms. About 1945, discussing with him what I felt as a new scope of vision, a more active sense of human solidarity, in his poems, I said, "I think your work in documentary films has helped, by forcing you to find terms in which to define your position plainly and explicitly." He shook his head and denied that his scripts had at all affected his poems. I had indeed put the matter too crudely, and he was right in rejecting my formulation. But I still think his film-work did help to make him think more directly about the political world and that it thus played its part, together with his reactions of pity and terror to the actual war, in begetting such poems as *A Refusal to Mourn the Death, by Fire, of a Child in London*. More importantly, it stirred his dramatic sense, made him want to find a cinematic sweep of objectively-based images, and these led on to *Under Milk Wood*.

Although he could not have read the Welsh verse and prose of

[1] In my first version I added more about Dylan's early political ideas but these are now well documented by C.F.'s *Life* and Professor Bill Read's book. It is worth noting, however, that in May 1934 he wrote to Pamela Hansford Johnson: "I could go to Russia with a Welsh Communist organisation." This suggests some close contacts with the CP at Swansea or elsewhere in Wales. In July: "Swansea is the centre of all revolutionary activities this week. It is the week of the trial of Tom Mann and Harry Pollitt. I have just left the Socialist Party, and offered my services to the Communists. I *was* in time for Mosley's meeting, and was thrown down the stairs."

his great-uncle, Gwilym Marles, whose bardic name he inherited as Dylan Marlais Thomas, he must have known from early years the heroic legend of G.M. as a radical preacher-bard who fought so hard against the landlords that he himself in 1876 was evicted from his chapel. Indeed G.M. is the foremost ghost among "the towering dead with their nightingales and psalms." And in his Swansea days, presumably to a considerable extent through Bert Trick, Dylan gained a secure knowledge of the essentials of dialectical materialism, which played a crucial part in determining his poetic technique. In 1938 he contrasted his own poetry with the sort of verse-composition that adds one logical point to another, using a single image and moving round in a circle:

A poem by myself *needs* a host of images, because its centre is a host of images. I make one image—though "make" is not the word, I let, perhaps, an image be "made" emotionally in me and then apply to it what intellectual and critical forces I possess—let it breed another, let that image contradict the first, make, out of the third image bred out of the other two together, a fourth contradictory image, and let them all, within my imposed formal limits, conflict. Each image holds within it the seed of its own destruction, and my dialectical method, as I understand it, is a constant building up and breaking down of the images that come out of the central seed, which is itself destructive and constructive at the same time.[1]

I quote this much-quoted passage because critics have often doubted it as a genuine statement of Dylan's method and because I believe that in it he is speaking with the utmost seriousness and setting out the exact truth of his method—in so far as a poetic method can be reduced to general principles in a few words. What Dylan here says is the ideal of composition he set before himself, and which he practised in his best work, when he is writing at his highest intensity and his mind is fully active. And there is not the least doubt that every word of his statement shows how thoroughly he had absorbed from Marxism those principles which illuminated for him his intuition and experience of creative process, and which confirmed him securely in the

[1] Compare his letter to C. Fisher, February 1935 (*Selected Letters*, p. 151), which is further important in showing that he must have reached his clear dialectical grasp at Swansea when closely in touch with Bert Trick and others of a Marxist way of thinking.

method he adopted. True, in later years, with his increased dislike of intellectualism and with the mixture of teasing mockery and take-it-or-leave-it challenge that he used as a defence against superficial or jargoning intruders (especially on his American tours), he would hardly have committed himself to such an explicit account of his way of verse-writing. He would have felt that it put him too much at the mercy of fools and professors. But that does not make it a jot the less revelatory.

It is worthwhile to glance at the script of *These are the Men*, remembering that Dylan would not have played a passive part in its conception and working-out. I have heard him and Phil discuss their scripts, and they were largely responsible for the ideas and treatments.[1] Dylan's value as a script-writer lay precisely in this fact; for there was nothing brilliant in the actual wording of his texts. He lacked the capacity to invent dramatic themes, Phil being much his superior in this matter; but he overflowed with illustrative or interpretative ideas. In *These are the Men* somebody else no doubt had the idea of using the Nazi film *Triumph des Willens* against its makers, though this too may have been Dylan's own suggestion; in any event the theme and the idiom may be taken as genuinely expressing Dylan's political positions. The film uses passages from a Nazi documentary on the 1934 Reich Party Congress at Nuremberg, and inserts a deflating commentary in place of the actual speeches. But what I want to cite here are the opening sequences.

(The mood of the opening sequence is quiet and slow. From a height we look down on to men baking bread, men going about their work quietly and efficiently, men of no particular nationality, just working men. We see them in the bakery, in the fields at harvest time, on the dockside, on a trawler, in an iron foundry.)

[1] I recall an amusing episode connected with Julian Maclaren Ross, soon after he had come to work with Dylan for Donald Taylor in Golden Square. (I had the impression at the time that Dylan, admiring J.M.R.'s stories of army-life, had been influential, through Taylor, in getting him out of the army into the script-job.) J.M.R., likeable and amiable as he was, was a compulsive talker who dominated any gathering with his often very entertaining chatter; but Dylan was now exposed day after day to the steady discharge of words in his rather loud inescapable voice. At last his nerve broke. I was near Soho early one afternoon and saw Dylan pallidly limping on the kerb. He had jumped from a bus in midcareer as the only way of throwing J.M.R. off, and had badly shaken himself in the process. We went into the nearest pub and he gradually recovered wind and morale.

Who are we? We are the makers, the workers, the bakers
Making and baking bread all over the earth in every town and
    village,
In country quiet, in the ruins and wounds of a bombed street
With the wounded crying outside for the mercy of death in
    the city,
Through war and pestilence and earthquake
Baking the bread to feed the hunger of history.

We are the makers, the workers, the farmers, the sailors,
The tailors, the carpenters, the colliers, the fishermen,
We dig the soil and the rock, we plough the land and the sea,
So that all men may eat and be warm under the common sun.

(Now we see behind the workers, behind the work they are doing,
the shadow of war. The men are still doing their jobs, jobs that are
done all over the world, pottery, carpentry, sleeper-laying, steel-
making. This is their peacetime work, but we see too what they or
their brothers all over the world are doing now—fighting on every
front.)

We are the makers, the workers, the wounded, the dying, the
    dead,
The blind, the frostbitten, the burned, the legless, the mad
Sons of the earth who are fighting and hating and killing now
In snow and sand and heat and mud;
In the streets of never-lost Stalingrad,
In the spine-freezing cold of the Caucasus,
In the jungles of Papua,
In the tank-churned black slime of Tunisia.

We are the makers, the workers, the starving, the slaves
In Greece and China and Poland, digging our own graves.

Who sent us to kill, to be killed, to lose what we love?
Widowed our women, unfathered our sons, broke the heart
    of our homes?
Who dragged us out, out of our beds and houses and work-
    shops
Into the battle-yard of spilt blood and split bones?

(We are back in the bakery again—the camera tracks forward as one of the bakers opens the fire-door—the camera still moves forward till the flames of the fire fill the screen.)

> Who set us at the throats of our comrades?
> Who is to blame?
> What men set man against man?
> Shout, shout, shout out their name!

(The flames dissolve into hands raised in the Nazi salute—the sound dissolves into the frenzied "sieg heil" of masses of men and women who crane their necks and push their fellows. From a great height we look down on the mighty crowd in the Nuremberg Festival . . .)

Dylan lent me the script for a collection of Declamations or Poetry in Action, which I made for Tambimuttu; so he definitely accepted full responsibility for the work. Somehow or other I lost the impulse to complete the book and so it was never published. What is specially characteristic of Dylan in his script is the stress on the solidarity of common tasks, on work as a uniting factor. Though his politics always remained rudimentary, they were based on this simple and fundamental idea: that work under the common sun united men and gave them their essential humanity, while everything that cut across the union—exploitation, racial or other divisions, war as the final monstrous expression of the alienation of men from one another and from the earth—was manifestly evil and needed no further exposure for its total condemnation. Brinnin therefore is partly right in his comments on Dylan, though he completely fails to grasp the depth of Dylan's convictions and the central part they played in his work:

> Dylan's political naïveté, it seemed to me, was a consequence of his promiscuous affection for humanity and of his need for emotional identification with the lowest stratum of society. His socialism was basically Tolstoyan, the attempt of a spiritual aristocrat to hold in one embrace the good heart of mankind, a gesture and a purpose uncontaminated by the real-politik of the twentieth century. While he expressed himself strongly on political matters and tended indiscriminately to support the far left, his attitude was a kind of stance unsupported by knowledge, almost in defiance of knowledge.

As long as, anywhere in the world, there existed groups of men pilloried by the forces of propertied power, Dylan wanted to be counted among their sympathisers. And yet no political manifestations of this ever showed in his poetry. Americans who had celebrated him as the romantic liberator—as the poet who had broken the domination of the once politically minded generation of Auden, Spender, MacNeice, and Lewis, would have been perplexed to find that he was actually far more censorious of the status quo than any of the other British poets.

The passage about spiritual aristocracy there would have made Dylan spew over Brinnin; and the assumption of his political ignorance merely shows up the ignorance of Brinnin himself. What is true is that Dylan's politics were at root the immediate politics of a clear-eyed and vigilant sympathy with one's fellows; and without such politics his poetry could never have come into existence or developed. Further, Dylan's love was not promiscuous or indiscriminate; it had its aspect of universal sympathy, as shown in the passage cited from *These were the Men*; but it also sharply excluded all who battened in any way, however abstract and hidden, on human suffering and division. It therefore excluded the major part of the intellectual world. There were very few contemporary writers indeed for whom Dylan had the least respect.

Dylan signed the Stockholm Peace Petition, the Rosenberg Petition, and actively supported the Authors World Peace Appeal. Doubtless there were many other such expressions of his downright political position; for I never knew him hesitate a moment before giving his support to such movements. He was always ready to collaborate with us in Fore Publications, though we forbore to ask him for poems, since he was hard-up and we did not pay. However, when Paul Potts (whom I had introduced to Dylan and who did much to help the Thomases in the last part of their Chelsea period) got together a collection for *Our Time* in honour of Lorca, Dylan at once offered *Ceremony After a Fire Raid*. He wrote a satire for *Circus* and was keen to join in our series of Key Poets (of which I shall say more when I come to Edith Sitwell) with its aim of "breaking down the barriers between poet and audience, and giving poetry a chance to re-discover itself as activity" (the last phrase was Tzara's); he allowed us to use his name and was going to give us the never-finished poem of which *In the White Giant's Thigh* was a part.[1]

He was friendly with Aloys Skoumal, cultural attaché round 1949 at the Czech embassy, who gained him an invitation to attend the foundation of the Writers Union in Prague in March. (MacNeice was also invited, but did not reply to the letter.) Skoumal has told me of Dylan, "Before he left for Prague, he came to our place in Willesden where he spent an evening with my wife and me. We talked about various topics, also about Wales. To my remarks on Welsh National Eisteddfods—I have attended one at Colwyn Bay in 1947—he reacted in a tone which was not exactly hostile but certainly rather sarcastic. Then I showed him some translations of his poems into Czech made by Offer and others during the war. He asked me to read a few stanzas of these, and in return he offered to read to us a couple of his poems in the original. I need not assure you how fascinated we were by his performance." At snowed-under Prague he enjoyed wandering about among the people and did not pay much attention to the official proceedings. One tale about him was that he got to know the wine-shops, into which he went on his own and ordered a double slivovice. He invariably paid with a five-crown note (worth about 6d. at the time), which he produced with a flourish and the magnanimous remark, "You may keep the change." Nobody remonstrated and Dylan was left with the impression of a lavish gesture. He enjoyed the company of the fine and jovial poet Nezval and of the large and equally jovial novelist Jan Drda. The latter, says Skoumal, was at Dobříš, the Writers' Home in the country, with Dylan. "There was still plenty of snow when they took him for a walk in the park. Properly speaking," says Drda, "Dylan Thomas did not seem to walk at all, he frisked and gambolled, he made the impression of a bear floating in the air." Another tale was that in order to protest against a dull literal-minded translator who had been allotted to him (I also once suffered from her), he climbed up on to the rail of the Charles

[1] John Davenport managed to get him £50 out of *Circus* funds to help him with this poem. Davenport was always a devoted friend of Dylan, who rightly had a great affection for him. I hope to write elsewhere on him and his co-editorship on *Arena*.

Bridge, clasped one of the statues that decorated it, and threatened to jump into the river unless he was at once given a new translator. The protest was effective.[1]

But if Dylan had no taste for official ceremonies, he was considerably moved by the new elements and forces manifest in Czech society. I have no doubt that the speech he is recorded to have given before the Congress of Writers was in fact what he said. He may have been jogged a bit by the translator; but he was never the person to let himself be cajoled into saying what he did not feel. When Jirina Haukova met him from the Ministry of Information and asked in some surprise why he had come, he replied simply, "Why not? I'm Left." He was not unduly perturbed by the fact that at that time any advanced kind of poetry was not likely to get into print in Czechoslovakia. "A real poet must stand everything, and it doesn't matter if he publishes or not." He merely felt himself at home, even if he disliked the custom of drinking at parties in writers' flats rather than in pubs or dives. "The faces in the crowd reveal the delight and pride that your people took in the birth of the new People's Republic, the beauty of simple people, proud and joyful, with the rhythm of history visible in every gesture." He was speaking of a film about 6 February 1948, but he was also speaking of Prague as he saw it. An oversimplified view in some respects, no doubt, but one with its deep truth—and owning a vital connection with his poetry and its secret dream. The situation had startled him for a moment into a happy statement which would unfortunately have been impossible in England.

He took the Peace Movements seriously and turned up at the meeting of writers held at Pearl Binder's house in 1950 to discuss the wording of our Appeal. I had arrived much too early and went to the pub across the road on the way to Hammersmith. Dylan came in. He had just returned from Persia where he had been

[1] Skoumal was a small imperturbably-cheerful man, a Catholic with a special love of our eighteenth-century literature, and of Celtic culture (hence his visit to Wales); he had a capacity to cite Swift in unexpectedly-apposite ways. He has translated into Czech *Gulliver's Travels*, a Swift Anthology, *Tristram Shandy* (the first Czech version, published 1963 and at once sold out), Conrad's *Nostromo* and a collection of his short stories, K. Mansfield's stories, etc.; he has written on Swift and Wilde, lectured on Yeats, Synge, MacDiarmid, O'Casey; is working on *Vanity Fair*. With his wife he has done the two *Alice* books.

working on a documentary film. There were upheavals going on in Persia and I said, "Congratulations on starting the revolution." For a moment he was disconcerted, then he gave one of his heaving laughs and expressed the hope that something shattering was really going to happen. At the meeting he had by far the most to say, arguing over every sentence of the Appeal and insisting that we must try as much as was humanly possible to get away from committee-jargon and make emotionally-direct statements. He dominated the discussion and all his amendments were agreed to.[1]

These points about Dylan's political attitudes and ideas are not irrelevant to the consideration of his poetry and the creative conflict there revealed. I have tried indeed in these reminiscences to keep to matters which I think are bound up with that conflict. To make the application of the conflict expressed in his life to the conflict driving on and yet limiting his poetry would involve a detailed examination of a number of his best poems; here I can only indicate briefly the way in which I think the application could and should be made.

Dylan, as I said earlier, was obsessed with the birth-copulation-death sequence or rather unity. Because of the concentration on organic experience, he might be able to see death as a birth, but he also was forced more and more to see birth (and copulation) as a death. The fear of death (impotence in body and mind) became more and more oppressive, weighing down as a solid mass that had to be laboriously and painfully displaced before he could find the words he needed. Now, with more details available about his early years, we can see how the lung haemorrhages from which he suffered as a child—with perhaps a recurrence in the late teens—had an indelible effect upon him. They left him with weakened lungs and a tendency to bronchitis; and upon them was added asthma, steadily worsened from about the age of fifteen years by

---

[1] Dylan makes fun of such activities in a letter (late 1949) to Davenport, "Dear Comrade, I was sorry to miss you when I was up in the smoke last week, I was quite looking forward to a good chat about *Arena* in the 'local' but you know how it is, I got caught up with rewording a petition against decadent tendencies in the cultural field, I expect you'll agree with subsection 4, it was my idea, I had the hell of a job getting it past, they thought it was a bit individualist, but that's them all over." He is perhaps recalling the AWPP meeting.

his chain-smoking. But these physical disabilities in turn were linked with a mother-obsession and came to express the sense of being smothered by the overlaying and inescapable motherflesh. His mother had pampered him to such an extent that when seventeen he was still incapable of cutting off the tops of boiled eggs. Her fussy enclosing affection, no doubt, was stimulated and driven to an extreme by her fears, guilts, and miseries over his infantile troubles. (His sister as a child had a liver-complaint and died of cancer of the liver when forty-seven. With someone so morbidly self-conscious of physical dissolution as Dylan, her troubles must have reinforced his fears and anxieties.) Psychologically, then, Dylan suffered something very like the mother-obsession of the asthmatic with its anguished sense of being held down, strangled, crushed. But, with his acute sensibility, emotional terrors far outstripped physical symptoms, drove him to drink, and made his hangovers abnormally wretched and guilt-ridden. He killed himself in order to escape death.

We can now better understand his self-identification with the withdrawn and frustrated father, which helped to carry him into poetry and at the same time sundered him from the family by making him all that his father had feared to become. His father surpassed, caricatured, tragically made a success, glorified and destroyed. In a sense he was taking revenge on his mother, on his own body.[1] He could fling off the coiling and crushing mother-sphinx only by flinging his own body off.

Along such lines as this we can analyse his inheritance, his patterns of repetition-compulsion. But we could find similar patterns in countless numbers of bronchial and asthmatic sufferers, who did not turn into poets with the tone and structure of greatness. The asthmatic pattern is there and must not be forgotten; but the poetry cannot be reduced to it. Dylan's long dialogue and duel with death as playboy, as ironic commentator, as lyrical and tragic poet, turned him into the mouthpiece of all men and evoked the innermost conflicts of our world. Such a development required both a social realisation and an aesthetic transformation.

---

[1] Note the element of revenge in the bragging confession, with its pang of genuine shame, which he wrote to Pamela Hansford Johnson after he had his first woman.

But in order to bring out how the widening of context and the deepening of apperception went on, we should have to turn to the poems themselves and make a sustained analysis of their method and scope. Here, however, I am dealing rather with Dylan as a person, with the raw material of the poems.

The childhood-world was for him both Paradise Lost and Paradise Regained. The hell of loss and alienation had then irrupted; the immediacies of organic contact which that world had contained still went on haunting him. His experience had shown him the hell extending and worsening in all the spheres of the surrounding world; yet that world also held "the makers, the workers, the wounded, the dying, the dead, the blind, the frost-bitten, the burned, the legless, the mad sons of the earth," with whom he could feel an entire and uncontaminated sympathy. His scattering of self in drink and copulation was a flight from the constricting mother, but also a return to her necessary and enveloping warmths. Caitlin had the thankless job of giving him a stable centre, without which he would not carry on, and yet embodying the mother-forces that drove him out of the home into desperate promiscuous satisfactions. She was his one true love, his redemption from the mother-sphinx, and at the same time she scared him for that very reason and touched off all his anxieties of being trapped and strangled.

In the postwar years his sense of an inner void grew increasingly acute; the more he felt great possibilities before him, the more he felt quite incapable of the concentration and comprehension which could put them into form. Brinnin is again half correct in saying:

. . . he and his unhappiness lay in the conviction that his creative powers were failing, that his great work was finished. He had moved from "darkness into some measure of light," a progress attended by the acclaim of the literate part of the English-speaking world; but now he had arrived, he was without the creative resources to maintain and expand his position. As a consequence, he saw his success as fraudulent and himself as an imposter. While he expressed such thoughts largely as self-deprecating jokes, he could not disguise their gnawing reality or force.

It is true that he felt lost, but not because his work was finished.

He was lost because he had begun splendidly and could not achieve a conclusion. His sense of being a fraud went far deeper than his fear of not being able to carry on; it was based in the conflict in his character and work that Caitlin had defined by calling him corrupt; it related to his written work as well as the works he could not write. The problem before him was not what Brinnin states:

> Would he continue, year by year, to be the roaring boy, the daemonic poet endlessly celebrating the miracle of man under the eyes of God? Would he, by some reversal of spirit, some redirection of his genius, become the wise, grey, and intellectually disciplined poet moving toward an epical summation of his lyrical gifts?

Such questions show a complete failure to penetrate the nature of Dylan and his work. The problem was to realise and control what was phoney and limited in the roaring boy, so that the creative conflict of the earlier work could be released into fuller dramatic forms with a wider human scope. Dylan was perfectly well aware of this. (Incidentally the phrase "under the eyes of God" points to the one blatant sentimentality in Dylan. He had no belief whatever in God or in Christ or in personal immortality, heaven, and hell; yet he spoke of writing "for the love of Man and in praise of God." No doubt he had his personal definition of God as something like "the totality of the living universe," but he knew quite well that the phrase would be given a pietistic meaning alien to his whole outlook. Brinnin cites him as saying that his aim was to produce "poems in praise of God's world by a man who didn't believe in God." One can imagine Dylan's blistering comments on any other poet who admitted to such an aim. I am not however criticising his use of religious imagery in the poems, especially of Christ's Passion; for such imagery is a precious and deeply significant part of the human heritage and does not necessarily imply that the poet using it is a Christian in any conventional sense of the term.)

Dylan wanted to develop dramatic and more objective forms of poetry; he realised that only by such forms could he break through the ring of obsessions, the tightening patterns which were strangling him. But for him the dramatisation could not

41

mean merely a change of genre, a projection of his unresolved inner conflict in a theatre of the absurd or of anguish. He declared that he wanted now to write only poems that were "happy," and in his declaration he showed his acute self-understanding. He accepted the earth and his fellows—in the terms set forth by his 1934 statement and implied by the opening sequences of *These were the Men*. A happy poem is not a poem without conflict; it is a poem in which the conflict is resolved. Dylan had come to realise that by the very intensity of his effort to remain lyrically concrete he had delivered himself over to the abstraction in a new and insidious form. To redeem and advance what was truly concrete in his achieved poems, he had to find the resolution of his conflicts in forms that broke through the limitations of the previous phase. Mankind had to become more than self and otherness.

A large proportion of his poems (some three-quarters), it has been shown, derived one way or another from what he had written at Swansea before he first left for London. What he did after his departure into the more challenging environment of London was to go deeper into the poetic themes, the world-system, which he had evolved in his early years: to bring out more sharply the inner conflicts and give the conceptions a new fullness and complexity of relationships—thus developing the dialectical system of imagic collision, fusion, division, branching expansion, and further fusion, which he sought to outline in the passage about his method cited above. But all the while he was dependent on the systems he had worked while still under the spell of his parental home, before he had let himself go into the world of experience. In the postwar years he was cut off from this body of material, partly because he had substantially used it up and did not want to go on repeating himself, and partly because the war had forced upon him the need for a decisively new arc of development. The small group of poems which he then managed to write proved that he was capable of breaking into new dimensions; but the prolonged travail of their production showed also how exhaustingly difficult he found it to make the new steps.[1]

[1] In those last years various burdens, the nemesis of his way of life, accumulated and drove him faster along the deadly path: his family of three growing children, the

Under Milk Wood was his attempt to break through into the enlarged and more objectively-based form. To belittle it in comparison with the more concentrated poems, which own a powerful dialectic of thought and emotion, is to misconceive its aim. Its simplicity of structure could not have been won without the struggle of the dialectic preceding it; and it represented the first necessary escape from private symbolism into a fuller world where the dialectic could achieve a new birth, with great new possibilities of expansion. The opera that Dylan planned to write for Stravinsky would have made an excellent next step.

> "His" opera was to be about the rediscovery of our planet following an atomic misadventure. There would be a re-creation of language, only the new one would have no abstractions; there would be only people, objects and words. He promised to avoid poetic indulgences: "No conceits. I'll knock them all on the head."

But he had reached the point where such a conception could only be a wild dream. *Under Milk Wood* had been completed under long and desperate pressure. The postwar years in general had seen Dylan steadily wrecking himself and dissipating his powers in an unavailing effort to escape the blind terror of death. He could not change the system of his life, the domestic hell and the flights which had become mere repetition of stale stimulations. He could not carry on to the new level the struggles defined in his poems up to and including *Deaths and Entrances*. He could only, by terrible and exhausting efforts, continue the same struggles and wring out a few more poems in which a painfully-won enrichment of old themes disguised the inner dearth. *Under Milk Wood* emerged belatedly as a sketch of the new artistic start of which he dreamed but which he had become incapable of securing. In the last eight years the nemesis of what Caitlin in bitter insight and impotence had called his corruption, took more and more charge of him. In a handful of poems he held the terrifying darkness at bay, reaffirming his sense of man's unity with nature and of the

---

need (after 1948) to look after his parents, the persecution by the Income Tax authorities, then the death of his father in December 1952—with the death of his sister in April 1953. (Though he cared little for his sister, her death could not but have added its quota of deadening fear.)

alienating curse that broke the unity. He was fighting a steadily-losing battle, sucked-under more and more by booze and his fear-hatred of money. In many respects he loathed going to the USA, and yet everything in him that Caitlin had called corrupt found the invitations alluring, irresistible. His death in New York was the logical result. Brinnin's book about the tours is the record not of Dylan in any fullness of the man and the poet, but of Dylan caught in the nemesis of his corruption.

To carry this analysis further would launch me into a detailed discussion of the poems, an adventure that I wish to keep for a separate essay. Here it is enough to conclude with a few more memories. Though Dylan disliked intellectual arguments, he was ready enough to tackle even literary or philosophic subjects if they came up by some side-approach in company that he didn't suspect. Once in a talk (1950–51) I cited a passage from Nietzsche, to which Dylan warmly responded. We wandered into a discussion of Nietzsche, Dylan showing himself well acquainted with *Thus Spake Zarathustra*. In the end—in the pub's pissoir, I remember with pictorial clarity—he remarked, "Why don't you write about him? You ought to."

"That'd be the last stroke to bring me down as a compromised Marxist," I said jokingly.

"To hell with that. Do it."

I said that I would. Some day I'll do it and dedicate it to him.

The last time when we had anything to say to one another was at the Savage Club. As usual, he ate no lunch and sat hunched in a dull haze over his beer while we others went into the dining-room. Afterwards, we somehow began talking of critics and poetry. He had had one of his second-winds and for the moment showed no signs of beer-immersion. We talked of Dickens, Eluard, and the things written about Dylan himself. I began talking of his work to him, which I hadn't done for years. Finally I said, "I'll write it all down. Better that way. Do you mind if I write about you?"

Dylan, no respecter of persons, answered, "Nothing I'd like better." He gave an owlish nod and began to slump back into a sozzled state. He had to go to some provincial town, I forget why. As we went out of the club, I paused on the steps, took out a pound note, and put it in his hand. He looked to see what it was, nodded without any particular emotion, and went off. I didn't know why I'd made the gesture; and I still don't know why. He was better-off than I was at that time. Perhaps I wanted to express the fact that, though by no means without my money-worries, I felt that money touched a deeper level of fear in him than in me. However that was, the action was certainly meant as a token of friendship, of love; something of a desperate token, an admission of failure to achieve the desired communication at conscious levels. I stood on the steps, also rather stunned with beer, trying to understand what I had done. Dylan had hailed a taxi. As he stepped in, he turned round and waved, a happy smile spreading over his face. I waved back.

LAST WORDS WITH DYLAN THOMAS

(This poem was written early in 1954. Reading some of the things written about Dylan and hearing some of the things said about him on the air, I felt bitterly how the reality of his life and poetry was going to be distorted—a process that had already begun, especially in the USA before his death, but was now hurrying on apace in Britain. I found out later that Philip had made the same point of anger in the note he wrote for the *Adam* issue on Dylan, but that section of his note was not printed. Looking back some twelve years later, I still feel that the poem has a valid point to make. It was printed in MacDiarmid's *Voice of Scotland,* in *Mainstream* in the USA, and (in translation) in *Plamen* of Prague, where Dylan has always been happily remembered; and also in my little book *Three Elegies.*)

So they got you at last despite your guiles of surrender
despite your sleight-of-hand with the apple-of-eden
despite your efforts to carry a piece of darkness
round on the palm of your hand

You walked a tight-rope even on terra firma
you walked the earth even on a tight-rope
you wore the mask of an intricate innocence

And now the people whom you most despised
write lies of praise about you

There was nothing in the world you hated but cruelty
and you loved almost everyone except the people who now
        praise you
Dylan walking in the midnight of a London
without the penny of a drink in our pocket
you assumed the mask of innocence over your innocence
and affronted the patronising world with a beggar's palm

You were a Robin Hood of tavern thickets
talking through a burnt-out cigarette
taking from the rich to give to the poor
            yourself the poorest
and dodging behind the wildwood of a baffling image

You wept in the cinema at people weeping
you wept and signed the Rosenberg Petition
you frowned and forgot to reach for another drink

You looked out over the wastes of death and wrote
            Light breaks where no sun shines
You looked out on Chamberlain from your hut of indignation
and wrote
            The hand that signed a paper felled a city
You denounced the guilty men of Nuremberg
in words heavy as clencht fists

But life was a sudden wind from the vats of cider
the distance where a girl dreamed in the cloverfield of her body
and grief was the lair of thunder in the oceanic shell
you smiled and reached for another pot of beer

You looked out from your bitter eyes of innocence
and knew it all and hid in your gentleness

We shall not walk again the London of a midnight

You knew it all, the map of our sharp-edged conflicts
and hoarsely whispered your indignant pity

I am for the people
I am against all who are against the people

But the map's contours burred in your angry tear
in the wheeling iris-lights of the lovely earth
you smiled and reached out for another beer

And life was a lifted wave with the naked image
borne on the curved shell of the mastered elements
the snakes of the wind in the tresses of blown gold
and the mouth of a sudden kiss come close and closer

I am for life
I am against all who are against life

You turned back to the childhood of a hayhigh sweetness
and climbed the stairs of water
seeking a thousand ways through the walls of murder
that closed the streets of daily life about you
into the endless spirals of the rose-heart

But because your face was innocent under a guileful mask of
        innocence
you always came on people

the dark tunnel of silence led to the friendly voices
the vortex of blind growth came still to rest
on the familiar faces of common people
worn by life as stones are worn by water
and you loved them even more than you loved the stones
the delicate maze of the revolving rose
broke into the clear face of your wife
and you were home again
in the daily streets yet closed with the walls of murder
the way of simple union and shared needs
the lionheart of honey the furious tooth of salt
the spinningwheel of the cottage-flower
the children's voices kiteflown in the dusk
the body of labour broken as bread is broken
and given in daily renewal
the lap of sleep and the ultimate round of dancing

But they got you at last before you had clambered through
they caught you halfway in the hole you had made in the walls

47

scraping at midnight hiding the mortar in pockets
they caught you helpless they broke you across the back
and broke you across the brow
and you smiled in your sleep

so near you had come
                    the flowers of endless gardens
not yet sown from the wayward aprons of wind
sent their warm lights upon you and you smiled

The murderers got you Dylan
and now they praise you in their church of death
and those who were waiting with outstretcht hands to drag you
up the jagged shores of safety
mourn and remember you another way

We turned to look at the dawn gone out of your eyes
and burning securely along the shores of the gathering peoples
and there your play with the apple has lost the sting of its guile

Edith Sitwell

I FIRST MET Edith Sitwell, for a moment, at the performance of *Façade* in 1926, to which Nina Hamnett had taken me; but it was not till twenty-two years later that I came to know her. In October 1944 we exchanged a few letters and she gave me permission to use some of *Façade* in the collection of Poems in Action which I mention in my Dylan essay and which I never published. Shortly after the war I saw her standing outside Unity Theatre, where she and MacDiarmid were to talk about poetry. She had expected someone to be waiting for her and could not bring herself to walk in unannounced. She had not anticipated the place's careless methods and stood with a look of dire strain on her face as chattering society-members hurried by. I turned and made a few steps towards her, but halted. I didn't want to appear to push myself upon her; perhaps also I didn't want to be staring into her overwrought face as she grew aware how anxious, indignant, and lost she looked—didn't want to identify myself with the organisation that had brought on her what was an ordeal of waiting on tenterhooks. So I went in and sent out the first officer of the society whom I saw. In the discussion she spoke well and with dignity, rather in accord with MacDiarmid (whom she seemed happy to be associated with) and betrayed nothing of the strain which she had showed outside. I wondered what strange proletarian den she had imagined she was intruding upon.

Shortly afterwards I met her briefly, but in circumstances of withdrawal that paired the encounter off with the non-contact outside Unity rather than with the acquaintance that was to follow. My friend the poet Maurice Carpenter, struggling with symbolic epics in the Spenserian stanza, had been writing to

Edith; and when his first child was born, he asked her to be its godmother. Edith agreed, and the ceremony was arranged to take place in the small elegant church of St John's Wood. (At the time Ann and I were living round the corner at 14 Wellington Road; and Leslie Hurry, whose father had been an undertaker in the High Street that ran down on the other side of the church, often told us how as a child he used to play on Joanna Southcott's tomb in the churchyard—though I never managed to find it.) The reason for choosing the church was that Maurice, for whom the baptism was a symbolic rather than a religious act, wanted the officiating priest to be Stanley Evans, who, as well as being an RAF chaplain, was curate here. Stanley, with whom I also was very friendly at this time, had some offices nearby, where I recall him presenting me with the Book of Common Prayer in the hopes that it would better my Marxism. He and his wife Stasia were living in a flat over a church hall converted into a People's Dining Centre for the duration, in Barrow Hill Road.

Maurice and his Mary arrived with the baby. We turned up as promptly. Edith came a trifle late in a taxi. Then we all settled down in the dim church. The afternoon was cloudy and grey. Expecting the priest at any moment, we all felt subdued and made no effort to be conversational. Edith replied politely to Maurice's remarks, but seemed sunken under the weight of the occasion. I felt that Ann and I were mere spectators in an event belonging to Maurice, Mary, and Edith; and I withdrew to one of the pews. As outside Unity Theatre, I did not want to seem to intrude in any way upon Edith, who had, it seemed to me, no reason to be interested in my existence. We all waited in an exasperated and fidgety silence. In my memory it seems to have lasted at least an hour, but perhaps it was only twenty minutes. Then at last Stanley dashed in, muttered something, and hurried into the vestry to don a surplice. I suppose he had been held up by some RAF work. Wrestling with the surplice, he got down to the job in a businesslike way. The baby squirmed in Edith's inexpert grasp and almost fell into the font. In a few moment's Stanley had completed the sacrament, and the howling baby was beginning to recover on Mary's bosom. Stanley chatted amiably and went off as fast as he had come. Edith seemed disconcerted by the whole affair. We faded away as Maurice was asking her to come to some small celebration and she was making signs of distress to any passing car in the hope that it might be a taxi.

After these misadventures, our friendship began on 2 February 1948 when she wrote me a letter of thanks for my review in *Our Time* of her *Shadow of Cain*. As always, when she was deeply moved, she wrote open-heartedly, with unrestrained warmth. "This happiness, and this encouragement, and this profound and wide understanding of all the implications in the poem, have come at a time when I have been feeling it impossible to work, and have been feeling a strange bereavement—I suppose owing to the increasing menace and deadening stupidity of the world. You might almost have timed this essay to the exact moment when it would be of the greatest help to me. For it has made me wish to begin to write again. Very little criticism is constructive." She added, "Leaving aside my gratitude to you for what you say about this poem, I am very moved by what you say about my early work. We *had* 'a tryst with the people.' But all that I am saying is completely inadequate. I am more moved, and more heartened, by your essay than you can know, or than I can express."

She had written care of *Our Time,* and asked for my address so that she could send me the copy of *Orpheus* with her Notes on the poem as well as her other two poems on the Bomb. She mentioned sarcastically that the reviewer in the *Manchester Guardian* had said of *The Shadow* that it was inspired by her interest in alchemical writing, and that something seemed to have happened, but he couldn't gather what. She remarked that he could not have heard of a certain event that took place at 8.15 on Monday 6 August 1945—"or, indeed, of anything that ever happened." She asked me to visit her with Ann in London, where she was to be from 22 March to 1 April (thus including Easter). She had to time her holidays so as to be able to help a lifelong friend "who nearly died under appalling circumstances during the German occupation of Paris." This friend we were to come to know as Evelyn Weil.

In my reply I mentioned that I hoped someday to make a fuller study of her work. On 6 February she fixed our meeting for

12.30 on Wednesday 24 March at the Sesame Club. A longer study of her work, she declared, "would be a source of the greatest happiness and pride to me. You understand what was in my mind when I wrote 'The Shadow of Cain' in a manner so extraordinary that you might have been that poem's author." (This was the kind of comment she was continually to make on paper or by word of mouth as I discussed her poetry or wrote about it.) And she added that she considered a work of mine, *The Anatomy of Spirit,* to be "of the very highest importance." I had not sent her this book or referred to it. I had written it in 1936 as the opening chapters of a study of Giordano Bruno; then, feeling that I could not adequately deal with Bruno without a knowledge of Renascence mathematics, I gave it to Methuens as a separate work. It was a slight composition, though perhaps it raised a number of large questions for which none of us yet have very satisfactory answers.

I never asked her why she mentioned the book, which seems to have been the only thing of mine, apart from the *Our Time* review and perhaps a couple of essays in *Life and Letters,* she had read before our meeting. If she had read it before she wrote *The Shadow of Cain,* I could claim that it had deeply affected her; for the last two chapters on Substitution Fantasies and on Spirit, are largely taken up with a Freudian-Marxist analysis of the idea of gold: the relation to faeces, money, hope of immortality (incorruptibility), the various unconscious connections and the rationalisations or sublimations. In my review, dealing with the complex way in which Edith handled the gold-symbol, I restated some of this analysis (without remembering it); and about the same time Hubert Nicholson, reviewing *The Shadow* for *Adam,* sent me a typescript of his note, saying that he had written it "with an uneasy feeling that I am muscling in on your territory; also I have pinched ideas and quotations from you; and have perhaps made some howlers into the bargain. I therefore throw myself on your mercy, as usual. Will you give me your judgement?" He had cited some passages from *The Anatomy of Spirit.* (Earlier in 1946 he had written to say that he had just read *The Anatomy,* "which has impressed me most profoundly. It is a wonderful book. I have just written to tell a friend about it and

remarked that it is better than the Bible . . . I have not read anything since I read the Communist Manifesto that has given me so
many things to think about." He wanted to know "Who read the
book? How was it criticised? What reverberations were there in
higher-Marxist circles? e.g. is it translated into Russian?" The
answers were simple: No one, not at all, not at all, and again not
at all.)[1]

It seems more likely then that Edith had got hold of the book
after reading Hubert's review, which pleased her a lot.

In sending me the material about her poem, she said that she
had explained badly, or incompletely, what she had meant about
Lazarus. "I think it appalling that what I can only call 'déprim-
ation' should be regarded as an *ideal*. Of course, one knows
nothing until one has experienced suffering, but suffering isn't an
ideal but a state through which one must pass. The ghastly
hierarchy that has just been abolished (temporarily, I suppose)"
of Fascism, "regarded suffering as an ideal, and now it seems to
me that everyone shows their wounds with pride—not because
of the fight which produced them, but because of the actual
wounds. Am I right?"

These words expressed something very deep in her. Despite
all the miseries and frustrations she had experienced, she carried
on essentially without selfpity. (I am speaking of her life up to
the period of her breakdown in 1960, after which I cannot speak
with any direct knowledge of her.) The wound in itself did not
matter and to display it was vulgar and poor-in-spirit. It had
virtue solely because of the struggle to which it testified —because
of the victory or resolution which reached out beyond suffering
into a new harmony and happiness.

At the time I did not realise how much of herself, of her deepest
aspiration, she had put into the words. Reading them now afresh,
wonder at my shallowness and I feel in their clear enunciation a
statement of principles which magnificently set out what were

[1] When I happened to turn up this letter in my papers, I was astounded at its
extravagant tone, but decided to quote it as a curiosity and as a complement of
Edith's remark. It is indeed possible that Edith did read the book at about the same
time as Hubert (early 1946) when Methuens sold off the stock at a reduced price and
copies were fairly plentiful in bookshops of the university towns, etc. If so, it
certainly played an important part in the formation of *The Shadow of Cain*.

to be the terms of our friendship. What I mean in saying this will appear as the story goes on.

I was delighted and excited to get her two letters; but, looking back, I feel that I did not at all sufficiently appreciate what I can only call the naked trustfulness of their tone and their expression. Edith had a splendid certainty in her emotional responses. If she let herself go, she let herself go, without reservations—just as if she felt herself insulted or attacked, she recoiled tightly into herself and threw out all her bitterly protective prickles. The fundamental pattern of her responses went far back into her childhood, but kept on reasserting itself all through her life. Now I can see that it was the number of times she had made this sort of candid and generous offer of her confidence, with a full trust in an equal answer of unguarded sincerity, and had found—sooner or later, usually sooner—a failure in understanding and openness, an ultimate betrayal of the gift of herself, which had contributed to the deep and permanent uncertainty and fear inside her, which however she always resisted and strove to master.

As to her comment that her Notes had stated badly what she meant to represent by Lazarus, I take it that she now feared the Notes appeared to make him out as the sole figure of total alienation and dehumanisation, of the mechanistic attitudes culminating in the atomic bomb. In the poem, on the other hand, Lazarus and Dives are seen as different or opposed aspects of the alienating process which unites them; and the final accusation is against Dives: "You are the shadow of Cain . . ." I had not dealt at all particularly with Lazarus in my review; Edith's comment was evoked by her response to that review in its entirety. She never ceased to repeat that she herself was unable to state as clearly as I could what the poem meant, and that her reading of, or listening to, my comments, gave her an uncanny feeling that I was the one who had written the work.

But since the review had thus released such a deep tide of emotion in Edith and in its way determined the whole of our future relationship, I had better give some idea of what I said in it.

2

I began by remarking that the development of Edith Sitwell "from a jangling fool-in-hell into a national poet with a great prophetic voice" might seem at first glance an odd thing; but it could be paired off with the way in which Tzara, Éluard, and Aragon had matured from Dadaism and Surrealism into their role as chief poets of the Left in France. "Though their styles have of course developed since 1920, their work makes up an organic whole from first to last." Edith Sitwell herself had early held to a position in which there were elements close to Dadaism:

> a determination to make faces and throw bricks at the world of the 1914–18 war. In that situation anger was the way to love, and chaos the only clue to a new cosmos. Edith Sitwell was deeply aware of the French Symbolist tradition, of Rimbaud, of the ferment of experimental methods in Paris; and perhaps along these lines of approach, plus her revolt against the war and county-society, she paradoxically discovered our own national tradition of deep popularly-rooted and imaginative poetry, which involves Skelton as well as Blake, nursery-rhymes as well as Shakespeare. It is therefore with her that the first important effort has been made to bridge the gap which the Victorians left between the people and the upper levels of verse. The Victorians, by a peculiarly withering and falsifying set of evaluations, deodorised our poetry and shut out all that was truly rowdy with the immediate voices of experience, all that was truly adventuring into new crystalline of the spirit. The final stage of Victorianisation came with the Georgians, who, often with pretty taste, reduced poetry to a suburban damnation.

Edith commented, "What you say of the Georgians is entirely true."

> The first act of the Sitwells, with Edith at the head, was to start a fronde against these vulgarisers. Often the main point may have seemed obscured in the dust of jeers and the delight of tripping up pontifical reactionaries like Squire; but the good work went on, and after the dust cleared, it became clear what a drastic and necessary work of demolition the Sitwells had done. For a while it may have appeared primarily a destructive process, like Tzara's Dada on the Continent; but as one gets it all into something like a clear focus, one sees that the poets who could feel the need to launch these

attacks had behind them a deep love of life, of all that bit cleanly into the truth of man. They were speaking for the forces of revolutionary harmony, the uncompromising levels of life; and their work as it moved forward could not fail to find that after all it had a tryst with the people, with all that in the people which held the revolutionary quick, the power and need of transformation.

It was the phrase here "a tryst with the people" that she eagerly seized on. (I did not at the time think of the encounter outside Unity Theatre, when a tryst with the proletariat had clearly shown itself in her face as something to be dreaded and yet not avoided— with the sober and intelligent, but not very fargoing, discussion that followed. I did not speak in the discussion, dominated by the emotion of withdrawal that had overcome me outside.) Edith had always deeply wanted the breakthrough into some new sort of union, a relationship of love that required no cautions, equivocations, reservations; and what she at once responded to, with enormous excitement, in my review, was the promise it seemed to give of a new audience, who would understand her wounds and her proud joy.

I went on to expand these points, which I still believe hold a profound truth, though the terms are deliberately simple and do not indicate the vast amount of problems which they raise. Then I came to *The Shadow of Cain,* with its theme:

our postwar world over which hangs the threat of destruction by nuclear fission. The division in man has reached gigantesque proportions, and the murder-madness of our society must face itself and be cured, or there is no hope. To express this point of conflict, Edith Sitwell uses a bare gaunt form, as if she were building up the ragged bones of a vast myth or making a terse political statement at a mass-meeting. There is little but huge space and clashing elemental lines of force (as in, say, Blake's *Urizen*); and yet in the midst of this desolation breaks a gush of life, a torrent of churning gold, which inundates the bleak chasmic space, and suddenly Man is there.

Thus, by spare means, she gets the desired effect of vastness and basic tension. She sees the social and personal issue in terms of Man's relation to Nature, which he has mastered only to bring upon himself this dreadful moment of choice. Man's scientific advance is not taken in abstract isolation, as it is by lopsided moralists who mourn that our scientific powers have outrun our moral resources. Rather, with true dialectical insight, Edith Sitwell sees the scientific struggle as the very essence of the moral struggle. In Man's relation to Nature, thus understood, we touch the ultimates of conflict, which are closer than breathing.

It was in statements such as this—as our later discussions made clear—that she felt I had been able to make explicit the meaning of her poem in a way which she could not do herself. And again in such statements as the following:

In this dim primeval universe of hers she depicts Man as a great fertilising force, who, grappling with the diverse energies of nature, has himself been rent, socially and spiritually, and who by the very meaning and direction of his conflict must strive for unity and the resurrection of brotherhood. And so, as the climax of the struggle, comes the moment when "the Primal Matter was broken, the womb from which all life began." And now is born the inescapable moment of final choice. "And in that hollow lay the body of our brother Lazarus . . ."

She develops her definition of this moment round the symbol *gold*. Gold which is light and the very quick of the transformative force; gold which is stability. And gold which in humanity has become the symbol of filth, of faecal horror and loss transformed into the money that murders and deforms. Gold that represents both guilt and redemption.

Out of this welter of conflicting meanings of *gold* she moves to her ending affirmation of Man fully resurrected into brotherhood. Man who overcomes the spiritual and social split expressed in nuclear fission, and makes it the source of a new fullness. "He walks again on the Seas of Blood. He comes in the terrible rain."

[3]

I don't recall in detail how I replied to Edith's second letter, but I tried to carry on further what I had written in the review about the reduction of men to things, to fragmented things, by the cash-nexus in its various economic, social and political forms, and about the incorrectness of treating mechanisation as a thing in itself, without relating it to the wider sources of dehumanisation. She replied, "It has given me a great deal to think about.

the rhythms of life *have* broken down: you are entirely right—slackened, loosened, like a pulse that is ceasing to beat. When we meet, I hope to have a talk with you about this. Inspired by what you say, I have started practising again, like a pianist—(I did that when I was young, practised technical experiments each day). But so far, owing to appalling headaches, I have only written three lines

> In the time of the wisdom of lilies, the brightness
> Of laughter and winds, I walked in the wet lanes
> Shining with Spring.

Not much to have done in three days . . . However . . . What you say is of great importance to poetry."

The three lines expressed her sense of grateful poetic resurrection. To gain a full sense of what the imagery implied we must look back to *A Young Girl* where the same complex is expanded to suggest the sense of inflooding life just before the moment of union comes, the breaking-down of isolation—"the white sun that is born of the stalk of a lily Come back from the underworld, bringing light to the lonely; Till the people in islands of loneliness cry to the other islands . . ."

I wrote her some account of the projected periodical *Arena*, which I had been discussing with John Davenport. We hoped to gather the best of postwar writing in Europe, in particular the work of those whom we called the Resistance Writers. We were thinking above all of France, where writers like Eluard, Aragon, Tzara, seemed to us to have remained true to the vanguard movements which begot them, and yet to have broken down the barriers between such movements and the mass of the people, thus deepening and universalising their work without loss of poetic individuality, without vulgarisation or lowering of standards. (I shall go further into these points when I come to the third section of this book.) Edith said that she was very excited by the project and hoped that our plans were going smoothly. She added, "You have a grand energy. By the way you have just received this unsolicited compliment from Tchelitchew, who is one of my closest friends." She had sent him a copy of my review. "And in reply he said in his very Russian English, 'Mr

Lindsay has such an extraordinary brain, a great understanding. He wrote with complete understanding in *Life and Letters* on Gibbeted Goddesses—where I find my ballet Errante, and the relation of this ballet to my Hide and Seek. It was *all* understanding.' " I did not know at the time the peculiarly important part that Tchelitchew had played in her life, or that nothing could have more confirmed her in her response to my review than such a tribute from him.

Meanwhile, at my advice she had read Lancelot L. Whyte's book, *The Next Development in Man,* and was much impressed. In the general analysis of this book I had found much wisdom, though I did not always agree with the terms of particular formulations; but what had overwhelmed me was its presentation of the unitary process of man and nature, and the way in which it tentatively set out new definitions and formulas of development—its rejection of Newtonian abstract symmetries and its search for the system of symmetry-asymmetry which real process reveals. All these aspects of the work affected Edith as strongly as they had affected me, and for the same reasons.

Edith also liked a note I had written for *Adam* on the *Selected Poems* of Edgell Rickword, which Greenwood of the Bodley Head had published at my suggestion. I remarked on the unfortunate abandonment of poetry by Edgell from the early 1930s. If he, with his strong Baudelairean sense of the City, had continued to compose and develop, Edith would not have been left alone in the world of poetry and we should not have been left defenceless against the take-over by the Audens and Spenders in the Thirties. As a result of that dereliction we in England had lacked the rich development of a true political poetry—by which I meant the sort of poetry represented by Eluard and Tzara in France. And so, when Edith returned to poetry in the war, she was picking up after a period of much confusion and flattening of the poetic impulse. "I wish I had any means of expressing what encouragement you have given me," she said.

The moment of our meeting was changed from 12.30 to 1.15, as she found she had to spend all the morning "in a most ridiculous way." At the same time she wrote to Ann repeating the invitation: an example of her careful courtesy. She explained that

the ridiculous way of spending the morning was in being photo-
graphed with Osbert for the benefit of her agents in the tour they
were making in the USA in the autumn; Osbert could manage no
other time. All the same, in her opinion, nothing could be more
absurd and damaging than such procedure.

A few days later she explained that she had been puzzled by
Tchelitchew's remarks as she had written them down for me.
Now with the aid of a magnifying glass and two sympathisers she
had made out above "my ballet Errante" the words "the theme
[of]." She herself had missed my essay on the Hanging Goddesses
in *Life and Letters,* apparently because at the time she was away on
one of what she called her Nursing Exploits: looking after some
member of the host of halt-blind-and-maimed with whom she
was always encumbered. "This is particularly maddening for me,
because at the time" (October 1946) "I was trying to study Greek
Tree-myths. However, this fire of light and knowledge is just as
wonderful for me now—just as inspiring." Meanwhile Tchelitchew had written again, saying that in my essay he had found
the myth of Errante, the worship of the Mother and of the Tree of
Life, which was closely connected with his painting *Hide and Seek*
(now in the Museum of Modern Art in New York). He said, "If
you see Mr Lindsay, tell him all this please. I can't thank him
more than to have given me the chance to understand myself."
Tchelitchew had been working on his ballet in late April 1933,
about the time that Lady Sitwell died; and this concurrence of
events had deeply affected Edith at the time. The fact that
Tchelitchew now insisted that my essay had at last enabled him
to understand his own work had in its turn an exciting effect on
Edith as of mysterious and fated interconnections. Reading my
essay now, she cried, "It is a great inspiration and excitement for
my mind, also. I only read it yesterday morning, but it will continue an inspiration—like a wild-fire—but *not* like the fires in the
poem I am sending you." This poem was *The Coat of Fire* which
she had composed some time before and now copied out for me
as an expression of the rather desperate loneliness and despair
which she had been afraid was finally blotting our her song.

My essay had dealt with the series of goddesses and heroines
in Greek myth and ritual who hanged themselves or were hung

upon a tree. Such figures were seen as forms of the mother-goddess; the myths and tales were commonly given a tragic twist by which the act of union or fertility was interpreted as murder or suicide; the series was ended by the male saviour-figures of Attis and Jesus, with the tragic twist supreme. I dealt with the cases in which dolls or masks were hung in the tree.

Edith was indeed moved by this account, which gave her a rationale for the way in which she had always by poetic insight penetrated through ritual and mythic forms into the concepts of pure natural process beneath them. Previously she had been drawing on her own deep intuition of the nature of the image, helped powerfully in momentary flashes by the thought of men like Goethe, Boehme, Oken. Now she felt that she had grasped all the relationships on a new level of consciousness. One of the poems in which her response to the essay on the Hanged Goddesses was openly shown was *The Madwoman in the Park:*

> The rubies of the heat high among the leaves
> Burn on Egyptian darkness; Reigns and Dynasties of light
> War in the leaves . . . There is no mask now of Erigone
> Or Helen, Dionysus, swinging from the branches,
> Moved by the young wind whose long dark hair
> Seems like the rain, the dying spirit of the air.
> There is only now the mask of our despair.

I had dealt with Erigone, Dionysus, Helen.

[4]

At last, on Wednesday 24 March, we met at the Sesame Club in Grosvenor Street, which was to be overwhelmingly the setting I henceforth associated with her. Once, when she could not get rooms there she stayed at Durrant's Hotel; and there were various meetings in rehearsal-rooms, in the Festival Hall, and so on. But the typical meeting was that in the Sesame. She often made half-apologies for living in a woman's club, but protested that here the food was excellent, unlike most such clubs. She kept up an assumption of totally ignoring the other residents, but she watched them carefully, and now and then with a proper display of caution would draw attention to some old lady and tell a caustic anecdote about her behaviour. With all her queenly manner she was acutely aware of others about her, and liked to know what was going on in the club. But she kept the other residents sternly at arm's-length, and always had ready one of her crushing retorts for the occasional member who tried to intrude on her privacy. Generally, however, her wish to keep to herself was well understood and respected; and with the staff she was uniformly on the best of terms.

Naturally there was no surprise in her person. Apart from our previous encounters, I knew her features thoroughly from photographs. Her large body rather lacked shape, but I was never at any time much aware of it except as the appendage of her strong and expressive face, with the prominent aquiline nose and the large cavities in which her shrewdly intent eyes were set—what she called her Plantagenet Face: an excellent phrase, for there was indeed a medieval quality about it, a mixture of gravity, fullness of life, repose, sharpness of spirit and earthy force. Nothing of beauty in the sense of smooth symmetries, but a great deal of beauty in the sense of a particular existence intensely and simply itself, constructing all its large and stubborn forms out of an inner grace in a graceless world. Apart from her face, it is only her hands, strong and beautiful, which I remember with vividness. The rather dead weight of her body was redeemed by the quiet life of her hands and the great force of life subdued to stillness in her sculptured heavy face. She looked best in dresses which, somewhat formless, had something of a medieval drape about them—or at least a Blakean notion of it—with heavy simple forms such as the gold barbaric ornaments which some wealthy American had made for her.

We had arrived too early, and filled in the time looking in the windows of antique shops before we walked in at exactly 1.15 and were despatched by the porter into the drawing-room where Edith sat against the wall near the door. I remember thinking that her brow was lower than I had thought. Then, as she rose, I was delivered from the confusion of trepidation and excitement that had been mastering me, and it seemed that we had always known one another. She had entered on her sixtieth year the previous September.

We talked of *Arena:* about what I felt had been the great cultural gains during the war, in so far as the idea of an antifascist war had gripped the people—Resistance poetry on the Continent, especially in France and Yugoslavia, and in England the vast increase of amateur activities in drama, dance, and music, with the response of hostels and provincial towns to CEMA groups, the Old Vic, Sadler's Wells Ballet, and so on. The new possibilities of writing based upon what was active and concrete in this release of the human spirit, something that made the ideas of peace and brotherhood cease to be abstractions and become at long last the valid material of art. (These were the enthusiasms that filled many of us at that time: Montagu Slater, Edgell Rickword, Alick West, and the others gathered round *Our Time,* which we had sought to make the mouthpiece of the new spirit—what we called, half in joke, half in delighted earnest, the Cultural Upsurge. The intellectual world remained totally ignorant that anything was happening. And still does not know what chances were then present and were lost.)[1] All that I said, Edith accepted without question as the expression of her own deepest ideals: what she had wanted and striven for all her life.

She was not in the least politically-minded in the superficial sense of that term. She always protested that she did not understand the Mechanism of Politics; and while such protests were in part the expression of a wish to protect herself bluntly against any appeals that would have drawn her into narrow partisanships, they were also largely true. She felt confident about making a moral judgement on any issue that came before her; she reacted with anger and outrage to all forms of cruelty and repression, and was much taken up with the movement against the deathpenalty; she knew where she stood on all essential points. But she felt that she did not understand the tactics and methods of the direct political field—or perhaps she simply suspected all the protagonists there of harbouring partial and unworthy aims under their large declarations. She was afraid of

[1] The only work dealing with this large and important development is still the compilation I made during the war, in the midst of it all, for the British Achievement series edited by Noel Carrington. I hope to tell the whole story in another book, with the climax in the big theatre conference.

innocently supporting any party, system, or group, and then finding that her name had been used to cover up activities which she abhorred. There was a mixture of innocence, craft and sound sense in her attitude.

But literature was a field where she felt quite sure of herself and her ability to distinguish that which was truly human from that which held the least falsity in its heart. She was ready to support all imaginative and deep-visioned writing, without concern for whatever political labels might be attached to its author. In this field she was unshackled of any fear of misunderstanding or being misunderstood. For instance, she had a total respect for Tzara, and would always, in any circumstances, have given her help in fighting for his work; but she would not therefore let herself be embroiled in any incidental political position of his. Later, the French writers of the Left, whom I had impressed with the quality of her poetry, tried to get her to attend some conferences; but though she was pleased at the invitations and always sent warm messages to Eluard and Tzara through me, she felt it would be a mistake to attend. She found graceful excuses for not going. Similarly, though much pleased, she declined an invitation sent through me to her and Osbert from the Union of Soviet Writers.

Such a project as *Arena*, however, she wholeheartedly welcomed and was ready to be identified with it in any way. I told her also of further works I had in mind: a book called *The Starfish Road, or the Poet as Revolutionary*. The theme was to be modern poetry: that is, poetry which truly reacted to the advent of the industrial town and all the steadily increasing alienations of bourgeois society. Poetry which, in this situation, sought to find the means of reasserting concrete human wholeness. Baudelaire as the first poet who understood what was going on, and rejected all romantic devices of escape from it or accommodation to it. The tradition he founded, with the varying forms it took as the conflicts matured, in Rimbaud, Mallarmé, Apollinaire. Then on to Futurism, Dadaism, and Surrealism, with a detailed examination of the contributions of Eluard and Tzara—and a glance at England after the breakdown of the Romantic Protest, with the rebirth of the true tradition in Edith and Dylan. In this development I saw Pound and Eliot as decoys and false prophets, who entered to some extent into the great tradition and at times produced work of considerable power or subtlety, yet who essentially sidetracked or distorted the many issues. Though there were passages by Pound and Eliot that Edith much admired, and though in earlier years she had attempted to invoke them as allies on the side which she championed, she many times in speech and on paper told me that she considered my analysis of them to be absolutely correct in her view. For personal and other reasons she was loth to be directly associated with it, but she encouraged me with all her might to make it and to print it.

I also talked on that first afternoon of a book I had been working on which was to be an elaboration of the *Loving Mad Tom* I had published in Fanfrolico days. Then an anthology of seventeenth-century Mad Poems, with a foreword by Graves and musical transcriptions by Warlock, it was now to become a much-extended collection of poems dealing with madness and various sorts of heightened sensibility, with a full commentary by myself. What would emerge was the way in which the later attitudes of the Romantic poets first of all appeared at the popular level. At the same time I was linking the seventeenth-century Madman with the medieval Fool.

The pattern of that first meeting was typical of most of my meetings with Edith. A preliminary drink and then lunch, during which the conversation was light-hearted and gossipy, with Edith revealing all that force of gay and caustic wit she could bring to bear on people she disliked or thought little of. Not that she altogether spared her friends. She was too clear-sighted, too keenly alive to the absurdity of the world, not to note their weak points or humorous aspects; but in their case her wit was tempered with affection, if only in the tone of her voice. On persons whom she came thoroughly to dislike, such as Grigson, she could lavish much power of inventive vituperation. But in such instances the person had ceased to be a mere limited individual and had been transmuted grandly into an archetype of stupidity or malevolence, playing his gross part in a world of Blakean myth. Often such villains were seen as having fallen out of their human estate and were reconstituted in grotesque animal terms. After the satisfaction of curiosity or vendetta at lunch, we retired to a corner of the drawing-room, or, if that room was crowded, one of the other rooms, and carried on serious discourse: that is, discussed poetry. If others were present at lunch, Edith uniformly asked Ann and myself to stay on after they had gone.

[5]

Before I continue with a detailed account of the intellectual relationship between Edith and myself, and the subjects that came into our serious discourse, I should like to develop what I have said of her personality and the sort of troubles and conflicts in which she continually entangled herself. Not that any sharp dividing line can be drawn between her personality and her poetry; and I hope that this point will become clearer as we go on. All the personal characteristics which I shall discuss shade off into aspects of her poetic self with its complicated struggle of liberation.

During the years of our close relationship I had a general idea of what life had been like at Renishaw, mainly drawn from Osbert's writings; but I did not realise how deeply and steadily she had suffered. She told me indeed much of what has now appeared in *Taken Care Of*. She said once that hardly a day passed in her childhood when her mother did not threaten to throw her out of the window or to commit suicide. Several times she repeated that kind of reminiscence with varying degrees of intensity, and at times was able to introduce her characteristic stoical humour. In 1959 she said, "If I'd been born in China, I'd have been exposed on a rocky mountain. But that's what I was." And yet, faced there with her vivid self, I did not fully assess what her anguished childhood had meant. That was a failure in imaginative comprehension on my part. For though she had forgiven her parents as far as a wronged person can forgive those who have offended, they still in many respects obsessed her. She could not forget their oppressive shadowing figures. I gathered that she had suffered much from bad tempers and tantrums, which were her inevitable reaction to such a family-world, her necessary outlets, and that they had left an indelible mark on her life. But again her book drove these points home. The raging lost mother and the lost megalomaniac father, hating one another in a frustrated system which gave them no valid release for their energies, and living in totally different worlds, had entered into being and created a ceaseless inner conflict. I saw enough of all this indeed to wonder at times how she had managed to preserve her sanity and her balance so well, torn as she was in such violently different directions. But as so often with important and adventurous creative intellects, the hellish discord from which she emerged dictated the terms of her creativeness. She had to surmount the discord and find its resolution, or she would be quite flattened or fly apart in pieces.

The struggle with her demented parents, carried on from her early years as her own personal drama in the depths of her spirit, became more than a struggle to maintain balance and to achieve a harmony or acceptance of life beyond all the infernal discords. It became a struggle with the world in which all distortions of the life-process, all stupidities and frustrating conventions, appeared as a new form of the parental attack. Hence her assault on the established world of culture; an assault which held in solution a total repudiation of all that world's social and political values. It was because I recognised this element in *Façade,* which linked it with certain aspects of Dada (especially Tzara's contribution), that she declared again and again that I understood her early poems as no one else had.

I realised from the poems themselves and from her remarks about her childhood (again clarified by *Taken Care Of*) that the beautiful surroundings in which much of her early years was spent had given her a deep response to nature. The happiness she had found in flower, tree, light, wind, water, had done much to offset the misery of family-life, driving her back on herself, but enabling her to identify that self with the movement of the elements, the colours and forms of plant and animal, the shapes and textures of growth. The elemental world revealed the freedom which was denied in her family-life; but it was not something seen as outside herself. She contained both the heaven and the hell; and if the family (and the society of which it was a refraction) seemed wholly hellish, yet the garden-heaven, realised as part of herself, was human too. And so there was the paradox that the so-called human world was essentially inhuman, while the so-called non-human world was human in its lovely hurries of growth, its rich freedoms. The potentialities she intuited in the sphere of nature gave her a criterion of human wholeness and happiness. No doubt something of this sort of thing can be found in all poets, all human beings; but the strength of the particular angle of vision I am sketching was peculiarly Edith's own. It provided the core of her imagery, with all its distinctive qualities, its elemental force and its concern for textural harmonies. Hence her continual ponderings on verse-textures, which at times seemed to make her treat poetry as a tissue of phonograms. The last thing she meant was such a reduction; and yet she felt driven to the textural analysis as the one sure escape from the false and tyrannous world. The larger significances of what she was saying were loud in her own mind, but she could not find the idiom which would have linked the textural analysis with all the implications of revolt it raised in her mind. What she recognised and hailed in the kind of criticism I made of her poetry, was precisely this enlarging idiom; and that was why she never ceased from saying that I spoke from the centre of her poetic process and was able to explain it as she herself could not.

At the outset, in my review in *Our Time,* I had made the link of *Façade* and Dada, and of the Sitwellian Fronde against the cultural establishment and the Dadaist demonstrations. We discussed this point many times; and she thoroughly agreed with my correlation. Indeed, in the end it helped her a lot; for it gave sense and significance to activities which she had in part come to regret. An aristocratic scorn had helped her to carry on her bourgeois-baiting, but she knew very well that in rejecting the bourgeoisie she was also rejecting a bourgeoisified aristocracy. (She responded so strongly to my *Men of Forty-Eight* in part because she liked the way in which it raised this sort of question in the characters of Boon and his Mary.) Though she felt to some extent ashamed of the element of personal petulance or neurosis in her youthful manifestation, she recognised the soundly-based element, and every now and then could not resist a certain unholy glee in the memories: as once for instance when she contrasted Sacheverell's retiring and unassuming character with what she called her own "vulgar violence and natural arrogance and swank."

She still felt the need to crush any person whom she considered guilty of presumption, complacence, or cruelty. Her life at the Sesame involved the keeping of the other old ladies in their proper places, and thus produced a certain tension, a fear that the correct limits would be transgressed. Woe betide the member who stirred the fear beyond the allotted point. Edith did not enjoy summoning up all her forces and making the necessary shattering reply; but she compelled herself to do it. As a result she might suffer a reaction for a couple of days. Several times I persuaded her to treat some critic's remark with the contempt it deserved. But when she felt the remark to be unduly stupid or insulting, she found it hard to ignore. She really wanted to be persuaded into ignoring it, but had to put up a fight for what she felt was the correctly chastising reply. A few times I could not persuade her.

But she was capable of the mildly crushing reply as well as the violent blow. In 1959 she mentioned that on the previous Sunday she'd appeared in a Brains Trust (on the BBC, I presume). Lord Wolfenden, the chairman, trying to draw her out, had asked amiably, "Are you interested in anything?" And she replied as amiably, "No, nothing." No further drawing-out attempts were made.

Of a young poet whom she had befriended and who then in her view had shown rank ingratitude when she was no longer of any use, she remarked, "A poet's virtues don't help him—on the contrary," and added contemptuously, "He's going round with his pack of boys. If he's sorry, why can't he write to me? Who could think I'm the sort of person who wouldn't accept an apology?" (This last comment was made in reply to another poet, then present, who tried to defend the ingrate as being too afraid to apologise for his behaviour.) Edith went on humbly, "Who am I to turn a deaf ear to the pleas of anyone whatsoever? It's an insult to me if someone thinks I'm mortally insulted and can't be approached." (A few minutes before she had been expressing murderous intentions towards noisy old Sesame-ladies, and had remarked of a dear friend and his lady-love, "She stinks, and he won't do anything about it. Surely he could find time now and then to give her a good scrubbing. It's not as if he were a really busy man.")

The many hardships and difficulties she had suffered in her youth and middle-age seemed to have left her in some respects stunned and numbed. They deepened her characteristic response of compassion, and gave her an unbreakable conviction of fellowship with all deprived and oppressed persons; but they did not break down her sense of personal isolation. She often said, "I am made ill by the thought of atrocities," and she felt deeply on questions of race, especially she had deep sympathy and liking for Negroes. She once said to me that she believed she had been born a poet, and nobody could be a poet who did not care about the great human problems. But, as I have said, she felt baffled by what she called the Mechanism of Politics. Because she held that a poet must be obsessed by the great human problems, she considered abstraction in any form of art to be an aberration. She several times indeed wrote of *Façade* as consisting of abstract poems or patterns of sound; but this, as I shall discuss later, was only a form of self-protection. Once I said, "If I were a painter, I should experiment with abstract forms and colours; but to be merely an abstract painter seems to me a kind of death."

She replied, "Yes, anyone who can be satisfied indefinitely with abstract experiments, is simply lacking in something—is just not all there." He revealed, she went on to say, a poverty-stricken sensibility in the face of the infinitely rich forms and manifestations of life in its full concrete mystery and human clarity.

With all her shrewdness and lack of squeamishness, she remained strangely innocent in certain respects. There was a virginal quality in her mind as well as a consuming curiosity about the sides of life she had never known or had known only from the outside. Hence the way in which she assiduously read such a newspaper as *News of the World*. (I believe that in her last years, as her creativeness lapsed, this aspect of her character grew much stronger; but, in saying this, I am not speaking from direct knowledge. At the end of the last lunch I had with her, as I was going, she turned to her secretary and said, "Get me some books of crime—horrors—or I'll go mad.") She was by no means lacking in experiences of common life. In the First World War she had worked in the Chelsea Pensions Office at 25s. a week; and throughout the 1930s (unless she was exaggerating in her accounts) she was hard-up, writing prose-works to make ends meet, as she devoted herself to looking after her old friend and governess, Helen Rootham, whose long mortal illness lasted from 1929 to 1938. Because of the invalid's need of close attention, Edith could not go with the family to Italy. She never went into details about all that to me, but I gained the impression that the family had behaved very badly. What she did often dilate on were the various odd lowlife characters with whom she came into contact during that period. She was pleased to have had such experiences, though she clearly had not enjoyed most of them at the time. Further, despite her genuine sympathy with the downtrodden and the deprived, she seemed to me to have always kept them at arm's-length, interested in the spectacle and admiring the stubborn element of endurance in the commonfolk she came to know—admiring also the manifestations of blind energy and hunger for life which she encountered, but standing always on the outer edge of the scene. The whole thing had dissolved into a sort of phantasmagoria, indistinguishable from her memories of Dickens' novels.

Tchelitchew, as far as I could make out, was the only person who had ever got behind her personal defences. I soon recognised a subtle change in her voice when she mentioned him, which made me look curiously at her face. There was a softening about it, especially round the eyes. For a swift moment there was a quality in her physical presence which I can only call girlish—though otherwise there is no term I should less apply to her.

The element of natural innocence was at times overlaid by an assumed innocence about the ways of the world. It was before her second American tour, I think, that she said she would like to have Paul Robeson associated with her in her appearances. She admired his voice and his character—as I know, because I had discussed with her my meetings with him in the Soviet Union in 1949. But in selecting him as her partner she also wanted to show her sympathy for the Negroes. I was present at a discussion when she went on for a long time insisting on the excellence of her idea, and seeming to be quite unaware of the implications of her appearing in the USA with a Negro, above all with one of such strong Left connections as Paul. (This was in the depths of the Cold War, it must be remembered, when Paul was already a marked man, though he had not yet been subjected to the thorough-going persecution he was soon to meet.) Geoffrey Gorer was the chief opponent of her plan, and argued on and on, saying everthing except: "You can't appear with a Negro—and don't you realise how politically compromised and compromising Robeson is." Edith went on blandly saying that she didn't see why she shouldn't ask Paul.

When she had looked at me, I said that she knew my opinion of Paul and that I thought her project a splendid one if it could be managed. I felt sure that even if Gorer didn't convince her, her agent in the USA would promptly quash the whole thing; and I was for the moment fascinated by Edith's attitude. At the end of the argument Edith still said that she was unconvinced, but I felt sure that she understood all the unstated points perfectly well, and that she knew she would have to surrender. However, by refusing to admit the existence of the political taboo, she felt that she achieved a kind of moral victory. She liked Gorer, who in this as in other matters kept on trying to make her see sense, realise the world she was in, behave correctly and realistically. But I felt that what he wanted to do was to knock the stuffing out of the essential Edith. In that he had no hope, and perhaps she enjoyed having a worldlywise councillor whose advice she did not mean to take. And yet in that she was to a slight extent deluded; for his effort to trim her into commonsense did have some effect. Her cautious side, which kept telling her not to get out of her depths in a treacherous world, was pleased to have a capable legislator at hand, who might go too far in his conformities but who was decidedly no fool.

There were indeed a great deal of matters that Edith thought it best to ignore. Partly because of that fear of getting out of her depths; partly because of a sort of magical conviction that by ignoring them she abolished them—or at least reduced their importance and relegated them to a lower world of hypocritical politicians and other professional batteners on the confusions, credulous stupidities, weaknesses and miseries of people. In 1950 she said to me, "Oh, how awful the state of the world is. Worse than ever. The state is, I think, almost entirely due to fear. Both sides seem incapable of believing that the other side at least means well—is not consciously and deliberately wicked." She, who had an acute sense of the world's evil, wanted to convince herself that evil was a kind of accidental possession. "I think," she went on, "Plato asked: Who would wish to be wicked? Some individuals do, I suppose. But I imagine it is rare, and even with individuals evil falls upon them as an illness falls upon them. Even Hitler, I imagine, did not begin by wishing to be wicked—it grew with power. Isn't this true?"

That was as close as she felt capable of coming to the political situation. Otherwise she wanted to abolish such things as the Cold War by treating them as vulgar aberrations unworthy of an intelligent person's notice. In the same way she did not like to refer directly to racial discrimination in the USA, but, keenly aware of it, wiped it out of existence by expressing warmly her feeling for the Negro. She praised my *Three Letters to N. Tikhonov* and my account of the Pushkin Celebrations in the USSR, but in tones that dissolved any political aspects into mere chance-ingredients intruding on matters of poetry.

And yet she unquestioningly accepted all my political and social analyses in works like *The Starfish Road,* though she did not explicitly refer to them. After Ann and I returned from Russia and the Ukraine in 1949, I talked to her at length about our experiences, above all about the conviction I had gained of people caught up in difficult yet joyous processes of transformation—something quite new, which had no parallel in our class-world. There was nothing dubious or questioning in her attitude to what I said; and she wrote *The Song of the Dust* in direct response. She called it several times "your poem," said that she thought it one of her best works, and was delighted when there was a chance of it being translated into Russian. Its essential meaning lay in the acclamation of the youth, the young spirit, of the USSR, and her own enhanced conviction of love.

This was the song I heard
When eastern light ripens the precious dew
In the bare rock and barren heart, and men pluck and
    bring home in stillness the great sapphire grape-clusters:

Beyond the ripening stillness
I heard the thunder of the growth of vines
And the great thunders in the veins of youth . . .

I do not want to limit the meaning of the poem to the specific relations that lay at its root; like all poetry with greatness in it, it has meaning at many levels; and there is here a Dionysian affirmation of life which bursts out with endless fiery overtones. And yet her response to the new life in the Soviet Union lies at its core, the dynamic moment of circumstance that moved her to write it. She accepted the direct reference to the USSR, for she accepted what I wrote of the poem in *The Starfish Road*: "She moves away from the exploration of the regressive forces; and out of the deep night of quest, of intuitive discovery of the rhythm of life, she rises to the clear morning vision of the new life in the lands where the forces of youth and freedom are stirring." She was happy to have me say that for her, but she would never have said it for herself.

In later 1951, at my request, she signed the Authors' World Peace Appeal. She said that she trusted me there was no political significance in the act. I felt a certain disquiet, and said that there were some persons for whom the word peace was a red rag, but that there was in my opinion nothing that could be described as party-politics in the matter. A. E. Coppard, it is true, had done much to start the Appeal, I think, after a meeting of the World Peace Movement. But he had soon dropped out; and though there were some Communists like Montagu Slater and myself involved, there were far more Pacifists, Quakers, and Labourites among those running it: for example, Alex Comfort and Naomi Mitchison. The Appeal was the one genuinely broadly-based peace-movement in Britain before CND. I attended a large number of the committee meetings, and I can certainly say that I do not recall a single occasion on which any sectarian advantage was sought or pressed by anyone. And some of the subcommittees, such as that dealing with Children's Literature (at that time American comics of an incredible foulness were pouring into the country), did very good work. I felt then that there could be no duplicity in asking Edith to sign an Appeal which a very wide body of our intellectuals, from Dylan Thomas to Herbert Read, had signed in all good faith; and I did not expect that any use would be made of her name except to include it among the hundreds of others.

However, it seems that some stress was given to her name on a leaflet. I do not know how this leaflet was composed and issued, and I never saw a copy of it. (There were several different sections, covering films, children's literature, and so on, with considerable autonomy. I think it was the Film Section which made the particular use of her name.) The leaflet was produced when she applied for a visa to the USA and caused her some trouble. She was extremely annoyed, but did not blame me. Rightly or wrongly, she was angry with a writer who she said wouldn't stop her "political cat's-cradling." (The leaflet was first brought to her attention by someone whose name she did not tell me, though I can guess who it was. This person insisted that she should order her solicitor to take the matter up; and she did as she was told. At the time she was suffering from double influenza.)

This was the only time that she was drawn into any action by me; and doubtless she felt that it confirmed her in her resolve to keep far removed from all forms of public involvement. As I have pointed out, she was more than ready to have my kind of political analysis of her work. That form of approach lay at the whole root of *The Starfish Road,* which she passionately desired to see in print and which she was anxious to support in every possible way. The book explicitly defined her work as belonging to the revolutionary tradition I discussed—a tradition which began in the dissidence of Baudelaire, his deep grasp of the alienating forces at work in the new kind of city-life initiated by industrialism, which reached open defiance in Rimbaud, and which then, via Apollinaire, developed into the mature comprehensions of Tzara and Eluard. She was proud to believe that she stood at the side of the latter two poets, and was ready, by writing an introduction for *The Starfish Road* and by defending it in any other possible way, to show that she fully accepted all the implications of this analysis. Whatever I wrote about her on these lines, in the reviews in *Our Time* and *Adam,* and in the essay I later wrote for *Life and Letters,* she enthusiastically welcomed. Yet she herself was quite incapable of making such statements. She had built up her own kind of defiant positions, based on her notion of phonograms and of organic correspondences, and she feared to fall into narrow formulations, leading to all sorts of misunderstandings and controversies, if she once tried to make a direct social or political statement. She came as close as she dared in her prose-work, *I Live Under a Black Sun,* with its preliminary quotation from Krupskaya about Lenin: "And observing these howling contrasts in richness and poverty, Ilyich would mutter through clenched teeth . . . 'Two nations.'" She could easily have used the wellknown remark by Disraeli about two nations, but preferred to turn to Lenin to strengthen her position. This neglected work of hers, published in 1937, is of great value in elucidating her use of imagery. By transposing Swift and his anguish into her own period, she brings out her own self-identification with him and her total rejection of the society of war around her. (Yeats showed a deep understanding in saying, "When I read her *Gold Coast Customs,* I felt that something absent from all literature was back again, and in a form rare in literature of all generations, passion ennobled by intensity, by endurance, by wisdom, we had it in one man once. He lies in St Patrick's now under the greatest epitaph in history.") *Under a Black Sun* reveals the desperate pessimism which was one aspect of her reaction to the contemporary scene; it defines the world of *Gold Coast Customs* on a larger scale without the belief that "the Fires of God go marching on." It represents the complete night of the soul which made possible the return of light and hope in some of the war-poems, in *The Shadow of Cain,* and finally—the highest point—in *A Song of the Dust.* (Incidentally, it reveals also the fear of madness which accompanied the violence of her reactions and revulsions, and the isolation she felt as she penetrated deeper into the night of alienation.)

The nearest she herself came to attempting the sort of analysis I made of her work was in the broadcast which she used as introduction to her *Collected Poems* of 1957. There she cited part of my essay for New Directions and made some comments of her own on *Gold Coast Customs*. But she still feared to make the final correlations which she wanted me to make for her; and she fell back mainly on her exposition of phonograms and on generalisations about symbolic correspondences. I had badly let her down by not publishing *The Starfish Road,* for reasons I shall later discuss. If I had done so, I believe that Edith would have stood by it as she had vehemently wanted to do. But the statement did not appear; and during those years she was getting at last more and more of the public recognition for which she had long waited and craved. She became a Dame of the British Empire in 1954, and had already received honorary degrees from the Universities of Leeds, Durham, Oxford, and Sheffield. (She used to put on the back of her letters her name and a triple "D. Litt."; but though I was ready to address my letters to Dame Edith, I ignored the D. Litts. she would also have liked.) She enjoyed all her honours; and though I would not suggest for a moment that they swayed her from her central positions, they did make it yet more difficult for her to state directly the social and political consequences that were implied by her poetic imagery. The illness of Osbert drove her further back into herself.

In this situation it was inevitable, I can see, that she would be converted to the Roman Catholic Church. Indeed, from the time she wrote *Gold Coast Customs* there must have been a strong urge to take this step. In that poem she had for the first time fully and plainly realised the terrible range and depth of the truths she had been setting out in her earlier poems. She brought her intuitions sharply and fiercely down to earth; and thus for the first time a definitive statement of all that was implied by the alienating process of bourgeois society entered our poetry. A great deal of this realisation came through the workings of her own mind in the creation of her poems, and through her response to Swift and Blake and to the tradition of Baudelaire and Rimbaud. I do not think that any directly political writings had affected her. The 1844 Manuscripts of Marx had not yet appeared in Moscow in their difficult German text. She had however read a good deal of

Hegel and the German Nature-Philosophers. She told me that the originating image of the *Gold Coast Customs* was the spectacle of some Hunger Marchers led by a blackened man who was jestingly acting the part of a skeleton or deathfigure; she felt that she was looking at a modern Dance of Death, and the fused image of London and the Gold Coast, expressing the final deprivation and dehumanisation of man, was born in her mind. (She had probably seen one of the many contingents swarming from all over England into London in early 1929.)[1]

Her thinking, as I have stressed, was emotional and intuitive rather than political and intellectual in the narrow sense. She was much taken up with the idea of revolutionary fires consuming a rotten society and clearing the earth for a better and cleaner growth; but always thought of the outbreak of fire as a sort of spontaneous combustion from below—something inevitable and finally necessary for the assertion of justice in the universe, but blindly violent and frightening. She still thought rather as Carlyle and Dickens thought. The Fires of God and the trumpet of the avenging angel, not the activity of organised persons, were what brought about the destruction and renewal. And so the image of Christ was central in her concept of revolutionary change, representing the final justice and harmony to be won, with Lazarus and Dives as the two social opposites whose blinkered and ferocious opposition brought about the impasse of violence miraculously resolved by Christ—by the reassertion of human unity on a new level. The very existence of Lazarus and Dives was the crucifixion of Christ. The resurrection of Lazarus was both a sort of mock-rebirth or parody of Golgotha, and a prefiguring of Christ's resurrection. It expressed the impotence of any efforts to change society and individual unless the full dialectical pattern were involved. (In political terms it represented the effort to achieve socialism without the ending of the class-system and the decisive elimination of the old power-centres. It scathingly expressed all that has come to be called the

[1] This, the Second National Hunger March, began from Scotland on 23 January 1929, in blizzard-weather. Contingents from all over England soon after began their converging marches on London. The First March had been in late 1922. An excellent account of these and similar demonstrations will be found in Wal Hannington's *Unemployed Struggles*, 1936.

Welfare State. That State was here seen as the worst possible thing that could happen to men, producing the limit of human distortion and spiritual disease.) In the same way, the system of Dives, the effort to maintain the rule of property and power in the traditional terms, could lead only to a total sterility and decay. Hence the insistence in *The Shadow of Cain* that the two seething and fermenting golds can only beget leprosy (increase alienation) unless they precipitate the death and rebirth of Christ.

The profoundly dialectical basis of her thought, here apparent, had been present to some extent from the outset of her poetic activity. Hegel and Blake did much to strengthen it and to make it more explicit, but ultimately it came from the deep poetic workings of her own spirit, the fullness with which she laid hold of reality—and by reality I mean something simultaneously human and natural, social and organic, personal and cosmic.

Edith then had based her whole outlook on the hope of revolutionary change without any notion whatever how that change could come about. She responded to the conflicting forces of her world with a conviction that they represented a worsening damnation unless the total transformation was somehow attained—unless her Christ was fully drawn into the historical process. But she held to these views solely by an act of faith, of poetic faith. She hung suspended over an abyss of fear and horror (existent Mankind: Lazarus and Dives), sustained in her desperate position only by her faith in the Christ in men, in their ultimate need to cast aside all limiting factors, all divisions rooted in property and power, and to be satisfied with nothing less than a pure integrated humanity.[1] (*Street Acrobat,* the poem she gave me for *Arena,* expressed her awareness of the balancing-act she carried on—though the Acrobat here is also the divided-man who ceaselessly swings between the outer and inner worlds without being able to integrate them.)

Hence the considerable solace I was able to provide her in the years 1948–53. She accepted my political ideas in their general

[1] Her rebirth as a poet after 1940 was linked with her turning more and more to long lines in which she could express a deepened element of meditation and a new vastness of scope. Walt Whitman, whose poems she estimated very highly, was an important influence, both technically and emotionally. She said to me once that the capacity to wield the long line was the greatest test of poetic control and power.

bearings, though she could not follow me into direct partisanships. Looking back, I see clearly that I should have been able to carry our relationship beyond this point. But I failed to do so. The failure was wholly mine; for after the way in which she had whole-heartedly backed my formulations, I should have gone ahead to publish *The Starfish Road* and struggle further for the worldview there expressed.

The lonelier and more desperate she grew, the more she needed to rely on her image of Christ, which steadily (for her) drew in more and more of life—which became in time all that mattered in life, all that had significance or ultimate reality. The activity of Christ (the concrete human universal), which she had intuited in both poetic expression and social change directed towards the actualisation of human unity, became solely poetic activity. And as such she could not sustain it. She had to find afresh the point of reference outside herself. If that point could not be found satisfactorily in historical process, it had to be found in the immediate Christ of ritual, of the Churches. And that meant in the Catholic Church; for in no other Church of Western Europe was there a traditional and universalising basis which she could find intellectually relevant. (Under different circumstances, the Orthodox Church would have similarly served.)

In saying all this, I am not trying to belittle Edith's decision. If in one sense I see it as a failure of nerve, in another sense I see it as a step to strengthen and consolidate her deep sense of human unity—the only step she could take if she did not see her way to become a conscious Marxist.

In begetting what I have called a failure of nerve, there were personal elements of despair and anger, apart from her general feeling of isolation and lack of understanding or appreciation. A certain person had shamefully let down someone whom she loved, at a crucial moment in the latter's life. She said to me, "If I had not become a Catholic, I should have murdered him." There was certainly a genuine and deeply-felt emotion in her words. But I am not suggesting for a moment that her conversion can be reduced to a need for finding a sure support outside herself in a moment of shattering grief and emotional disorder.

In our discussions on the matter (which I think began about April 1955) she always took the position that in the last resort there was no choice for anyone facing up to the realities of our world except Catholicism or Marxism. She was naturally aware of antagonistic elements in the two creeds or worldviews; but she did not consider these a necessary part of the situation. The last thing that could be said to have moved her to Catholicism was anti-Communism; on the contrary it was precisely what Catholicism shared with Communism that attracted her. Without owning any programme or thought-out idea of a final harmony between the two systems, she felt that the image she had fostered of the unifying Christ was not only capable of finding its point of harmony with the struggle for a classless society, but also *must* find that point—or else be proved a lie. There was no conflict between the immediate apprehension of Christ and the struggle to actualise human unity in the sphere of history.

I have mentioned that, despite her deep sense of the reality of evil, she remained often naive and simple-minded when brought up against the world of facts. Once I stupidly drew her notice to some photos of British soldiers, one of them an officer, holding heads that had been severed by the headhunters who were used in fighting the Communists in the Malayan jungle. She strongly denied that Englishmen could be guilty of such things; the photos worried her and she several times returned to them, trying to prove there was some optical illusion. Yet in other respects she often took for granted that things were moving as viciously as they could in the worst of all possible worlds (that of the alienating process); and she gladly accepted the vision of evil in writers like Faulkner or Céline as well as others less-talented. And at the same time she could be sensibly realistic. She said to me when we were discussing the Khrushchev disclosures of 1956, "Neither Communism nor Catholicism are disproved by the existence of bad Communists or bad Catholics." Though that fact did not exonerate one from needing to expose and get rid of the bad members of a movement or group, who used the noble words for the purpose of power-politics or personal ambition.

Naturally she discussed only generalities with me in this matter; but once or twice, when a young Catholic poet whom she was helping was present, the conversation drifted on to lesser matters of religious gossip. She and the young poet discussed Jesuits and their ways in somewhat unflattering terms; and Edith told of a Jesuit from Glasgow, who unceremoniously invaded the Castello di Montegufoni when she was there, and who, noting the profusion of works of art, tried to make up a bundle on the spot for the adornment of the church with which he was connected—I think as priest. In Edith's account he was an uncouthly pushful fellow, and had to be sat heavily upon, though even then he was not reduced to any undue state of contrition for his bad manners. (It struck me that with a certain Jesuit democracy of spirit he might have thought the artworks would be more useful in illuminating the Glasgow slums than in decorating the lonely Castello.) Another time Edith discoursed of "a maddening sacerdotal ass behaving like a divinely-inspired district-visitor setting to rights a very bad slum." This priest had interfered in some way in her affairs. Again, in 1959, after enthusiastically discussing Sacheverell's recent prose-work and his refusal to accept any religious positions, she said, "I oughtn't to approve as a Christian, but then I'm not a good one. I don't go to church often."

To sum up then, it seems to me that while Christ originally appeared in her poetry as a necessary image of human unity, of the resolution of the omnipresent alienating process, she came to feel more and more the need of the image as an external reality, outside as well as inside her poetry. It was no longer sufficient to feel that somehow, sometime, the drama of her imagery would become externalised in world-history. To bring her to this point, a multiple series of pressures were required: increasing age and lack of resilience, deep uncertainties and anxieties, a sense of having quite failed in poetic impact (despite the minor tributes and honours that came her way).

[6]

She was always heavily aware of her body, I think. Once I said to her, "As Nietzsche remarked, one is young as long as one isn't aware of the weight of one's body." She gave me a blank stare, with no flicker of response. Something unusual in a person who

84

normally showed herself so keenly aware of all the overtones and undertones of any comment. Only later, when I read her account of her childhood—how she suffered from a curvature of the spine and weak ankles, so that her parents handed her over to an orthopaedic surgeon and she was long imprisoned in what she called a Bastille of steel; even her nose was tormented, till breathing was difficult, and the muscles of her back and legs were semi-atrophied—only then did I understand the comparative deadness of movement in her body in general beside the life in her hands and face. She had never been unaware of the weight of her body.

Oddly, in one of the few letters of mine of which I have kept a copy, I find the phrase of Nietzsche repeated. (The verses were an inscription in a copy of a work on local archaeology I had written, *Discovery of Britain*, 1958):

> It's a long time. The clotting universe
> settles and drags like bats on the mind's rafters,
> befouling the table of hospitality;
> and *Time* grows palpably, maliciously,
> with age, no longer an unresistant medium
> in which we soar or drop or hang suspended;
> it darkens, viscously, and clogs the veins
> of thought; and we are aware of *Hyle,* Matter,
> the thickening woodland treacherous with dogs
> that Plotinos knew.
>   I scribble this in metre
> because a certain beat can charm the snake
> whose swaying head keeps all thoughts directed
> warily outward, while the thorns and weeds
> tangle behind the eyes and cut us off
> from the one spring of renewal;
> and I am tired of the presumptuous bones
> clad in no resurrection, rattling in graveyards
> of busy prose and darkening repetition.
> I want a world of bodies before they grow
> aware of their weight, and all the flowers are sudden
> as thoughts clasht from the dialectic cymbals:
> something where nothing was, yet not surprising
> because there is still no break between chance and choice.

Edith hated the term poetess. She also insisted that writing serious poetry was a work of severe and sustained physical strain as well as spiritual concentration; a great stamina was needed, of a kind that woman did not usually possess. And she declared that "in the past, with the exception of *Goblin Market* there has not been a technically sufficient poem written by a woman.[1]" (She forgot Sappho. But one of the things she often regretted was her lack of knowledge of ancient Greek. She used to say to me, "What a great refreshing source of thought and feeling you must find in the Greeks. I feel what they must have been, but cannot know it.") Certainly during the years I knew, when her strength was failing, she found the struggle to write poems very exhausting. "I have finished tinkering about with that poem, and my mind is no longer acting."

She found standing for any length of time a wearying business. In mid-1949 she said that she had spent the whole of a month "on her feet," getting at Tchelitchew's letters for Yale University, and was consequently worn-out. She told me once of the agony she suffered as a girl when left alone with some minor member of the royal family, whose title I forget, but who was as shy and young as she was. So the minor piece of royalty did not think of telling her to sit down, and Edith, unable to withdraw, remained speechless and suffering on her feet for an interminable length of time till some rescuer appeared and broke the spell.

When she fell down, she could not get up again unaided. Many accidents that prostrated her in this uncomfortable and undignified position occurred, of which I recall two—both at Montegufoni. In 1956, as she was on her way to lunch, she slipped on the waxed floor of the drawing-room, and on account of her bodily stiffness she landed with a crash full on her face, which was badly cut and bruised. Osbert came in with a guest to find her stretched on the floor and spattered with blood, her head on his secretary's knee, with the young butler and his wife holding ice to her head. Again in 1960 she had two accidents,

[1] At a lunch in July 1959 to which I took my niece Cressida, as my wife Meta (with our son only a bit over three months old) could not come, she talked to Cressida about poetry, praised *Goblin Market* and stressed the inequality of Emily Dickenson. Speaking of those Victorian days, she added, "All right for the men. They walked on our faces with their boots then."

with the result that she could only sit up in bed, when propped up by somebody's arm and suffering agony. In the second accident she came down flat on her spine on a stone floor and lay there for five hours, unable to move, until someone chanced along and found her.

During all the years I knew her, she was fighting against some illness, plagued by some nuisance, or distracted by some call on her sympathy. In April 1949 she was complaining about a long preface to write and two books to correct while she was suffering from a violent cold accompanied by sinus. The sinus was caused, she thought, by the lack of electric light at Renishaw. The rooms were so dark that she had to correct the proofs by a dim oil lamp—"such as is used, presumably," she commented, "by the Esquimaux—no wonder they look as they do." The cold was so bad that every time she sneezed she expected to find the windows blown out. (When she was suffering from a cold, she gave up writing letters, as she had a terrible dread of germs and feared that she would infect the person to whom she wrote.) She said that she received the first issue of *Arena* by second post just as she was going out to be boiled alive in aid of her rheumatism.

When in New York in 1950, she had a wretched time. First she thought she was getting flu, then found it was only a chill. But she sprained her foot and then by making a false movement she strained every muscle in her back, she declared. She went on working but couldn't put her feet on the floor. An osteopath was called in and he cured her. But promptly a man whom she insisted was well aware that he had influenza visited her and transferred his germs to her. For several days she had a temperature of 102°, then was left with "every kind of complication," including a poisoned gland that had to be removed. As soon as the infection was gone, she continued working—and all the while, she told me, she was in great mental distress. In August that year her eyes were so overworked by proof-reading that whenever she took up a book her eyes poured with tears. In November a tiresome young man with a violent cold came up and breathed on her, so that she was laid up for over a fortnight with acute bronchitis, which was thought to be turning into pleurisy. Pleurisy did not eventuate, but the tissues of her right lung were attacked. She remarked to me, "I must say that the American nation, much as I love it, is uncivilised in the way it goes on breathing cold germs on defenceless people." Then, remembering her similar complaints about English folk, she added, "Still, our nation is nearly as bad, if it comes to that."

It was later that year, or perhaps in 1951, that she said she had had bronchitis four times in three months and had been coughing all night, with damage to the tissues of her right lung. The illness burst on her like a bomb in the middle of the night—to use her own phrase—and she fled from the Sesame, at the doctor's orders, to Renishaw. Ann and I had been asked to lunch with her the next day; and as there was no time to get in touch with us, Osbert came along and acted as the Sesame-host. For three weeks, Edith later said, she was lying in Purdah with her mouth wide open all the time. Three weeks? she mocked at herself. Surely that was a reminiscence of Elinor Glyn.

In 1951 she had an accident in the USA—I think in New York. She tried to dodge out of the way of a motorcar that had come quickly round a corner; but with her stiff frame she failed, caught her foot in a tramline and hurtled across the road, eventually falling with the usual crash—her head under a motorcar that was slowly backing. Luckily the car didn't hit her head, but her knees were badly cut. In February, her lung was again being threatened with bronchitis, and then a tropical bug of some kind got her in Mexico. She felt sure that she was nearly dying. When she arrived back in England in April she said that she had been ill all the time in the USA and now she was again on the verge of bronchitis. In late 1952 she told me how she had gone off to Italy in haste after a series of rows in which she had been innocently involved by a relation; then she injured the hinges of her right knee and was in too great pain to work. When she mustered the courage to stand up, she had to stay still for five minutes in anguish before she dared to move. The one compensation had been that the jungle of zinnias in the garden, when she stood in its midst, was neck-high.

This sort of thing went on all the while. She was always just recovering from, or about to succumb to, attacks of bronchitis, influenza, fibrositis. But I fear that at the time, though I sym-

88

pathised with her, I did not really do it enough. When someone is continually complaining about illness, yet does it with a stoical dry humour and appears in vigorous health and full of energy on all the occasions when one meets her, one tends to write off the complaints or at least to treat them as highly exaggerated. No doubt Edith did exaggerate at moments, and at moments used her illnesses as excuses for not doing things she disliked or lacked the time for. But I now feel sure that what she said or wrote was substantially true, and that she maintained her high flow of spirits, her eager interest in all matters of poetry and thought, at the cost of a ceaseless and wearying struggle. That she lived so long and managed to keep working over so much of her years, under such difficulties, is the proof of her tremendous toughness of body and spirit, her determination to carry on till she had completed the full arc of her poetry in its organic development.

The nuisances and the sufferers with whom she was surrounded gave her hardly less trouble than her own body. I do not think there was ever a meeting, after we became intimate, when there was not a story, or two or three stories, of pests and infesting fools. The plaguing individuals nearly always had some kind of malady, mental or physical; otherwise Edith would have had no mercy on them. But as things were, harassed and pitying, she was perpetually in semi-hiding or momentarily emerging to attend to the petitioners. At times she explained the reason for their pleas. The sufferer had once worked at Renishaw or had come into Edith's orbit during the penurious years when she nursed Helen Rootham. But more often the person afflicted with imbecility or illness seemed to have come mysteriously out of some limbo for no other purpose than to haunt her.

I give a few examples. In May 1949, a person whom she called "an awful new lunatic" had fallen in love with Osbert without ever having even seen him, and was threatening to come and live at Renishaw. Edith said that she was writing by every post with declarations that the only alternative to the marriage was suicide; and Edith was replying that she was an hysterical ass. In July, as she was struggling to finish two books and was working from morning to night, every girls' school in the country was asking her to come and give away prizes. Late in

1949 she and Osbert found out by chance that Grey de Ruthyn, who, two miles away, was considered their nearest neighbour, was desperately ill with pneumonia and had no one to look after him but a doddering old housekeeper. He had been left for five delirious nights with no one to attend to his fire or give him a drink. Osbert at once called in a specialist. In 1949–50 she said that she had been half dead with exhaustion over Christmas after shouting out *Gold Coast Customs* for two and a half hours daily, with two performances at the end, and then she had found herself caught up as buffer between two combatants in a really appalling row—the whole thing steeped in what she called the most ghastly misery and misunderstanding. (Later in 1952 she was complaining about the lack of a microphone at a performance—of which of her works I have failed to note; the heat and the irritation affected her so much that she almost fainted in the midst of the whole thing.)

Early in January 1950, she complained that she was being badgered to go and lecture in the north of Skye, travelling alternately by train (with sixteen changes) and boat, or else to attend local sales of work. She was further being plagued to death by Japanese, composers, Indians, and an old woman who had mistaken her for the widow of her father's fifth cousin, and who in the past (at the time of Lady Sitwell's imprisonment) said that she couldn't invite Edith into *her* mother's house. Next came persecutors described as a synthetic Indian and a Swiss female explorer who was plodding after her in the most remorseless manner, a kind of *primum-mobile* fidget. In London she had to look after Evelyn Weil, whom she expected to be soon stone-deaf, as well as two penniless women (one of whom had had her gas cut off). Edith was spending much time in trying to find jobs for the luckless pair.

But though Edith poked fun at herself and her suffering friends or dependants, she clearly did get a certain satisfaction out of attending them in their broken-down and hopeless situations. Her most characteristic emotions were, I think, uncertainty about herself and compassion about others. She also felt strongly the emotion of *noblesse oblige*. As I shall mention later, she was ready to cut short a London visit and inconvenience herself in order to attend the wedding of a girl at Renishaw. At one time in 1952 a dear friend had had a dangerous operation; then on the day that Edith heard she would recover, news came that the woman who had been housekeeper at Renishaw for thirty-five years (the wife of Osbert's soldier-servant) was lying mortally ill, in great pain and delirious, nursed by her husband. She died. About the same time Edith heard of another friend dying. She wanted to rush back to Renishaw but couldn't. (At this period for some months the only work she could do was on *The Road to Thebes*, a poem which she discussed at all its stages with me.)[1]

But sometimes the Renishaw connections too were mere botherations. Edith was plagued by the daughter of a nursery maid who had left Renishaw when Edith was eleven—about sixty years before the time she discussed the matter with me. Edith had never seen the woman all those years, but was still pestered by her. When Sir George died, she had written to say that she would at once come and live at Renishaw in order to help Osbert and Edith, adding that she would bring her bike and run messages. Where to? Edith asked. To heaven, presumably. During the war, the daydreaming woman had been, in her own account, engaged to a Lieutenant Dick Strong, who was awarded the VC but died in action before he could receive it. Edith diagnosed an addiction to Girls' Weeklies.

Evelyn Weil, a harmless distracted old lady, was the only one of countless lost-souls whom we met. Edith treated her with a firm and kindly hand, and could not have been more patient. But with her the account of the pests and the pensioners shades off into that of the friends and acquaintances we met at the Sesame.

A landscape looks different when seen from the top of a hill from what it did when one was moving through it and able to see only bits at a time. Death has the effect of throwing the whole personality of the lost one into a stark and unified perspective. Now, and only now, I realise how deep was the fear that Edith felt of life, her uncertainty, and her lack of any stable conviction in her work. She was in essence the rejected one, unable to believe

---

[1] In 1959 Edith said that on every London visit she always took out to dinner one of the servants who had waited on her for many long years.

that there was any place for her in life or art; she suffered from a total doubt of herself. And this was the agonising anxiety that she wrestled with, from her earliest childhood on.

But fear and doubt, with the sense of complete estrangement, could not by themselves beget a poet. She was excluded, but she knew what she was excluded from; she knew the paradisaic garden of transformation and communion. She struggled always to regain the garden. Like Tzara, but in her own way, she saw poetry as action; and her deep anxiety gave her both a passionate sympathy with all who in any way suffered her own fate of exclusion from the sources of life, and a fierce need to fight against the excluders, who battened on suffering as the necessary material feeding their hungers for power and privilege.

She desperately needed her poetry to be understood and evalued critically but positively. If these facts are borne in mind her fascination with the lost ones of the world can be properly put in focus, as well as what I think I may call the drama of our relationship and of my failure to carry out the full championship I had offered and meant to carry out—above all my failure to publish *The Starfish Road*.

[7]

I am sure that no emotion went deeper in Edith than did pity. At one lunch there was a third guest, a rich American woman, for whom Edith apologised aside to us. A plump gaudy harmless aimless prattling person, who seemed to own not the least link with the world of Edith's poetry except perhaps as a rather minor and incompetent understudy for Lady Bamburgher with her interest in the latest grin, the latest game, the latest love, and with that foul plague-spot, her romantic heart. Edith had been unable to get rid of her, not liking to hurt her feelings. So we all went to a base-ment studio where Edith was trying out her speaking part in the setting of *Gold Coast Customs*. Humphrey Searle wasn't there; the pianist was, I think, merely someone provided by the musical publishers in whose basement we were. Edith read the verse with her usual eloquence and rhythmic control, till we came to the passage:

What is that whimpering like a child
That this mad ghost beats like a drum in the air?
The heart of Sal
That was once a girl . . .

Her voice began to break. She tried to carry on, but burst into tears, sat down and wept. It took some time before she was quite herself again. Lady Bamburgher made clucking noises of helpless sympathy, and herself sniffed. "I should have read the poem through aloud to myself," said Edith at last, "a couple of times before I came along. Osbert always advises me to do that. It saves one from being caught up in a sudden leap of emotion like that. But I didn't have time."

"No, of course not," said Lady Bamburgher. "I quite understand." She opened and shut her bag, and relapsed into her death-slack ease, settling her face into the correct grimace of someone receiving a dose of the higher culture. Ann and I said nothing. The reading continued, with no more tears.

Mostly the lunches or dinners were uneventful. Usually we saw Edith on her own; but now and then we were drawn into one of her larger entertainments. Once X. came, bringing his newly-married wife. Shy and talented, with the best of public-school manners, he had married an Irishly talkative impulsive woman, and was obviously and mutely happy about it. There were several others present. Mrs X. had clearly felt that the meeting with Edith was something of an ordeal, and had fortified herself against the occasion, so that she was a trifle boisterous and in her voice bogmist and whisky were mixed a little hoarsely. I had not met her before, but she had known Phil well and was relieved at finding at least one straw at which she could clutch as the deep waters of the event closed over her head. At the long dinner table Edith had put her next to Spender, but after a glance at his scared face she quietly got me to change my place and I sat on Mrs X.'s other side. Mrs X. began to enjoy herself and to feel that she had unnecessarily feared an encounter with dragons, but she still kept an eye on Edith at the head of the table. Somebody turned the conversation on Kenneth Patchen and described him as fat and bedridden, a poet in difficulties, who deserved help. Edith then remarked of his book, *Memoirs of a Shy Pornographer*, "But surely if one is a pornographer, the last thing one wants to be is shy."

Mrs X., whose ears had pricked up at the mention of pornographers, was so surprised and relieved at Edith's comment that she burst into merry laughter and could not repress a shout. "Edith Sitwell says if you're a pornographer, don't be shy about it!" She was so enchanted indeed at such a pearl of wisdom, which somehow was not the sort of thing she had expected from Edith, that she kept repeating it loudly for the rest of the dinner, while Spender squirmed. She felt that such an admission of common humanity among highbrows, could not have enough publicity. Edith smiled appreciatively.

Upstairs, after dinner, she told me again what Edith had said, and for some reason which escapes me, she launched into an interminable anecdote about Napoleon and Josephine, with Josephine saying, "Well, if we're not married, there must be hundreds of thousands in France who aren't." This too was considered a witticism worthy of indefinite repetition. Spender had now fled. Edith smiled appreciatively.

After the others had gone, Ann and I stayed on at Edith's request. Edith said very sweetly to Ann, in a grateful voice, "She didn't seem to mind us, did she?"

After that Mrs X. became a good friend of Edith.

Not so happy was one of the afternoons when she had a large party in the front room of the first floor at the Sesame. The villain of the event was a young Catholic convert who had been in a monastery—a Trappist house, I think; certainly one with a strict discipline. I had met him once or twice, and he had impressed Edith with what seemed his dedicated humility. Now, as Ann and I were going up the Sesame stairs, he came in and ran hastily past us with a smiling nod. We thought he was only just arriving. But in fact he had been at the small lunch-party and had demoralised it by dropping things on the floor and then trying to caress the legs of the lady next to him—someone who was not in the least likely to appreciate such a tribute. About halfway through Edith had become aware that something was going wrong, but for once did not feel adequate to the situation and did not like to accuse an ex-Trappist (or a Trappist on holiday, or whatever he exactly was) of unduly amorous behaviour. She wound up the lunch as quickly as she could. But then a scene developed in the upper room to which they adjourned. The ex-Trappist, with whom another male member of the lunch-party began to remonstrate, turned noisy and wanted to commit suicide by jumping out of the window into the street-traffic or at least to discard his clothes in full view of Grosvenor Street. The resulting scandal would have made it difficult for Edith to continue as a Sesame member as well as hardly constituting a good advertisement for monkish disciplines. However, after much pointless argument, the young man was persuaded to adjust his clothing and depart. Edith thought she had got rid of him and tried to calm her shattered nerves before the guests of afternoon-tea arrived.

But then, as I have said, the young man, after walking round several blocks or something of the sort, decided to return and complete the attempt in which he had been frustrated. This time he remained quiet, and though I saw him once or twice leering with what seemed to me an ineffably blessèd happiness, I did not suspect him of anything unseemly. However, he had in fact attached himself to Miss Y., one of Edith's dearest friends, and followed her round the room, hissing with quiet persistence in her ear, "I want to lay you." A minor drama, of which I was aware, was afforded by Mrs Z., disliked and disapproved-of by Edith, who had somehow gatecrashed and who was in hot pursuit of a young Australian pianist, a very fine performer, of whom Edith was very fond. Edith had told me of the various devices tried by Mrs Z. to waylay the pianist and penetrate into his flat. In the intervals of a discussion with me on African music (about which I knew nothing) she was now watching her chances of penning him in a corner, so that our conversation was rather distracted, and every now and then she darted off on seeing her quarry momentarily disengaged, only to return to African music when she was baffled by his quick movements or Edith's baulking of her predatory swoop.

Every now and then Edith drifted my way with anxiously dragging face and murmured dispiritedly, "I can't bear it any longer." I thought she was merely referring to the large crowd of guests, or at most to Mrs Z.'s dogged pursuits. So I made a few sympathetic noises and remarked that everything ends sometime. Mrs Z. licked her lips, gave a complacent glance down at her plump breasts, and then turned a rapid brown eye on the pianist, who was taking care not to get himself wedged against a chair by the wall, with no line of retreat. The ex-Trappist beamed benevolently on the world.

When we lunched with Edith a few days later, we heard the full tale, which took about an hour to unfold in its detailed recital of miseries.

That was certainly the major mishap which I witnessed. I was not present at any of the evenings when Caitlin Thomas felt impelled to retort to Edith's admiration of Dylan by her most fractious behaviour. Edith mentioned a few disastrous events of this sort, but never showed the least animosity to Caitlin. In November 1950 I find that she wrote, "I am horrified by this revelation about Dylan," but cannot recall which particular revelation she had in mind. Revelations about Dylan tended to have much the same theme, drink and women. Edith may have referred to one of the tales coming up in the trail of Dylan's 1950 tour of the USA; but I think rather she was speaking of the wife of a certain academic, whom she intensely disliked. "It was very bad of him to treat Caitlin like that. Please tell me more: I am anxious to know all the details. Last time I saw D., he complained that C. thought he didn't love her any more, and said it wasn't true." Edith always clung to Dylan's assurances of his one-and-only-great-love for Caitlin, and felt that somehow this was a large umbrella-virtue which could cover up a host of lecherous peccadilloes.

On the one hand she was ready to accept almost any sort of behaviour from someone like Dylan, who, she was convinced, was a great poet. (She similarly thought that a liking for drink was a quite unimportant facet of the character of Sidney Goodsir Smith, who delighted her both as a person and as a Rabelaisian scribe.) On the other hand, in almost all other respects she was a strong adherent of the proprieties. I was with her when a well-known poet, who had left his wife and had been invited to lunch, got his mistress to send a complicated wire in the hope of inveigling Edith into replying to her and including her in the invitation.

Edith saw at once through the attempt and said, "Well, that's the end of him." She ignored the wire and had no more to do with the poet. Again, she was distressed when another poet used a dinner-party of hers to ingratiate himself into the arms and affections of an American novelist, whose husband had become a nuisance. Myself, I was surprised only that the novelist could exert such charms, for, until this episode, the poet had always seemed securely homosexual. A short while before, this novelist, whom Edith had only seen twice in unimportant connections, rang her up to say that her war-casualty husband had taken something or was going mad. He was threatening her and liable to do anything, so Edith must immediately find a doctor. The day was the August Bank Holiday. Edith didn't know what to do. So the woman came to lunch and wept throughout the meal, to the considerable interest of the Sesame old-ladies, because Edith went on refusing to invite her to Renishaw, where she would have disturbed Osbert. The husband then turned up in wrath and a terrific scene followed, at the end of which the husband was found to have fallen asleep, to the astonishment of the avidly-listening and crowded room. When he did come to himself, he was unable to stand on his feet or speak.

Edith said to me, "I was just a little annoyed. I mean it is rather tiresome to have that kind of thing happening in one's club."

The scenes then proceeded for several days. All this while Edith rose at five in the morning to read proofs and to carry on with the script of her film (for which incidentally she had no contract).

It was amusing to hear her imitate the man with whom she was working on that film in Hollywood. Her clear and noble enunciation was not much fitted for imitations of American accents. "That is the scene," he would say, "where you have those cardinal-guys threaten the King with everlasting damnation. And you have the King say to them: That's okay by me, boys! You can tell your boss the Pope that I am the King of England. And to *hell* with his damnation." She commented, "A dramatic scene! I had worded it slightly differently." However, after her script-accomplice had done his best thus to horrify her with Hollywood vulgarity, she caught a glance of his eye and realised that he was acting up to what he thought she thought Hollywood was like. He was gleefully enjoying the attempt to agitate her and make her protest at such barbarity.

Though we lunched or dined with her more often alone than with other guests, we could not but meet many of the others she invited. I was never present at the same time as Dylan; I have the impression that he did not see her much in these years leading up to his death. Among those whom I did meet at the Sesame were Osbert and Sacheverell with his wife; Sir Kenneth and Lady Clark; Arthur Waley and Beryl de Zoete; Bryher; Humphrey Searle and his wife; Gordon Watson; Gascoygne; the Gorers; John Lehmann and Spender; Robert Herring. The only persons whom I took along were the Whytes and Randall Swingler. Though I did not get to know them well, I was always pleased to see Kenneth Clark and Arthur Waley, both modest, learned, and gentle in character. I showed Clark my Turner essay in *Life and Letters*, and he gave me some advice as to how to carry it further. Two small matters stand out in my mind, suggesting his amiability. We were discussing the exhibition of Yugoslav Medieval Art, and the question of the symbolism on the Bogomil stone-tombs came up. He mentioned the upright hands, and I asked how he interpreted them. "Perhaps a symbol of authority," he said, and flushed apologetically, feeling that with my political views I might feel touchy about authoritarianism. What I did feel was a slight embarrassment that he should think I could be embarrassed by such a theme. Another time he stood aside to let me go first into the lunch-room, and then said humbly, "Sorry, but my many years as a civil servant has made me impossibly polite." Waley with his long melancholy face was a more withdrawn person, seldom emerging from his friendly cave to show anything of his erudition, but quietly interested in what anyone else had to say. His friend Beryl de Zoete was in any event capable of talking for two.

The one aspect of Edith's entertainments of which I did not altogether approve was her way of keeping in with persons who did not really interest her but who had influential positions in the literary world. Thus, Pryce Jones always expressed the warmest interest in what I was writing, and wanted to hear all about it.

Yet he was editing in those years the *Times Literary Supplement* (which is assumed to notice anything of any value at all), and that periodical did not review the novels in which I was attempting a series, *The British Way*. The first three appeared during the period in question: *Betrayed Spring* which, with the background of the Great Frost of 1947, dealt with the setback to the active spirit of change carried over from the war-years; *Rising Tide*, which was based on the Dockers' Strike in 1949 and which I wrote after much discussion with many of the men who had played leading parts in the struggle; and *Moment of Choice*, set in textile Yorkshire of 1950–51 and concerned in parts with the peace movement. However, space was found for a leading article which did its best to make fun of the third book, saying that it opened well and suggested an Anthony Powell dealing with the industrial scene but then ceased to be a serious novel because it dealt with the London riots on Mayday and became embroiled ludicrously with political issues. I am not suggesting that Pryce Jones was himself personally responsible for this sort of treatment of my work; I know nothing of the way the *T.L.S.* is run. But I could not help identifying him and his weekly; and I resented the silence or the attack only because of his affability. If he had said that he didn't like my work, or had ignored it, I should have failed to note what the *T.L.S.* did or didn't do, since it was behaving in no way differently from the other respectable and responsible organs of opinion in the Cold War. Thus, it also published a long review of my *Byzantium into Europe* (anonymous, but obviously by a certain Cambridge don) which made the book a pretext for demanding the exclusion of Marxist scholars from universities, and which condemned it as a mouthpiece of the Moscow Foreign Office—though I had no connection with any university and many of my main positions were certainly counter to those prevailing in Russia at the time. Edith was enraged by the review and told me that she was tempted to write one of her savage retorts, but held herself back with the thought that as she was no scholar she would lay herself open to a scornful reply and would do more harm than good.

Edith got much pleasure from entertaining, but was not easy to lure from the Sesame. While we were still at St John's Wood, we tried to get her along to lunch; but her excuses, which kept putting the event into the future, made it clear that she much preferred us coming to the Sesame, and we gave up trying to make some return for her hospitality. After I came to live at Castle Hedingham, she several times made detailed plans about coming down for the day; but they always faded out for some reason or other. How she managed her lavish parties, small and large, at the Sesame, was a bit of a mystery—especially after she once mentioned to me how she had been drawn into backing a theatre-performance for £425 and defined that sum as nearly more than £100 over her yearly allowance. Even when her earnings as a writer were added, she clearly must have kept running into debt. Though she could live cheaply enough at Renishaw or Montegufoni, her London expenses must have been high. I think there must have been no time of her life, after she left home, when she was not beset with money-worries.

When we first came to know one another, she had been afraid that I might be aggressively left and that she would have to be careful in her introductions. She soon, however, realised that such caution was unnecessary; but she still took care not to invite me at the same time as Roy Campbell, for whom she had much affection and admiration. She discovered that I did not take him seriously as a Franco-fascist and that I considered many of his attitudes to be the confused expressions of a fellow-colonial who attempted to build up political principles out of personal like and dislikes. Thus, because he looked on Spender contemptuously as a namby-pamby Little Man, he identified support of the Spanish Republic with effete liberal illusions, backscratching cliqueism and so on. True, out of this kind of pettybourgeois rage much genuine fascism did indeed come; but Campbell himself seemed to me primarily a sick man, a very poor thinker, who had ended by being demoralised by his resentful fancies, despite the vigorous pictorial element in his best writing, his grasp at a certain level of the life of the senses. Edith had much enjoyed his assault on Grigson, but she became less happy about his vendetta against Spender. (The more confused part of herself, which was rooted in her capacity for violence and anger in the face of the "enemy," had its links with Campbell's emotional positions; but she would never let herself be dominated with these immature elements, as Campbell did.)[1]

Once, when Spender and I were having a drink by the bar in the Sesame before lunch, the attendant came from a near telephone and said loudly, "Mr Roy Campbell wants to speak to you on the phone, ma'am." Edith rose in considerable confusion and dismay, and was put out for the rest of the lunchtime. She told me later that she had felt dreadful. I told her not to worry; I was sure that Spender was not so petty as to object to her friendship with Campbell. However, the episode rankled guiltily, and she did her best thereafter to divert Campbell from any thoughts of attack, by fists or pen, on Spender. She got him to cut some three thousand words of scathing scorn out of his autobiography. Campbell had been convinced that Spender was continually attacking him in lectures and thus preventing his work from being printed in the United States. Edith managed to convince him that this was a delusion, and in late 1949 he even drove, at her urging, to a printing works in a vain attempt to stop an attack on Spender which he had written for some periodical.

[8]

I should now like to return to our discussions on poetry, to the nexus of shared ideas that in the last resort constituted our friendship. Much of this inevitably consists of comments by me on her work, and by her on mine, but I think it will be found that the narrower and more personal aspects of the exchange between us all the while dissolve into larger issues; and I trust I am not mistaken in thinking that the way in which I am thus able to link those larger issues and the personal exchange, with its (for us) considerable excitement, has the effect of communicating a degree

[1] I never met Campbell after the 1920s. Once, about 1948, we were both supposed to speak on the same platform at some poetry meeting, and on the way there, as I walked behind Bernard Bergonzi and some others, I heard them saying, "There ought to be sparks flying when Lindsay and Campbell collide." However, he did not turn up. I doubt if the sparks would have flown, as I learned from several sources that he was friendly to me; and once, when J.D. wrote to him with a project intended to do him a good turn, he replied in a letter of furious abuse, cursing him and all the other left writers he could think of, but explicitly excluding me from his fulminations.

of light and warmth which would be lacking in a more objective presentation of the ideas and attitudes.

First then I should like to carry on by giving in some detail our discussions during the rest of 1948. For their tone and their material I shall rely on her letters, which preserve in a clear concentrated form the sort of things we talked about, and the general direction taken. She told me that she would have liked to give us *The Coat of Fire* for *Arena*, but it was already in print for the April issue of *Horizon*. She was, however, at work on a new poem; and if it turned out as she hoped, she said that she'd send it to what she called our new and exciting adventure. Ann and I had gone off to Paris to see Eluard and Tzara, but Edith was again visiting London in June. She asked us to keep her arrival an absolute secret, as she was being plagued and badly disturbed by a poor girl who had had a mental collapse and whom the medical treatment had left in a most trying condition. Here was yet one more of the suffering pests whom I have mentioned as perpetually haunting her and increasing her own malaise.

"How lovely your translation of *Daphnis and Chloe* is," she wrote in one of her three April letters. "The beauty is most extraordinary. It certainly cannot be more lovely in the original. And as for the essay at the end! There is *no* living writer who gives me more to think about, who is more feeding to the mind, than you. You have the most amazing vitalising quality, there is never any dead matter. I am so grateful to you for having given me this lovely work."

It is naturally pleasing for me to be able to cite such comments of hers on my work; but I do not give this and similar passages in this essay for that reason. First, I want to establish the closeness in thought and feeling that existed between Edith and myself from the moment she read the review in *Our Time* and wrote to me. A closeness that continued for many years, as my narrative will show. Secondly, it is only by thus establishing the close and continuous texture of our intimacy that I can demonstrate how entirely she agreed with my analysis of her work, and the dynamic way in which that analysis reacted back on her, giving a firm consciousness to what had previously been largely intuitive and fragmentary in her thought. Generalised accounts of our conversations would have nothing like the life in these statements in her own clear, tense, and vigorous words. Nothing less will convey the steady excitement, the effect of persisting intellectual discovery, which we shared through those years. Finally, though many of her comments deal with my works, they are none the less revelatory of herself. Not only of her quick and penetrating sympathy, but of that part of herself which was stirred and released by my works. And so, though I am well aware that readers are liable to be irritated at an author citing passages which praise his own works, I trust that in this case they will forgive the transgression and forgo the irritation. For me to make generalised comments on our friendship and exchange of ideas would be impertinent and meaningless. The actual words of her responses bring out, as nothing else could, the candid warmth that was always alive in her and struggling to emerge, and the intellectual energy, the keen vivid spark that was struck out by ideas which stirred her essential self. And so I cite those words as the only way to convey that deep element of her which I was fortunate enough to evoke in all its guileless impetuosity and generous fullness of response. I think that the reader who can then approach the narrative as simply one of a friendship through which Edith reveals her deepest likes and dislikes, the whole field of her poetic sympathies and emotional impulses, will be able to set the particular points of discussion in a perspective that deprives them of their less important personal aspects.

Now, as to the objective value of her comments. Edith, for reasons which I shall later touch on, was highly susceptible to flattery, extremely eager for praise and recognition. One way or another there are perhaps few poets and artists of whom that might not be said; but Edith, because of the peculiar suffering of her earlier years, was in some respects abnormally anxious about her position. Every artist who makes important advances into the unknown of life and art is driven on by a linked certainty and uncertainty, confidence and despair, enormous assurance and intense dogging anxiety. In Edith's case the fears and doubts had been deeply accentuated by her troubled lonely childhood; while playing their essential part in the complex of violent forces that turned her into a poet, they also made her liable to moods of uncertainty beyond even the common measure. Hence her voracity for praise, which for a moment dulled the ache of doubt.

But though the element of vanity was thus present in her response to any appreciation, she was in the last resort far too clear-sighted and well-balanced to be taken in by praises which did not have behind them a comprehensive understanding, an intellectual basis, which she could respect. When it became clear that she was being much affected by my ideas and writings, many of the persons surrounding her interpreted her attitude as the mere result of flattery. I had praised her work, therefore I was a serious thinker, etcetera. The fundamentally insulting view of her intelligence that many of her friends had was expressed by Stephen Spender in an exchange we had over my *Life of Dickens*. Spender and I had been on good terms for some years; and we were meeting at the time now and then at Edith's Sesame. Then he reviewed the *Life* in a New York paper. I did not mind that the review was hostile; what upset me was the manner of the writing. I felt that he had condemned the book in a doctrinaire way as bad in itself because I was a Marxist; I considered that this was a pandering to the whole cold-war atmosphere thickening round us at that time; and I was particularly hurt that Spender, friendly on the surface, should have written this sort of thing in an American journal. So I did what I have never done before or after about a denigratory notice of one of my books—and heaven knows I have had enough of such notices. I wrote a letter to Spender protesting against the tone of his review, and saying that I had done my best to write a book in which there were no narrowly partisan viewpoints. (I could have added that the book was denounced in the *Daily Worker* as a lot of Freudian nonsense.) In passing I mentioned a number of different persons who had praised the book—not to prove it was good, but to show that it was not dogmatically or sectarianly conceived—and cited Edith among the others (who included Angus Wilson and Desmond MacCarthy). Spender in his reply singled out Edith and said that she would praise any work that flattered her. He referred, I presume, to the fact that it was dedicated to her.[1]

Edith was surrounded by persons, who, while polite enough to me, lost no chance to tell her that she was ridiculously overvaluing my judgement and my work. I could name several of these councillors of hers who for one reason or another felt sharply antagonistic to my ideas (and politics) and who did everything they could to undermine our relationship.

I give these facts in order to make clear that Edith knew just what she was doing in maintaining our friendship and in saying what she did of my ideas and writings. That she was unaffected in the least by the attacks on me demonstrates how firmly grounded was her sense of our affinity. Like everyone else, she made her mistakes; and with her wholehearted responses she could be at times swept off her feet in ways that she later regretted. But she was incapable of maintaining in the most passionate tones an intellectual and emotional relationship for several years, unless her whole being was truly implicated. After her death, a close, and intimate friend read through the mass of letters from her which I have kept, and remarked, "I know very well the sort of thing which Edith said when she wanted to be kind, and which had no real significance. What she says in these letters is said with every fibre of her being. They enclose the whole Edith as no other letters of the postwar period do."

Edith knew, then, that I had no reputation in any of the fashionable or dominant sections of the literary world; but insisted on taking our relationship in the world of ideas with the utmost seriousness. She had very high standards in this sphere. For instance, she asked me to take out a quotation from Cyril Connolly in my *Starfish Road*. Yet she liked him personally, and

[1] Our correspondence, I regret to say, then divagated wildly into generalisations, ending in a query from me: "When you joined the Communist Party in the time of the Spanish Civil War, what was your idea of Capitalist Crisis?" and an epistle which I could hardly decipher, posted by Spender in Berlin. I trust I am not being unfair to his article; what I record is its effect on me then, and I may have been hypersensitive in view of the period's pressures. He was, I know, trying to be conciliatory and fair in many matters. Thus, he once asked me if Randall would regret an article he wrote on Virginia Woolf at the time of her death. I said yes, and Spender then said he'd cut an attack he had meant to make on him in this relation.

on that level she later dedicated a short poem to him. I could cite more examples of this sort of thing.

She was thinking about the *Mad-Tom* book, which interested her a great deal. "I have never before encountered anyone with such universal learning. It is so invigorating and inspiring to me." She had completed the poem for *Arena, Street Acrobat,* and apologised for her handwriting, as she had been suffering badly from fibrositis in her right shoulder, plus what she called the upset of a terrific rumpus with an American poetaster and Messrs Routledge. She had expressed interest in my last novel and the one I had in the press. With some misgivings I sent her *The Subtle Knot,* a slight work dealing with a group of London students who have survived the war and try to get together again in a dramatic production—*Everyman* in the crypt of a bombed church. Edith found it "a beautiful study of these wandering, lost people wrecked by those terrible years—and sometimes by their own nature. And it has most extraordinary passages of beauty: 'wind and the sea and the golden sheafs of light.' It is also quite terrifying. The part about Stuart telling James to go away and put out the light, couldn't be beaten for horror of that kind. One is left with the feeling of shock, as though one had seen it happen, and had passed through the night that preceded it. Mrs Murray," a secret drinker, "is perfection. (I had a Mrs Murray in my life once.) It is at once so dreadful, and so funny—(it isn't funny, of course, to the unfortunate victims of the Mrs Murrays—not while it is happening). But it is impossible not to enjoy (in a book, anyhow) the innocent surprise about the bottles, 'What an extraordinary thing.' " (I tried to bring about a dialectical relation of the actors with the characters they play, so that they become what they act and act what they become.)

She was very pleased with a sarcastic passage about the Logical Positivism of *Polemic*. "Sometimes, looking at that kind of paper, one wonders why such people do not go mad from sheer boredom! Incidentally, I had a pretty sharp dust-up with the editor of that paper," Humphrey Slater, "who, immediately after asking me in the most pressing terms for a contribution, published an exceedingly scurrilous and violent attack on me by a Mr Grigson.

Having done that, he then allowed this gentleman to attack Dylan, and wrote to *me*, of all people in the world, a cosy, matey sort of letter—as from one friend to another—asking me if I would reply to it!!!" She sent several corrections for *Street Acrobat*. During the days of its composition a traction-engine had been lumbering up and down outside her room. She also sent me *A Poet's Notebook* and repeated her excitement over the thought of the *Mad Tom* book.

Street Acrobat showed elements of thought gained both from Whyte's book and from our discussions on post-Galilean science. In the last lines the reassertion of new life was the expression of the new hope she had been gaining. She felt in a new way that the dichotomy of false heavens and comfortable hells could be broken, with the ending of the abstract science of the Bird-men.

Our next meeting was fixed for Wednesday, 9 June. Edith was to be only three days in London, and would have to spend most of the time "in the most melancholy occupations. This, and one other event, will be my only pleasures." We suggested that she might like to come and lunch with us, in our house almost opposite Lord's in Wellington Road. Edith replied that she would come in September to see us there. And now she explained the briefness of her visit to London. She had meant to come for a week, but now she found she must hurry back for the wedding of the daughter of Osbert's old soldier-servant (who was still looking after them at Renishaw). The girl wanted her to attend, and so her plans had been curtailed. The melancholy aspects of the visit were now defined as the need to call on a woman whose serious illness had involved the amputation of both legs; now her hands and arms were going wrong. Further, Edith had to look up a woman who had just come out of hospital after nearly killing herself with some poison. The agent had to be seen about the American tour, and clothes for the tour had to be tried on. "I am in rags." And so, "altogether, the lunch party to which you and your husband are coming," she wrote to Ann, "and an hour or two with Tom Eliot, are the only peaceful moments I shall have during the visit."

On the same day she wrote to me, with further comments on her melancholy duties, one tragic and one maddening, and added that she wanted also to see a friend who had just remarried after losing his first wife in very distressing circumstances. "I have to see them, or hurt their feelings." She repeated how interested she was in the book to be called *The Starfish Road* (after a poem by Tzara). "My gratitude to you is very great. I look forward with avidity to the book, which will be of great importance to poetry. Oh, we need a man like you to write about poetry." She was much intrigued to find out what I would say of Lautréamont. "What a curious mixture of genius and high-falutin bathos." But the main part of her letter was taken up with remarks on my novel *Men of Forty-Eight* (written in the winter of 1940–41, but held up till this year by Methuens, for whom I had done it). "I opened it on a superb, a really *magnificent* passage, about 'this tramping beat, this thunder of humanity,'—and about 'crying a hymn to the smothered lightnings of man.' I think it is sublime. That of course is what all great art does—what Beethoven does—and what sounds in all great art. I cannot tell you with what excitement I look forward to reading it. I will write to you when once I have. It is very strange that the book should have been delayed, to come out in this particular year. I don't mean that the practical reasons were strange—but that it seems as if the moment had been planned from outside, as right, whilst, perhaps, the other moment was unripe. What fiery poetry shines in your prose, and burns there. But it is always of the theme, and never 'prose poetry,' but a grandeur born of the theme."

A few days later came her fuller verdict. "I am overwhelmed by *Men of Forty-Eight*. It is a book on such a scale, and written with blood and fire. It is *tremendous*. I have now read it through, and have read several passages over and over again. It must be read, in its entirety, I think, at least three times before one can grasp everything, although I feel that I *have* grasped everything. It is quite wonderful. What tremendous *living* and writing have gone to the descriptions of the revolutionary outbursts—the word descriptions is wrong, because they burn and live on the page, and the sound comes up to one in thunder, these tremendous tumults, like the 'drums and tramplings of a hundred conquests' that de Quincey spoke of, the almost unbearable tenderness, beauty, and sadness of 'Spring over London'—the fire of the terrible speech of Boon towards the end—the poetry of it all: (such phrases as 'the homeless dark': how wonderful that is), the tenderness in some cases, a pitiability or ardour in others, of the characters, the noble poetry about the sun-warmth, and that grand quotation from Heracleitos!! The book is profoundly impressive, and as moving as it is impressive. I hope the reviewers will realise what they are reading. I don't see how they could help it."[1]

In gathering material for the background of the book's hero Boon I had read a large number of memoirs of the period, and among the details I selected were some that chanced to be connected with Edith's ancestors. "By the way, it will amuse you to hear that I am the great-grand-daughter of the old man who took Nelly's portrait down (see page 213). But my great-grand-mother (whom I remember) wasn't *really* sympathetic. She had it hung in his dressing-room to punish him (as she was quite au courant)." This was the Dowager Duchess of Bedford with whom Edith as a child drove out in the afternoon and who looked as if she would crumble into a little silvery dust. "She comes in several of my early poems, in *The Sleeping Beauty*, where she is the Dowager Queen, and in *Colonel Fantock*. She was an aged terror!" Edith ended, "My grateful thanks, and my great admiration."

Next Wednesday she tried an omnibus gathering of those whom she considered her main left admirers: Miles and Mary Carpenter, Hubert and Barbara Nicholson, Ann and myself, and Miron Grindea. Not that Grindea was rated as left, but he had published things by Hubert and myself in *Adam*—and at that time I was the president, with Prof. Joad, of his excellent but incoherent organisation for doing something excellent but incoherent about international cultural relations. (I tried to reorganise it, as I tried also to reform the format of *Adam*; but in both matters Grindea, small, agile, and grimly indomitable, took not the least notice of my efforts.) Edith told me that she had also asked a terrified young man from Cambridge, who had been ill, of what she had no idea;

[1] The reviews in fact were the usual pointless meanderings; and Alick West's treatment in *Sunlight and the Mountain* was a little worse. However, a young Russian, who teaches at Balashov on the Volga, has written a penetrating essay on the novel; so I suppose I may count myself lucky. Tributes from such diverse points on the spiritual map as Renishaw and Balashov help a writer to feel that he has not entirely deluded himself as to what he sought to put into a work.

she had ordered him to come along only if he were quite cured. He was the kind of lad, she insisted, born to have mumps. "I have been very severe and explicit on the subject," she said, and I am sure she had been. She had a terror of contagious diseases, even the mildest cold, and one never dared to go near her if one were liable to sneeze, cough, or sniff in the least degree.

The meeting had its comic side, even without the terrified young man from Cambridge, and needed all Edith's tact to keep it going. As we sat later in a large circle in the drawing-room, Hubert in a rather impertinent voice asked Edith a question about her parents. Perhaps he had made a special effort to nerve himself, and it was his strain that made him sound so aware of bad manners. Perhaps he felt that he would sacrifice himself to bring the conversation down to earth. Edith did not turn a hair, answered politely, and changed the subject. Grindea rose and kissed the tips of Edith's fingers with truly Rumanian courtesy as he said goodbye in a whirl of international commitments. I knew we would see no more of Hubert at the Sesame.

Since she had read *Men of Forty-Eight*, without comment Edith dropped Mr Lindsay and called me Jack. Ann and I had finally decided that we must give up trying to maintain an expensive house in St John's Wood, and we had partly removed to a cottage on the estate of Lord de Lisle and Dudley at Penshurst. The place had been found by a dogged young woman writer, who was convinced that she only needed to unearth a fully congenial spot in order to produce great works of literature. She began in one of the watchtowers of the Napoleonic era, and, failing to be inspired, was gradually working her way northward; some years later I learned that she had reached Yorkshire. Having tried Cooks Pit in vain, she offered it to Grindea and to us, and we both accepted; so she said we had better share it. Grindea did come along once and leave a toothbrush in a tumbler as a token of occupation, but otherwise he forgot about the place. We began gradually moving in, together with Tony Adams and his wife Barbara, and I set to work on a second version of Catullus and the *Life of Dickens*. One Sunday afternoon, after walking up from the village-pub, I was alone in the cottage and wrote a piece of music for Edith, which I called *Sibylla Ultima*. She was pleased at it—

getting my letter as she was on the point of leaving for Newcastle, where she was to stay for the night and then go on to Durham next day for her Doctorate. "I have never known anyone with such an exciting and inciting mental energy. It is like an unquenchable benevolent volcano. And it must make any artist in the various arts who knows you, feel inspired to work. I really long, too, to see *The Starfish Road*. There, again, it has a most wonderful name; and what a history of the name." She had been reading my versions in the *Companion to the Oxford Book of Greek Verse*, and was sending me *The Chain-Gang*, with a message from Charles Henri Ford in New York, "Tell an admired Jack Lindsay that anything I can do for the paper [*Arena*] in America I shall be most happy to do."

She returned to Renishaw to hear of the sudden death of a close friend; and a few hours later Georgina rang up to say that Sacheverell was seriously ill—though not as seriously as had been at first feared. The two shocks had made Osbert, unwell for some time, fall ill as well. Edith was unsettled, too disturbed to write; but she managed to play *Sibylla Ultima*—she hadn't touched a piano for some time—and found it "as beautiful, original, and strange as I had hoped it would be." She wanted to dedicate a poem to me but would have to wait, she said, till she had composed one "which is in the least worthy of you. And worthy of the Sibyl." She was going to have the Sibyl bound up by a man in Sheffield whom she thought the finest book-binder in England.[1]

The Chain-Gang, later called *The Stone-Breakers,* sought to define the force that would break the stony heart, the stone still sealing Christ's tomb and preventing the resurrection of human unity. To see that force incarnated in the workers damned for ever to stone-breaking, who will someday end alienation, turning "the red sea of the heat" of division and exploitation into the redeeming sea of the "infinite Blood of Christ."

I had now finished the first draft of *The Starfish Road* and had promised to send it to her. Dennis Dobson was publishing a

[1] My music is merely that of a poet working out certain rhythmic effects; I have no ear and no knowledge at all of the theory of harmony. The only admirers of it have been Edith and Bernard Miles, who even rashly stated once that if I wrote a play on the Peasants' Revolt for the Mermaid, as he asked me to do, I could compose the music for it.

work of mine on Marxism, which I had called *The Fullness of Life* but which at his request I renamed *Marxism and Contemporary Science*. Dennis was keen also to publish *The Starfish Road*. He had seen the manuscript, and I asked him to send it on to Edith, who had offered to write an introduction. (I had also asked Alick West to write one, as I thought he would say something quite unlike what Edith would say.)

On 23 July she said she had been meaning to write for some days before she got my letter on the book. She had been struggling to finish a poem for a Continental magazine run by a friend of Eliot's, she declared, without an idea in her head, while writing two broadcasts that had to be done by 15 August. So she felt nervous, and in the words of Tchelitchew, who compared himself to his pet tortoise, "I crowl and I crowl." "Sometimes I work at lightning speed. But now I have got to drag something out of the depths to the light, and it doesn't like coming." She wanted to send me a book by Maurice Barras, and said, "I should regard myself as deprived of one of the things I want most, in all my life, if I were to be deprived of an essay by you about my poetry. It has been understood by you as if [you] had actually lived through all its processes." She then asked me to do an essay for a collection about her work being brought out by *New Directions* in New York. James Laughlin had asked whom she would like to write about her latest work—the other essays having been got together three years before and then mislaid. "And I said, of course, *you*. Please do not be angry. I would be more grateful, more deeply grateful than I could say—and I know what I am asking, because I know how busy you are—if you could possibly find time to add, perhaps, a little to your review of *The Shadow of Cain*—so as to make the essay longer— (could some of the new book be added?)." She went on, "It would mean a very great deal to me, and to the success of the book." The essay would have to be done at once, as she thought the book was on the point of going to press. In its history there had been a continual tug-of-war, broken by frequent mislayings of the manuscript on the part of various combatants, with moments when she had felt herself "driven to the verge of dementia by the crosscurrents." However, what remained of the collection was now safely in the hands of Laughlin, "a strong silent American."

Ann and I were going to Paris in September to see Tzara and Eluard. Edith was staying in London from 30 August to 8 September; then from 24 September till 16 October, when she left for the USA. "I do hope to see a lot of you both." She underlined, "Will you please not tell anyone I am coming? As I want a little quiet." In my previous letter I had remarked that as I wrote I had on me the eyes of a small Cypriot warrier moulded in clay in the eighth century B.C. Edith answered, "It is wonderful, what you said about the exquisite creature who looks at you with those eyes made wise by the centuries. Strangely enough, I have such a communicant here. The stone head of a boy, sculptured by Michaelangelo's teacher. I have never seen anything with of such a heavenly youth and divine yet earthly innocence. I watch him always when I am in the room. He shames wickedness. I do hope *The Starfish Road* arrives this afternoon."

[9]

The essay which I hastily wrote for *New Directions* was a restatement, in less simple terms, of what I had said in the *Our Time* review. After stressing the way in which Edith had brought our poetry back into the mid-European stream, I spoke of her vision of hell that penetrated to the depths of our reality.

But because this vision of hell was poetically realised, it bore at its own heart the potences of heaven. The poetic act is the marriage of heaven and hell, as Blake knew. The harsh edges turned into the delimiting factors of a new harmony true to the human condition. The trauma, exposed to the Apollinian light, provided the basis for a new health. The dissociation, dominant in the world, was overcome and made to yield the secret of a new integration. An integration, not a phoney bit of wishful-thinking based on the veiling of the deep conflict, but proceeding out of the heart of that conflict.

Both heaven and hell receded into the small and complete garden of childhood; and the gigantic struggle of alienating and integrating forces in the world was telescoped into the formative process of the senses in the magicked child. The return to the pure sources expressed the healing of the trauma, and now out of a delicate unfolding of dream-movement the poet dared to pass through the complex maze of associations into the realising structure of symbol.

In symbol the poet gets to the root of the uniting factor in man. And so from this point Edith Sitwell moved back into the world of actual men and women, able to hold fast to her gains (the free poetic image truly based in the human condition) and yet able to express sympathy . . .

I pointed to *Gold Coast Customs* as the turning-point. It stands

for the moment when the stark realisation of hell (*Façade*) mates with the lovely dream of lost Edens (*The Sleeping Beauty*), and out of the marriage of heaven and hell the Earth of Man is simply, terribly, exaltingly begotten.

In this movement a new enrichment of the time-planes occurs. Two moments of horror—one primitive, one contemporary—are fused, but not in mechanical superimposition. The effect is of violent contrary movements, a nausea-sudden fall back through levels of time into a ghastly and hopeless centre of fear, and a forward-movement out of the engulfing past into the crisis-moment of renewal. Cain, Dives and Christ (basic symbols for Edith Sitwell of the human condition and the forms of social struggle that make up history) now appear. Cain or Dives seems victorious; the seamless garment of man is rent and divided up among the hirelings; and yet the Whole Man lives on and reasserts himself, in the toil that makes break and the pang that makes poetry. "The fires of God goes marching on."

Speaking of the war-poems, I said:

The battle of men is realised, not as something projected on to the detached screen of the universe, but as a storm of potences which reaches everywhere. A form of pantheism? Yes, but not quite according to the definitions in the manuals of philosophy. Pantheisms have usually been of a passive contemplative nature; and this attitude is essentially active. Man and nature are felt as one only because man is discovered at the deep polarising levels of his basic conflicts and integrations, of the process that makes him man. The philosophic affinity is rather with Marx who says that, in the development whereby man's natural existence becomes his human existence, "nature has become man for him."

After stressing afresh that *The Shadow of Cain* does not see the scientific processes of nuclear fission in abstraction, but as the terrible moment of choice confronting alienated man—the human essence of division and dissociation reflected in matter itself—I resumed the argument:

The Shadow restates in the new historical situation the conflict posed by *Gold Coast Customs*. But because of the new breadth of realisation, the necessary involvement of physics as well as history, the contrasted-and-united planes are not only those of primitive and contemporary life. There is a vast geologic recession of planes, which gives the element of cosmic bleakness that I referred to (at the opening of the essay). And this massing of huge simple convolutions and retreating diagonals of force is one with certain dream-structures of space. The crucial evolutionary moment, the moment of fundamental scientific discovery of the nature of energy-matter-process, the moment of human change and renewal (in both individual and group)—all these moments are fused together in the imagery and rhythm of the poem.

It opens with a broad statement (in Hegelian terms) of the issue from the focus of physics, which is linked with the picture of geologic phases of convulsive movement—we are the molecular level as well as in a dream-space. Man emerges (as in a primitive myth such as that of the Zuni). Man in his primitive ritual finds his precarious unity with the vast forces; and through the imagery of the birth-trauma relates his own experiences to his intuitions of elemental change. Beyond terror, he arrives at regeneration; the panic power breaks into the realisation of human renewal and the rejection of division:

And the great rolling world-wide thunders of that drumming
    underground
Proclaim our Christ, and roar: "Let there be harvest!
Let there be no more Poor—
For the Son of God is sowed in every furrow!"

And so we are suddenly in our own world, where the deepest processes of spiritual transformation, symbolised as Christ, have appeared as the knowledge of nuclear fission, a new deepening of the knowledge of good and evil. But the evil has got out of hand.

> The Primal Matter
> Was broken, the womb from which all life began,
> Then to the murdered Sun a totem pole of dust arose in
> memory of Man.

The forces of terror have gained control; and we go falling, falling
aeon after aeon. Life is split to the core. And there

> in that hollow lay the body of our brother
> Lazarus, upheaved from the world's tomb.

The poor man, the maker of bread who is also the living wheat-ear,
the murdered man around whom the forces of redemption most
powerfully play. To him hurry "the civilisation of the Maimed, and
too, Life's Lepers." They cry for salvation, in the midst of terrible
pressures of regression. "Then Dives was brought . . . He lay like
a leprous Sun."

> Like a great ear of wheat that is swoln with grain
> Then ruined by white rain.

There lie the two dead men, who are Man, with their conflicting
forces, their opposed symbols of *gold* (Gold that is quick of light in
the corn, alchemical moment of transmutation and the healing of all
sores, money the faecal defilement and the fires of corruption). And
the golds fight and unite; the opposed forces are broken down into
a new unity; the fission in man, reaching down through all levels, is
made the basis of a new wholeness. Because the horror is faced and
understood at all levels, Christ arises out of the split sepulchre and
womb. A Judgement Day of all that distorted and divided; an
achievement of peace, plenty, brotherhood.

In discussing this essay with Edith, I explained further what I
then grasped of Marx's *Economic-Philosophic Manuscripts* of 1844,
and I pointed out what an admirable commentary on *Gold Coast
Customs* would have been the passages in *Capital* where commodity-fetishism was analysed. Marx, like Edith, had felt driven
back to Africa of the past, where the alienated human essence was
lodged in the fetish, in order to express the extremity of man's
subjection to things in bourgeois society—a subjection which
involved, as its last indignity and distortion, the thingification of
man himself. Edith fully accepted this relation to Marx.

Reconsidering now what I had written, I feel that I paid too igh a compliment to nuclear fission and the physics on which it was based, as if they expressed a full grasp of the processes of transformation of matter. Today I see them as lopsided and hopelessly incomplete, reflecting almost only the negative side of the situation, the descent into ever greater division. To grasp scientifically the nature of transformation from the integrative aspect will require a quite different approach.

Still, I feel that I said something in my essay, though not enough; and what is said, is not precise enough. And looking over the book, *A Celebration for Edith Sitwell*, edited by Jose Garcia Villa, I feel how remarkably lacking in clarity or depth of meaning has been anything written about her work. Here among the contributors are Spender, Bowra, Prokosch, Horace Gregory, Kenneth Clark, Gordon Bottomley, Arthur Waley, L. P. Hartley; but little idea emerges of what her work expresses, why it is important, and what are the means it uses. We find comments, at times interesting, but always marginal. Not for the first time I am driven to ask myself if I am deluded in what I find in Edith's work, and if there is not some centrifugal confusion, a pervasive blurring of images and meanings, which has begotten this indefiniteness in the responses. And then, not for the first time, I come to the conclusion that it is rather because of the fiery certainty of her attack that the smudged reactions appear. She has indeed her misfiring passages, hectic, repetitive, and tired; but these do not affect the core of her achievement. In the last resort she has not been understood because she has been saying things that people do not want to understand. We have only to think of the vast amount of exegesis of Eliot, Pound, or Dylan Thomas, which, though often wrongheaded (in my opinion) as to the conclusions it draws, is yet helpful in enabling us to get inside their minds and methods; and then we feel what a blank silence or well-meaning mumble surrounds Edith.

[10]

On Monday 26 July she remarked, "There is now so much I want to say that I find it is difficult to begin. I am overwhelmingly grateful to you for writing this essay about my poetry for Mr

Laughlin: it *is* good of you. Nobody could exaggerate my excitement at the prospect of this: for nobody is inside my poetry as you are. *The Starfish Road* arrived on Saturday, and I have been magnetised by it ever since. It is obviously, even at first glance, a book of the highest importance, and that not only from one point of view—that of the actual criticism of, and insight into, the work of the writers discussed—but from a far more universal point of view." She was acknowledging the receipt of the manuscript to Dennis Dobson, and said she would repeat what she had said to me about it. In two or three days when she felt more able to get at grips with it, she would write in more detail.

"It is an electrifying book. It is the mental history of an age—as I see the book. I shall say that also. It would be quite impossible for me to exaggerate what I believe the importance of this book to be. Really, you have got the most extraordinary gift for seizing and lighting essentials—the essence. And it is a book for everybody, if they have any mental life at all—not only for people interested in poetry. Of course I don't really know the *details* yet, as a whole. But what you say about Auden and the rest of those boys is profoundly true—and you are the first person to say it. What you say about my poetry gave me almost a shock—it is so true of what has been in my head. I nearly go *demented*, sometimes, at the utter lack of understanding of my early poetry. Only you have understood it. I have, as I say, the belief that this is infinitely the most important book of its kind to be written." She then commented on two versions of Catullus I had sent: "so beautiful; and so far away, and yet utterly near." She ended with some comments on what she called her rhinoceros-like lecture-agent in America, who had insulted the American Poetry Society, telling them they would "have to pay goodness knows what before they are allowed to as much as look at" Edith. Angry letters had been reaching her, saying "almost in as many words, that I am egging on the rhinoceros to grind the faces of the Poor."

What I had said about Auden followed on from my analysis of the Objective Correlative as set out by Eliot as the way in which the poet externalised (or socialised) his inner life:

118

The next generation of poets—that mainly known by the names of Auden, Spender, Day Lewis—emerged without any clear sense of values, but strongly influenced by Eliot's desiccating methods, especially his notion of the Objective Correlative. Auden in particular made this device his aim, expanding it on lines that might be defined as a meek version of Dali's paranoia-art [discussed earlier in the book]. The artist is conceived as a misfit, a neurotic, whose protest against a society of alienation takes the form of a compilation of symptoms, simultaneously the clues to his neurosis and his alibis, his evasion of full health (conceived as a successful fitting of oneself into bourgeois society). The lists of Objective Correlatives reveal the structure of his alternating or opposed symptoms.

This attitude of Auden's dominated the young poets of the Thirties; it gave them an easy way-out, an appearance of close contact with social causes and movements, and at the same time a protection against true participation. It provided the form of phoney intellectual-conscience that promptly failed to function the moment that any real choice of struggle was forced on it, as happened in 1939. For this reason the activity of the poets on the side of Republican Spain was mainly illusory, a utopian phase when it seemed possible to be a good liberal and a good rebel: to challenge the bourgeoisie on moral terms without going over to the proletariat.

It was Eliot's Objective Correlative and Auden's development of it as a method of neurotic (artistic) protest, which deflected most of the young poets from any effort to understand the nature of Edith Sitwell's work. That at the point of strain (1939) Auden would move over to an openly split position, of religious idealism, could have been inferred.

then went on to discuss the place of Dylan Thomas as the exponent of the revolt against the Eliot-Auden synthesis.

Edith always thus picked out any comments of mine on the destructive role of Eliot and expressed her particular agreement with them. Both in writing and in conversation she fully assented with my elaboration of the sort of argument set out above.

Three days later now, on 29 July, she wrote again. "I think *The Starfish Road* a really terrific book." Her only lament was that "it is dreadful to think it must be at least a year, under present conditions, before it can come out." (What would she have said

if she had known that in my shilly-shallying the book was neve
to appear?) She enclosed a copy of the report to Gordon, ther
manager of Dobson's. "The book is so packed with profound
sayings and insights, so sun-lit, I could only speak of essentials to
Mr Gordon. It really is a wonderful book. Dear me, yes!" She
suggested only that a sonnet by Baudelaire, which I had trans
lated, should be left in the original. "This is in *no* way a reflectio
on that most admirable translation. But Baudelaire lies *in* the
French language as very few poets lie in their language; and it i
therefore a good thing, I think, to have the actual *material* there
The translation gets every wave of meaning and feeling, it is
sheer matter of texture which is unproduceable in anothe
language; I feel the same, always, about de Nerval." She als
wanted me to omit a quotation from Connolly about Aragon
which I had put in because of the part he played in getting
Crève-Coeur and *Les Yeux d'Elsa* published in England. She felt
certain regret about the need to discuss some of the wilder mani
festations of Dadaists and Surrealists, which she could not bu
link with some of her own earlier baitings of the bourgeoisie. "
see that if you are to write a history of the movement, you ar
obliged to write about their demonstrations. But I wish they had
not made them—just as I wish I had not done a great deal that
did do when I was young and high-spirited."

She added that she thought Sacheverell was a really great poet
one of the greatest of the last hundred years, great as Keats wa
great, "in exactly that warm, sunny, pagan manner." She insisted
that she wasn't making this claim because of his being he
brother, "because I am incapable of being influenced in *poetry,* b
that, a personal relationship." (I was able to reply truthfully that
thought Sacheverell underrated, that once I used to carry hi
Hundred and One Harlequins about with me, and that he indeed ha
a wonderful grasp of certain musical and idyllic effects. I did no
add that I could not accept the comparison with Keats, who i
his greatest work has a passionate concentration, a dialectica
structure and range, which no one could claim for Sacheverell.
However, Edith concluded by saying that she realised Sachevere
did not come into the scope of my analysis. "I am excited by th
book to the very marrow of my bones."

The report on *The Starfish Road*, which she gave me to use as I wished, ran as follows:

To me, it seems one of the most highly significant and important books that have been written for many years. Indeed, I think it would be impossible to exaggerate its importance—and that, not on one level only, not only as the history of the growth of the poetry of our time. It is a history of the development of Man's spirit, and the reasons for that development, and the book seems to me to be of the highest general interest.

At that moment I broke off to have a good laugh as I thought of the happy hunting ground the book will be in the future to all lecturers, and writers, on almost every conceivable subject dealing with our present and future cultural and moral state—(using the word moral in its larger sense). Everything falls into its proper place, is seen in its proper perspective. The true importance of Baudelaire, Rimbaud, and other poets of the time is seen, perhaps for the first time, in its fullness. The first chapter and the Conclusion are really magnificent in their sweep and their extraordinary comprehension. The tragic raison-d'être of the Dadaists is seen, and the part about Paranoia Art is very important. The part about Tzara (the chapter on him) is of great beauty, and of the highest interest—(it does not throw a light upon poetry alone, but on the whole world). The whole state to which modern poetry is arriving—working—seems to me to be summed up in the phrase of Mr Lindsay's about the poetry of Tzara . . . "The bitterness gives way slowly to a new love. The love for the pure sources. Gradually the inner tensions are found to coincide with the tendencies of history." There couldn't be a more important statement.

Then take this, from page 152: ". . . these are the poets who stand at the pivotal points of a vast and decisive spiritual change in man, bound up with social, political, and economic revolutions. They cannot therefore but give an important new revelation of the creative element in man." The book is packed with vitalising, fertilising ideas and pronouncements, and is extremely exciting.

It is, for one thing, the only revealing and understanding book, so far as I know, that has been written about the "revolutionary" artist's task—to quote Mr Lindsay's own phrase about Tzara: "Starting from the deepest levels of the disrupted unconscious, he began the task of building man up anew, building him up from the *elemental levels*."

121

I said, earlier in my letter, that everything falls into its proper place. Messrs Auden et Cie do. They have been given a completely exaggerated importance by certain people—or were given it a few years ago, because, as Dr Johnson said (very unfairly), of Gray, "He is dull in a new way, and that makes people think him great." Mr Lindsay isn't deceived, although he writes of them with perfect fairness.

The chapter on Eluard, a beautiful poet, is very fine. The translations from Tzara, Eluard, and Aragon are admirable. But, as I say, the book has an infinitely wider scope than the literary one. And it seems to me of an even added importance at this time.

Here, as always in Edith's comments on my work, it will be seen how eagerly she embraced the concept of revolutionary poet in the terms of my definition. Roughly, what I was saying was that the revolutionary poet of the modern world—that is, since the advent of industrialism with its rapidly extending fragmentation of man—was a poet who entered into the dark night of alienation, extenuating nothing and realising the full horror of the fragmenting and dehumanising process, and who only then proceeded with the task of recreating man, rediscovering his wholeness, and linking the new forms of integration with the social and political forces making for the end of division, the overthrow of bourgeois society. She accepted this position without the least fraction of criticism or evasion, though she had always sheered away from creeds that imposed a social function or role on poetry from the outside. She felt that in these formulations of mine the rights of the poet to his necessary freedoms were maintained.

Two days later, on 31 July, she sent me an excited telegram, with a following letter, about the essay for Laughlin. "Your understanding is the most extraordinary I know. I am amazed always by its depth, its sweep, and its comprehensiveness. Because every overtone is seized—not only the foundations and what Jung (I think) called 'the suns below the horizon.' That you should have written this essay about my poetry is a very important thing in my life as a poet—one of the most important that has ever happened to me. And not only that. It has come in a moment of my life when I have been feeling great personal and creative

despondency—being dead tired mentally—and this great illumination and belief is as much needed by my creative self, as water is
by a plant, and sun is by a plant. It is so amazing to have one's
poetry understood in its completeness, and in every vein and
impulse. Sometimes when reading a criticism of my poetry by
other critics, I think: 'I *might* have meant that—but actually, I
didn't mean *quite* that.' But with you, never. You are one of the
only two people who know what my early poetry means—Arthur
Waley is the other. And you are the only person who knows what
The Shadow of Cain means. What you have written about that
poem is a wonder of insight. You might have been the mind and
heart that wrote it. Only, *I* cannot explain it as *you* have done.
There would be no possible excuse for anyone who has read this
essay, to pretend they do not understand every shred of meaning
in the poem."

In late September she was to broadcast a talk about *The
Shadow* and her later poems in general; she asked if she could
cite the paragraph in which I summed up the poem's conflict and
resolution. "It is very nobly written, and I cannot explain that
part as you have done. What does not my work owe to you. And
what will not the work I shall do in future years owe to you."
She thanked me for some "strange and beautiful lines" I had
sent—translations from the ancient Sibylline Leaves. "I suppose
being a great scholar helps to make you the great critic you are.
Being a poet doesn't necessarily make a man a great critic. Look
at one whom we all revere as a poet—but who only sees other men's
poetry through his own eyes." (She was referring to Eliot.)

She took up her letter again to say that she had received my
reply to her comments on *The Starfish Road*. "I repeat, that I
think it is one of the most important books of our time." She
said that she agreed with what I had said about the Dadaist
manifestations and the need to record them in discussing the
movement. She said that she had read my essay twice again, and
was breaking off because she had to have the letter registered in
Sheffield on account of the Bank Holiday.

On 9 August she apologised for being slow in writing. She had
felt "seedy" on account of fibrositis in the spine and right arm—
"so useful for a writer!" I had sent her a setting of some lines of

hers about "Shadow like a lovely lady," and she said she had only read it visually so far, as she was still abed. Once, many years ago, she had played the piano with ease, but now felt strange before it. I had made some remarks about my Australianness as at least one main reason for my role as Total Outsider in the English literary scene; and had mentioned my period of domination by my father Norman, and the break in 1930, when for some years I obstinately persisted on the starvation-line, unable to find any way of living as a writer but determined to take no other course, whatever the consequences. "I am sure you are right, and that the key-thing *is* that you are an Australian. That extraordinary vigour and speed, the particular sweep and all-comprehending grasp of your mind, and a kind of heat and fire that comes from the sun—these I am certain are the result of this. How strange that you should ever have been dominated, even by the remarkable man who was your father. I should have thought your mind would always—no matter at what age—have been the dominating one. The 1930 break must have given you an added strength and purpose . . . I ran away first when I was five, but I didn't know how to put my boots on, I had to walk in my socks, and didn't get very far, and was captured and brought home by a policeman. I finally got away—though only on ticket-of-leave when I was twenty-five. But complete—or *almost* complete freedom has only come in the last few years. In some ways I think it is the best thing in the world to be a slow developer, and that one should pass through all contemporary influences." (I had made these points.) "You say you are outside all cliques! My God, so am I, and it is terrifically important, from one point of view. But, as you say, it adds to the up-hill aspects. I know, for nobody would have anything to say to my poetry for years and years—indeed, until 1942! Meanwhile, all the 1930 boys in their brown shirts with Liberty in large red letters all over them were scratching each other's back and rolling each other's logs as hard as anything. Nietzsche had a violent, invigorating effect on me as he had on you. I am furious at the misunderstanding of him, and the vulgarisation you speak of. I am glad you are writing the autobiography of your early life."

How Nietzsche and my autobiography come thus together was

the result of my brooding over what Whyte had to say of Nietzsche in *The Next Development*:

> The subjective tradition of Europe restricted further development, and its decay was inevitable. The isolated subject had to die before being re-born as part of nature. This meant agony for countless individuals all the world over, who experienced the dissolution of values in their own and their children's lives. The death of such a grand tradition was bound to lead any high genius who experienced it to visions of unequalled and intolerable intensity. That was Nietzsche's situation . . . His arrow to the farther shore can only be followed by those who can stand outside their own failure. Europe cannot accept Nietzsche because he represents the death of the European tradition.

I tried to make out how it was that we in Australia, under my father Norman's leadership, had sought to base on Nietzsche a rebirth of the grand tradition. Somehow, the raw colonial aspects of our situation made us able to feel Nietzsche as the reviver of what in fact he expressed the death. Our positions were illusory, derived from transitional and contradictory tensions that could not last for long; but we felt the situation, in the illusory form we gave it, none the less intensely. Starting from this point, I began the quest into my childhood, boyhood, and youth, which in due time was to beget the trilogy, *Life Rarely Tells, The Roaring Twenties, Fanfrolico and After*.[1]

Edith said that she would like very much to be introduced to Whyte and his wife. "I wouldn't speak; but should listen to you and him talking. Silence is one of my few gifts." I did later introduce her to the Whytes, though I forget the exact date. Edith liked Lancelot, and their friendship continued till her last days.

"The end paragraph of your letter is profoundly illuminating. As I've said before, I think you have an all-embracing all-comprehensive as well as creative mind. There is no work of yours that I have seen that I do not find exciting in the highest sense." And she repeated, "It's odd; I've been nearly dead,

[1] The originating essay, which was printed in *Meanjin*, preserved the discussion about Nietzsche as the starting-point.

mentally, for many months, and now have a violent upheaval of my mental life. It is like a geyser coming out of the earth. Perhaps I am going to be able to write again, soon. When do you go abroad? I do hope you will be back before I go to America." She asked if I had an agent there. If I hadn't, she would like to take *The Starfish Road* across for placing.

Three days later she was complaining that she had had to go back to bed with a racking headache due to her spinal fibrositis, and was only just getting about again. She had, however, managed to get to the piano and had played "haltingly" the second piece of music I had sent her; she found it "lovely and haunting." She repeated her hopes that we would be back in England before she left for America on a tour which she was coming increasingly to dread. "I can't stand all the yapping about nothing."

Soon afterwards she was discussing dates for a meeting, disappointed that we would be away during the first week in September, and hoping that we would all be able to meet when she returned to London before her departure. "I am writing two lectures and a broadcast, and the whole Continent of America is up in arms against me." She wanted to know how I was getting on with my *Life of Dickens*. The same day she wrote again. I had casually cited a passage about Renishaw which I had noticed in something written by Harry Pollitt. I forget just what he had said, but I felt sure it would please Edith, as it did. "Osbert will be so delighted to hear about Mr Pollitt. Though it makes me so angry to think of what he must have gone through as a boy that I can hardly breathe. I am afraid it must have been my odious parents whom he saw. Nothing to do with me—I disown them! They were firmly convinced that miners had a grand time and ate duck and drank champagne every Saturday night (though why the hell they *shouldn't*, I don't know! My parents had both). Please tell Mr Pollitt we aren't like that. And Osbert is a grand landlord, and a father to the whole district."

I did hand on her good wishes to Harry at a social in Hampstead in some sort of art-gallery, where he happened to be present and where Ann read *Gold Coast Customs* in her wonderful voice, pure as flowing water and rich with a sea-depth of emotion. I watched him listening with his shrewd canny eyes, a bit puzzled and at the same time affected. "Aye, the lass's heart is in the right place," he commented, nodding his head and taking a good swig of beer.

We did not see Edith before she departed; for we had flown to Poland for the Wroclaw Conference, after which we spent some time in mid-Poland, Warsaw, Cracow, Zakapane (with a visit to Auschwitz), then at Prague, finally at Paris with Tzara. I shall perhaps tell that story elsewhere. But here I must mention that I was deeply affected by the Conference, by the ruins of Warsaw and the desolation of Auschwitz. The Peace Movement that sprang from Wroclaw was largely abortive as far as England was concerned; but I was ready to support it or any other peace-movement whatever, whether it was endorsed by the Communist Party or not. I at once supported CND and sent in my name to the Committee of a Hundred as soon as I read of their formation, though they did not think it worth using. I gave my name in 1962 as a signatory to the suit filed by Linus Pauling against bomb tests in both the USA and the USSR. I did all I could to help the Authors' World Peace Appeal. In 1948 or at any later date I have never been able to see what the political affiliations of any peace-movement matter; if the cause is peace, it is a good one.

I had written on Edith for *The British Ally*—as one of several accounts of writers which I did for Wright Miller and Calder Marshall. At that time the Russians were looking for excuses to attack *The British Ally;* some journalist misinterpreted my plain words about *The Shadow of Cain* and described it as a poem in defence of the atom bomb. I was infuriated, and wrote a reply; but as Wroclaw came about soon after, I thought that here was a good chance to take the matter up directly. At Warsaw the delegates often dined at a large restaurant which was almost the only tall landmark left in the devastated city at that time. One night I saw Fadeyev seated at a near table, and near the end of the meal walked over and sat with him for coffee. I had already met him a few times in London; but had been put off by the dour face he wore at that time. At Wroclaw he had caused trouble by describing T. S. Eliot as something like a hyena with a type-writer; and though myself a foe of Eliot, I had been as annoyed at this attack as were the rest of the English delegation. Now, however, he unthawed and I saw his pleasant smile for the first time. Perhaps he had been drinking enough vodka. We got on well. He agreed that a disgraceful mistake had been made, and promised to see that amends were given. Edith was pleased when I told her the story. It was the night, I recall, when news of the death of Zhdanov arrived; for Jan Drda, the huge Czech writer, was sobbing on the stairs, and I was astounded that anyone could mourn such a politician, whose views I intensely disliked.

[11]

So ended 1948. The kind of discussion which it had seen was to continue for many years; but I shall not attempt to carry on my account in a chronological way. Rather, I shall deal with the more important points of our collaboration: *Arena, The Starfish Road,* and my writings about her work.

As I have said, she enthusiastically supported our quarterly *Arena,* in which Randall Swingler had joined Davenport and myself. The aim was to gather what seemed to us the best of the postwar work in England and abroad. The critical values in question, and the way in which we felt that the growth of Resistance or antifascist writing during the war linked with the prewar vanguard traditions, will be clearer when I come to discuss Aragon, Eluard, Tzara, and I shall not go into them here. It is sufficient to mention that the first issue of *Arena* in 1949 included Edith's *Street Acrobat,* five of Jean Cassou's *Sonnets Composed in Secret,* Tzara on the Dialectics of Poetry, Pasternak on Shakespeare's Imagery and Rhythm, Eluard's *From the Horizon of One Man to the Horizon of All,* Camus' *Archives of the Plague,* with stories by Tikhonov and Endre Illes, an essay by myself on Catullus and another by Alick West on Shaw, poems by Malcolm Lowry and MacDiarmid, and critical assessments of B. Traven by D. Lynn (South African) and of Camus by M. J. Lefèbre (Belgian). One might have thought that with such contents the issue would excite some interest. It fell totally flat. No bookshops took it; the only review, that in the *Daily Worker,* consisted of an attack on the Editorial Note. That Note was written by myself; and I cite part of it, as it expresses clearly enough the sort of thing

128

which I had discussed with Edith in connection with *Arena,* and which she ardently accepted.

Arena neither seeks to label our culture as "decadent" nor to acclaim it as securely progressive. We believe that the culture of our world is rent by intense conflicts, and for that very reason is full of the most violent potentialities for good and evil, for integration and disintegration. We believe in particular that countries like France and England which have well back in their past undergone successful bourgeois revolutions, have passed during the last hundred odd years through phases of culture which are of the utmost importance for the future. (The one flat period, in the visual arts, for instance, that can be simply labelled decadent or moribund in any sense is that of nineteenth-century academicism and naturalism, in which the tradition of the Renascence is seen petering out, with the folk-roots cut away. But at once a series of counter movements, often sectional and limited, begins struggling to find the lines of renewal, the necessary breakings-down and the points of new organic integration.)

Looking back from 1966, I find it hard to recall fully the sectarian positions general among Marxists, which, with the emergence of the Cold War, had hardened into the dogma that the Bourgeois West was totally decadent. Hence the opposition to *Arena* in the CP and the way in which I was trying to fight a battle on two fronts. The bracketed statement above about academicism was polemical, meant to infer that Soviet art at that time was drawing on the one development of western culture which *was* hopelessly decadent, while labelling as decadent those in which there was genuine conflict and contact with reality.

The Note went on:

The work in which *Arena* is interested is the sorting-out of these confused and often vital trends of resistance—the clarification of the valuably formative from the false and the merely fashionable (a feeble conformity trying to exploit what was for a moment a genuine adventure). This work includes a give-and-take between Marxism in its critical aspects and the free play of the creative elements in our culture; it aims at separating-out and strengthening all that genuinely reveals the artist's prophetic function, his capacity to reach ahead into various aspects of the integration that his world lacks but needs for its advance. And that means also showing how this function worked out in the past.

Christopher Caudwell posed with fine precision the issue at stake. The critical problem is to realise what "is the lie at the heart of contemporary culture, the lie which is killing it, and deeper still is found the truth which is the complement of the lie, the truth which will transform and revitalise culture."

The notion of the dialogue between Marxism and the other elements in a culture, acceptable a decade or so later when the exposure of Stalinism had been made, was an unforgivable heresy in 1949. Emile Burns told me that I was absolutely wrong and should drop my formulations; when *Arena* appeared, his words were echoed in the review by Derek Kartun, then a leading light of the *Daily Worker,* who left the CP in 1956 and dropped flatly out of politics.

Edith said to me of the first *Arena* issue, "I think you have every right to be proud of it. The vitality is extraordinary, rising up from the pages."

Further issues of the first year included poems by Neruda and Julian Tuwim, essays by Aragon and Sydney Goodsir Smith, stories by Vittorini, Montale, Alvaro, Angus Wilson, Lowry, Leonov, Nagy Istvan, Dan Davin, and others. But reviewers and booksellers remained quite unimpressed. A similar fate overwhelmed our attempt to start a cheap series of good poetry. Randall and I were the editors. Edith gave us several poems for her booklet; George Barker gave us his *Confessions*; Dylan Thomas was ready to contribute when he had something new. (Davenport got Barker and Norman Cameron for the series.) Stanley Snaith, whom I had known in the old Franfrolico days of *The London Aphrodite* and who had been befriended by Gordon Bottomley, happened to come into the office, and I was pleased to make up one of the booklets from his poems. I also added *Twinter's Wedding* by Jonathan Denwood, which I think may be called the last long sustained folk-poem in English (in the old sense of a peasant poem genuinely rooted in the songs, customs, and festivities of the countryside: here, of Cumberland). His brother Marley had given it to me before the war and I had long wanted to find an occasion for getting it into type. Randall, Jack

Beeching, Maurice Carpenter and myself also had our booklets; and Tony Adams designed the series admirably, as he had done *Arena*. But though one or two reviewers did notice us this time, the booksellers were implacably hostile, and sold hardly a couple of dozen copies—orders which they reluctantly passed on to us. Even Edith's booklet hardly sold at all. (The price was a shilling.) Later on, under another imprint, George Barker's poem was to attain its modicum of fame, but not while he was a Key Poet. Similarly, no one took any notice of Malcolm Lowry's prose and verse in *Arena,* though later, when he appeared elsewhere, he was to be highly praised.

In 1949 I wrote the first version of my first autobiographical volume, *Life Rarely Tells.* The version was substantially the same as the book that appeared in 1958 under that title, though I added a little and to some extent reorganised the material, omitting an excursus on the psychology of Kierkegaard and Nietzsche. I asked Edith to read the manuscript. She read it and was so excited that she could not wait to write or to talk about the work. She sent me a telegram of congratulation. What she said to me was as follows: "It is one of the most moving, important and illuminating books about a young creature's spiritual develop-ment, indeed all development, that I have ever read. I think it very wonderful. It moves me deeply. I have never read a book that was more alive." She said several times that she was much moved by the account of the discovery of poetry and the first tentative movements of my own expression, as well as what she called "the meetings with the beings who are islands in seas one cannot navigate." (Such beings were Plato, Blake, Shakespeare, and so on.) She was particularly fascinated by one passage, which had no particular relation, however, to such matters and which described the shooting of flying-foxes in a mangrove swamp. The detail about my uncle shooting off their claws so as to bring them down from their perches (to which they clung even in death) hit that nerve of pity and outrage which was so quick in response in her. She said, "I think you cram every moment of your day, cram it with eternity and not with today, as Kierkegaard said."

She had been very interested in my discussion of the "crisis in the symbol of authority" and the obsession with the "unknown murderer" in men like Dostoevsky, Kierkegaard, Kafka, Nietzsche. It seemed to her, in her phrase, of great life-importance as well as literary importance. She quoted back to me my own statement: "We can fight the existentialist because he condemns men to hell, and yet recognise that in so far as he truly reveals hell he is revealing the pang we must all feel, the division we must overcome." She called this a primal truth, and she added, "I shall fight the idea and the ideal of hell always. Perhaps that is why I, when I was young, like you, when you were a boy, was obsessed by Nietzsche. But this book of yours has depth after depth."

As soon as I told her that I was working on a *Life of Dickens,* she expressed the greatest interest; for Dickens was one of the writers she most enjoyed and admired. In late July 1949 I sent her proofs and she at once commented, "It seems to me the only important book on Dickens that has been written." She made several detailed observations; but I shall omit these here and deal rather with the fuller remarks she made when she got the bound book. I may mention, however, that she was especially intrigued with some of my correlations: for instance, that Dickens was writing about Mrs Todgers and the Voice from the Tomb at the very moment he was telling his mother-in-law how he was being haunted by Mary Hogarth—and the associations of Tom-All-Alone.

I dedicated the book to her, as one who like Dickens had "carried on the great tradition in a dark age." (The phrase was his, and had seemed to me to show how essentially conscious he was of what he was doing, and what he was up against.) She told me that the dedication moved her deeply. "As for the book! What a pride to have such a book dedicated to me. I think it is the only great book about a great genius considered as a man *as well as a* medium for inspiration, that has ever been written. I can think of no other. Wagner's book on Beethoven is a great book—but it does not deal with the man, only with the artist. And Boswell's Life of Dr Johnson is not the life of a great genius, but the record of a very wise and shrewd old man, a terrific character, but no genius. But even that old fool Desmond McCarthy says you have made him realise Dickens' greatness to the full. What a wonderful, wise, recreative and humane book it is, to be sure. Your genius for leaping straight to the heart of the matter is shown everywhere. The book is, also, almost unbearably moving. The part about his childhood, and his love for his sister, is of an appalling sadness. The child, the youth, and the man, are as alive as they must have been to themselves—as the whole being was to *him*self. The book seems to me even greater than when I read it in proof. What an amazing gift you have for illumination by quotations. That letter to Maria, written when he had met her again and was trying to avoid her, contains the daily history of every writer . . . And how the man's fundamentally humane nature (to everyone excepting his wife and his sons!!) appears in that letter! Few people who are trying to get rid of somebody who was once loved, do it so kindly, with such anxiety not to humiliate."

She went on in this vein, and throughout our relationship maintained an equally high opinion of the book. "The works are so illuminated by you, down to their deepest roots, that no one—not the poor silly little boys and girls who say, openly and without shame, that they 'can't bear Dickens' will, at least, have in the future no excuse for not realising that they are unable to bear one of the greatest masters who ever lived. That old owl McCarthy, in his review, which is, anyhow, a grand send-off for the book, and will set flocks of people rushing for it today (I am told a review of such importance and length in the two Sunday papers sells books more than anything else) puts, as a small cloud in the midst of his otherwise clear sunshine, the fact that you do not think *David Copperfield* the greatest of his books. *Of course* it *isn't*! It is dull—dull—dull—in comparison with most. When one thinks of it compared with *Bleak House, Little Dorrit, Our Mutual Friend* or *Martin Chuzzlewit*. The whole of your criticism is of the most undeceivable kind. I am profoundly excited about the book. I cannot remember a book that has excited me more. I am deeply and endlessly proud of the dedication, and as endlessly grateful."

To grasp the point and emphasis of some of Edith's comments here, one has to remember that in 1949 Dickens still had a low reputation in the intellectual world. In May 1948, Priestley, with whom I had been discussing Dickens, wrote to me, "For the last twenty years there has been something withdrawn, invalidish, over-introverted, about highbrow criticism here, which is mostly written by people who did not want to share experience with ordinary folk. A further point is that many of them have never really read anything. When you talk to them the gaps in their reading are appalling. David Cecil told me the other day that in an argument with Cyril Connolly, who said that Flaubert was a greater novelist than Dickens, he finally discovered that Connolly had never read Dickens." That correctly represents the situation, I think. Now such narrow attitudes are hardly tenable, or at least they have to put up a better pretence of being aware of a wider and more rowdy world.

Two more works of mine which Edith welcomed were *Song of a Falling World* and *Byzantium into Europe,* a study of Latin verse from about A.D. 350 to 600. Of the first she said it had opened up a wholly new world to her and was her constant companion. She commented in detail on many of the poems but instead of lingering over her remarks I shall pass on to the second book, which had an incomparably greater impact. She read it in proofs. "The life, the fire, the learning, the vistas, the sweep of it! They are extraordinary. And what wonderful phrases there are." She repeated that she could not exaggerate her enthusiasm and was overwhelmed by "this terrific excitement of a new world that you have brought into my life. (And which is actually giving me a new spiritual vitality. How selfish one is! But this book is *exactly* what I was needing to renew me.)" As she read, she had to linger, she said, reread and fully absorb. But "the book is already forming a great pattern for me." She was full of such declarations as that "I do not know *when* I have been—not only so enraptured, but so vitalised and renewed and have had so much new blood of the spirit given me by anything as by these wonderful works and by that great book, to which I am now going back with fervour."

A little later, she was again so caught up in emotion that she sent me a wire about the book. And then she followed up her first expressions of pleasure with reiterated praises. "I am so entirely overwhelmed by the splendour of this book. I can only say that you may feel the writing of it makes it worth while to have lived—would have made it worth while, even if you had not had the great personal happiness of loving and being loved by Ann. I *am* overwhelmed." Things were rather difficult for her at the time. As usual, she had to go out and help a friend in difficulties; but she was so gripped by *Byzantium* that she sat up all night reading it. She had become so exhausted that she fainted. "Nothing could possibly give the faintest idea of my excitement about this wonderful, this extraordinary, this infinitely *important* and beautiful book." She told me that she would be going back to it at the Sesame as soon as night came down. She would have peace till the nightclub opposite got going. Meanwhile "I can see the flames of its wonders in their full splendours."

She maintained this attitude all the while I knew her. Almost the last words she said to me were, "I still carry *Byzantium into Europe* with me wherever I go. I can't bear to be without it."

I showed her fuller translations of many of the poets I mentioned, especially of Paulos the Silentiary. She loved his poem on St Sophia, and was much struck by the odd epic, *Hexameron,* by George of Pisidia. A phrase, which I cited in my book from Porphyry about "pure fire compressed into holy forms," had a remarkable effect on her. She long brooded over it, as if it provided the key to secrets of her own imagery which had so far eluded her; and kept on returning to it, finding new suggestions and stimulations. (In some reminiscences she wrote for the *Observer* in her last years, she cited it in the midst of her account of Roy Campbell, in which she denied that he was a fascist. I had the feeling that she mentioned my book in order to balance her words defending such a right-wing character.)

Did she then simply read all of my works with such a fiery eagerness that any criticism of their faults was burned away? Not by any means. Where she could not give this wholehearted acceptance, she said nothing. The first experience I had of this sort of silence on her part was over my novel *Fire in Smithfield,* which followed *Men of Forty-Eight.* I confidently expected that she would like it a lot, if not so much as the previous work; but she never referred to it, and I at no time asked her for an opinion which she did not volunteer. In this case, however, I feel sure that her silence did not arise from any aesthetic dissatisfaction;

for, judging by her other responses, this was the sort of work of mine that she would have thoroughly enjoyed. No, I feel that the explanation was she felt I was trespassing on her own ground (Princess Elizabeth and Bloody Mary) and was afraid that the book would be too anti-Catholic. So she did not read it.

However, her failure to make any comments on *Betrayed Spring* and the following novels of my series *The British Way* certainly arose from a lack of interest in the method and material. I sent them to her, and she ignored them. But when I sent her *The Passionate Pastorial,* an eighteenth-century comedy of nakedness in a forest-setting (based on Ashurst Forest near Penshurst, in the midst of which I was living), she promptly read it and expressed her enjoyment. It was typical of her that she was so taken up with a poacher (a rather minor character in the book) that she at first skipped through to read all the passages about him; and was moved to tell me a story about her great-great-grandfather. A Negro slave had run away from a cruel master and hidden in a cave not far from Renishaw Hall, where he lived by stealing and killing the sheep of the great-great-grandfather. The latter found him out and captured him, but instead of sending him back to the master he bought him and refused to charge him. Then he sent the fellow back to the part of Africa from which he had been taken. Such a story stirred Edith's pride.

When my *Life of Meredith* was published, she said that she thought all the conclusions absolutely right. Meredith had been neglected and undervalued, and she felt that the book restored him to his just place. She didn't, however, care much for his poetry, which she considered too jagged and raw in texture. "The body of poetry isn't his body," was how she expressed it, but she found "shining beauty" in his prose. The main character of the *Egoist* she thought could not have been bettered as a portrait of her father as a young man, before his later eccentricities came upon him. (This point she often repeated. She knew and admired the *Egoist* very highly.) When I quoted to her a passage in which Meredith said of a performance of Lady Macbeth's waking that it suggested someone stricken mad at the moment of resurrection, she was much affected and wanted me to write a letter to the *T.L.S.* embodying the quotation so that no one else could get in first with it. Apart from the fact that I thought it very unlikely that anyone else was reading Meredith, I had no interest whatever in staking that sort of claim; and Edith's insistence on the need to take such steps seemed to me to come from the less independent side of her personality.

But though a few details of the study of Meredith excited her and she stated emphatically her agreement with my thesis, she did it soberly and without anything of the enthusiastic expansiveness of her comments on paper or by word of mouth about the Dickens book.

She was then far from a simple acceptance of whatever I wrote. She expressed uncompromising partisanship of certain books, she ignored others, and she was cool in her judgement when she did not feel touched to the quick.

[12]

But now I must come back to *The Starfish Road,* and to my writings about her work. After she had seen the manuscript, she kept on asking about it, expecting it to be published. In January 1949 she wrote from the USA, asking for it (with underlined words) so that she might write her preface. "I had hoped to have it two months ago—have indeed, looked for it every day. Perhaps it will come while I am in Florida, where I go on Saturday. Today, I am going to do *Façade,* at the Museum of Modern Art. This terrifies me. I *wish* you and Ann were going to be there. Again, you are one of the only people who understand what I was trying to do."

Later in the year, after I had written an essay on her work in *Life and Letters,* "You are one of the only great critics of poetry there has been. As I said in my letter, you rank with Coleridge, and with Swinburne (who I think was a superb critic). Indeed, above Coleridge in your understanding, because there are certain things he could not understand—phrases in *Hamlet,* for instance. Whereas you flash straight to the heart of the matter, in every case." She repeated once more her opinion that I alone understood her early work, and went on: "I am more profoundly grateful to you than I could ever express, for what you have done,

137

and are doing, for my poetry. And the idea of your writing a *book* about it fills me with happiness and pride. Again, more than I could ever express."

Yet again she restated what she had said about Coleridge and Swinburne, and this time ended: "You get at the innermost life of the poems. Really, I don't know anything like it. It is almost terrifying. It is certainly *life-giving*. (I had felt, lately, that my poetry was dead in me. But you have brought it to life again. I feel it stirring.)" She went on yet again about my insight into her early work "as though you had been inside my mind. She told me, "Nothing *nothing* has given me such happiness for ages, and when I say ages, I mean ages. What do you think it would mean to me to have a *book* written by you about my poetry? I could hardly hope for such a thing. It would reward me beyond all my hopes, for my long years of struggle and misunderstanding and abuse."

Then again I find her repeating, "I *could not bear* to be deprived of your book. I really do not know what I should do were I to be."

In January 1950, she told me, "Nothing has *ever* given me more. It was so extraordinary, the effect it had. It was to me as if I were young again, and had just had my first book published. I don't think anything else has ever given me more excitement and a feeling of vitality going to begin again. (I have been dead for some months.) All in the essay is so extraordinary. Not only your profound understanding of the *import* of my work as a whole, the essence of it—the giggling maid, for instance. It has *exactly* that condensation into essence of time and place that I was trying to get. I can never, really, Jack, express my *very* great gratitude, my profound appreciation. Osbert was made as happy by it as I was—and am." He had in fact sent me a telegram of thanks.

In February 1950 she asked if my essay could be used as a preface for the book of her early poems that Duckworths were issuing; and she hesitantly suggested that she would be pleased if I agreed to cut out what I had said of Eliot and Auden. Appearing in *Life and Letters* (or in a book like *The Starfish Road*), such comments could not be connected with her; but if they were put in front of a book of hers, they would seem rude and harsh towards two persons she liked. (She had met Auden in New York and rather liked him, though she did not know him at all well.) "Tom is a great friend," she said, "Wystan also is a friend, and I think it would hurt their feelings terribly." At the same time she insisted that she was completely in accord with what I had said. "What you say is utterly true about Tom's dog-collar. But there one is. Life has withered him, and it is tragic."

I of course agreed, and she was grateful. Later in the letter she spoke of the matter again. "What you say about Tom is entirely right, and it does, indeed, need saying, and it was said with the greatest brilliance and insight, as is always the case with you. It is merely a question of personal friendship on my part." She felt that perhaps her attitude showed a weakness, an element of falsity. "I don't know, really, whether personal friendship ought ever to come in matters of literature, but, although one would never lie, there are cases where perhaps one cannot speak."

By mid-1950 I had begun to sheer off *The Starfish Road* and was extending my analysis back into the eighteenth century, following up trails I had opened in an essay for *Life and Letters* on Turner's verses. I was developing a huge work, *The Sunset Ship,* which in due time I also shelved—though a small part of its material was used later in my edition of Turner's poems, also called *The Sunset Ship,* and in my *Life of Turner,* in 1966. The rest still remains in manuscript. As with *The Starfish Road,* I made no effort to get any of it published, satisfied with my one reader, Edith, to whom I showed most of the chapters. She was almost as excited as she had been by the other work.[1]

Again, in early 1951, she wrote to me from New York, "I am absolutely *longing* for *The Starfish Road*. If there is anything of any sort I can do in any way at all, please let me know." In April, back home, she commented on some of the new chapters. "*The*

[1] For instance she wrote, "The Turner eighteenth-century imagery work on which you are now engaged excites me very much. Nobody was ever more born to write about imagery than you. As I have said so often, there is nobody who has such wonderful and fertile energy as you. It is most truly dynamic in the real meaning of the word, allied, as it is, to the most acute understanding." She was particularly interested in the section on Smart and his *Jubilate*. She understood and fully accepted the method, which linked the development of the poetic image with the struggle against the mechanistic philosophy of Galileo-Newton and with the social forms of exploitation and alienation linked at every point with that philosophy. (Essays on Edward Young and on Savage, which were forerunners of the fully expanded positions of *The Sunset Ship,* had appeared in *Life and Letters.*)

Starfish Road is *magnificent*. What a sweep and grasp—what a delving into the very roots of the matter." She was especially pleased with what I had said of Thomson and Smart, in a revised version of the book, dealing with their ideas and images of light, and then of colour, which emerged as active elements in their poetry and its philosophy—elements opposed to the Newtonian mechanism which reduced life to quantities. She said that she considered the comparison I had made of Smart and Thomson along these lines was "one of the greatest pieces of criticism of the last hundred years or more." She spoke in the same vein of my accounts of Baudelaire and Lautréamont. Baudelaire had been one of the abiding central influences in her poetry, in her whole poetic thinking. Lautréamont, whose relatively minor stature she recognised, however, exercised a considerable fascination for her, and several times she urged me to carry on my analysis of him at greater length. Of Mallarmé she said, "Nobody, I think, has ever written so finely about Mallarmé as you. It is really violently exciting. You have really found the life-principle of that flower"— the Spectre of the Rose, she meant.

But as I have been saying so much here about *The Starfish Road* and giving only very generalised accounts of its method, perhaps it would be as well to cite the beginning of the analysis of Mallarmé as an example of what Edith so passionately accepted and praised. After discussing what was implied by Charles Cros' description of him as "a broken-up Baudelaire, whose bits could not fit themselves together again," I went on to deal with what was implied by a "musical" poetry, the development of the reverie-method in *L'Après-Midi,* the breaking-up and reconstitution of a scene or situation in terms that were felt to have poetic purity. Then I continued:

Mallarmé saw his work as an effort to "separate, on the basis of different attributes, as it were, the twofold condition of words, crude and immediate on the one hand, essential on the other" (*Divigations*). The crude word is that which has no aim beyond the moment and is lost in the action it accompanies or promotes. "As though one were to take a coin and silently put it into another's hand," adds Mallarmé, with a simile which shows how he equates action here with complicity in the bourgeois scene, the cash-nexus.

The crude word facilitates relations only in the same way as money does; it binds in a false relation, in alienation. The essential word penetrates behind the false relationships, into an uncontaminated truth: "I say: a flower! and beyond the oblivion to which my thought consigns any contour, in so far as it is something other than the known calices, there musically arises, the very idea in all its sweetness, the absence of any bouquets."

In all this there is something that is new only in the intensified focus. All true poetry lifts the elements of common experience to a new unity and grasps at the essence of language, at the kind of deep integral process by which language has been born and developed. The poetic word is neither the word of normal communication nor some "poetical" abstracted counter, a special language. It is the common word at a higher level of concentration, with a multiplicity of reference gathered to a single point. Mallarmé means all this, but he also means something else—and though he seeks metaphysical explanations of this something, it is in fact simply his sense of the deep split in life caused by the alienating process of his world. By bringing together the two questions, the nature of the poetic word and the opposition of the creative process to that of alienation, he achieves his new intense awareness of the essential "word."

His position thus embodies a deep truth and an unrealised element of the alienation against which he fights.

He is above all aware of the concrete nature of the essential word, its basis in the total life-process of men (at the heart of which lie both the full organic process of body-spirit and the productive activities that make man man). "Approaching the organism that is the repository of life, the word with its vowels and diphthongs represents a kind of flesh" (*Les Mots Anglais*). But because of the unrealised division in his thought—which cuts the organic process away from productive activity—he sees this "flesh" of the word as an abstraction; the total music as a silence. That is, he sees the essential word as an activity totally lacking all the nexus of relationships that are crude—that reflect the contaminated relations of the bourgeois world which constitute actuality.

Here then is the basic contradiction, which drives him on and which he is yet never able to overcome. All the while he is aware that the word is "flesh" as well as abstraction, is a force linked with the "new" in life as well as a metaphysical silence. Thus, he declares, "Every soul is a melody which the problem is to renew."

His notion of verse as incantation carries on this contradiction.

For it sees verse as both a magical act raising up phantoms or lies, *mensonges,* and as the concrete apprehension of reality:

"I maintain that there is a secret equivalence between the old methods and the magic that poetry will always be. I state it here, and I admit that I personally in my essays have perhaps stated it to an extent that goes beyond what my contemporaries are able and ready to enjoy. To evoke the unnamed object in a deliberate shadow, by allusive never-direct words, which all amount equally to expressions of silence, is to attempt something that comes close to an act of creation; this act of creation achieves plausibility within the limits of the idea that the sorcerer of literature exclusively exploits, till he succeeds in educing the semblance of an illusion. The verse is conceived as an Invocation! And no one will deny that the circle which is forever closed and opened by rhyme has a similitude to the rings that a fairy or magician draws on the grass . . .

"The verse, which out of several vocables remakes a word entire, new, strange to the tongue and like an incantation . . ."

But, in using the simile of the magic circle, the fairy-circle, he forgets that behind such forms lies the dance-circle of the primitive group, which has a continuous history from earliest tribal days right into the days of the folk. The magic circle is only a special (and in its later phases a broken-down or decadent) form of the dance-circle. What is vital in Mallarmé's thesis about the opening-closing circle of rhythm reaches back to the communal dance; what is frustrating in it halts at the magician's diagrams.

The form in which the question of belief is raised is again typical of the contradictions already noted. The poetic word or image is a lie, is supremely real. It is something to be accepted as more real than the "crude" world, where words are indistinguishable from the cash-nexus; it is only a phantom of momentary magic. Yet in fact, in Mallarmé's poetry, the quest is for a new richness of contact, not a devious statement of total loss; he seeks to grasp the ghost of the rose which evokes the rose, to express the momentary unity-and-conflict of emotion and its setting, of man and his world, but not to lose experience, to drown it in a metaphysical silence. He makes his verse the pledge of a new, pure, and satisfying union:

> To plunge me deep in pure delight
> without a pathway, understand,
> O dreaming girl, by subtle cheat
> to hold my wing within your hand.

Freshness of dusk invades your flesh
at every pulse of feathered play:
as delicately the prisoned beat
thrusts the horizon further away.

O giddiness, Space pulls and strains
shuddering still like a great kiss
which, mad at being born in vain,
cannot leap out or sink in peace.

Feel how the wild shy paradise slips
like buried laughter in release
out of the corner of your lips
deep in the universal crease.

The sceptre of the shores of eve
stagnant on eves of gold is here:
this white closed flight that you oppose
against a bracelet's ring of fire.

The diverse elements—the image of the bird (heart) in the hand, the
fluttering kiss, the sense of standing at the centre of life and of
energies radiating outwards to press the very horizon back, the
edenic renewal of life and the impact of hurrying time, the opposition
and unity of far and near, stable and unstable, free and enclosed—the
setting in the firelit room with the reflections on the bracelet on the
girl's wrist as she lifts her hand, the hand in which is centred the
emotion and sensation of union—and the final fusion of the two
landscapes (the sunset-horizon and the bracelet-circle in the enclosed
room)—all these elements, to name only the obvious, are truly
unified in the poetic conception, the movement, the syntax.

From here I went on to analyse the relation of his ideas and
technique to the choice-and-chance of the poetic act imaged as a
dice-throw, the impasse of *Igitur*.

[13]

I feel also that I should give here some further account of what
I said in the essay on her poetry which she used as an introduction

to *Façade and Other Poems* in 1950.[1] I began by arguing that one could link the confusion and trivialisation of contemporary poetry in England with the failure of poets and critics alike to make any sense out of her work. (I feel that this thesis is even more true fifteen years and more later than it was then; for then there was Dylan struggling inside the great tradition.) I briefly analysed the Romantic Movement and its breakdown in England after Byron, Shelley, Keats, and the way in which dissociation or alienation triumphed there, while the fight against it passed above all to the French poets—despite a few lonely dissidents such as Hopkins. (I should have added Meredith.) I tried to show what the Victorian betrayal of poetry had meant, and its effects in Edwardian England—with the irruption at that point of Edith on the scene. Her relation on the one hand to Baudelaire and Rimbaud, and on the other to our native tradition, from Langland and Dunbar to Blake and Beddoes. Her relation to nursery-rhyme, folksong, mumming-play. I took two simple examples ("Jane, Jane, Tall as a crane, The morning light creaks down again," and "The gossiping naiad of the water, In her sprigged gown like the housekeeper's daughter") "to show the new way in which she uses the symbolist 'derangement of the senses' for integrative purposes. The folk-theme of Jane brings out the immemorial aspect of the girl getting up at dawn for a day of labour; the image of tallness, again traditional, gets its particular emphasis from the strange feeling of gawkiness and giddy half-awakeness it evokes; the sense of going down in the chilly early light is one with the creaking of the stairs; the folk-rhythm conveys the treading, the familiar steps of descent, and rivets the various elements of imagery, the angular sense of strangeness-to-oneself moving in the dawn. Or take the other lines" which I had quoted as an example of her peculiar Englishness. "The sprigged

[1] To round off the tale of things I wrote about Edith's work there was a review of her *Shakespearean Notebook,* and a talk I gave at the PEN congress in 1954 (Amsterdam) on her poetry. Of the first she said that my notice, that by John Russell in the *Sunday Times,* and a third by Kenneth Muir, were the only ones that grasped the book "and knew what I was trying at least to do. But then yours is one of the only extraordinary understandings of this age, as I have said, not once, but a thousand times" (19 January 1949). (Also a brief unimportant passage in my *After the Thirties,* 1956.)

gown brings out simultaneously the social setting, the exact tone of the summerday, the patterns of waterlight."

I then discussed the omnipresent element of conflict in her work, its personal, social and aesthetic aspects all fused; her splendid revival of free, controlled Rhythms, tense, organic, liberating—breaking through all set and flaccid patterns, all dead symmetries. The link with the dance, and so again with folkforms, ultimately with immemorial ritual. The link further with the rebirth of Joy in her poetry, a tremendous contribution without parallel. But because of the penetration into conflict and contradiction, the confrontation of this Joy always with the actual hell of alienation, the pang of the crucified body. "So, despite moments of pure release into happiness, there is deeply imbedded in the method the need to express the wrong done to life, the twisting of the loveliest things into sources of pain and discord. The rich springing bell-sweet rhythms of love-of-life are jangled into the ironic sense of hell, a persisting agony of tension. Life seems fighting to escape into a lyric space, yet for ever forced back into suffering and pang. The elemental pattern of joy and loss, life and death, becomes the accusation of a world based on the lie; it breaks through, it accuses, it splinters the surfaces to which the lie clings; and the deep simple pattern coincides with the life of the world, smashing it up and yet bringing it together momentarily into the promised delight and untainted union. Black Mrs Behemoth and the young springwind that threatens the useless candle-life and blows on to new worlds. A feeling of danger and unapprehended menace: the flat painted shapes of the world caught up in furious gyres of compulsion and suddenly deepening, so that nothing is what it seems. A conflict expressed in every detail of form, in the clash or sweet drone of sound and its throbbing textures. *Façade* is the climax of this phase, with its clear bright rhythms, its topsyturvy mocking picture of the damned world and all the lovely scrolls of elemental energy, the sweet flow of change and the knots of terror. The mad façade falls down and the reversal of all things begins."

Edith always expressed herself particularly delighted with my analysis of *Façade* and its allied early poems; she rightly felt that if these were not understood, nothing of her worldview, her techniques, her imagic method, her poetic meanings, would be grasped. I went over a large number of the poems with her and she agreed entirely with my interpretation of them. Someday I hope to write down this detailed examination. Here, in the essay, I probed into two of the easier poems, and made the statement: "I should like to combat the idea that these poems," *Façade, Bucolic Comedies,* and such early poems as *Mandoline, Singerie,* and so on, "are in any ways nonsensical, i.e. collocations of haphazard words and images. True, the associations are often glancing and rapid in the extreme, but the total effect comes from a highly organised basis of sense."

Take *Dark Song.* Here the image is that of the hard-worked servant-girl sitting in a semicoma of exhaustion before the fire. In her tiredness her bodily essence asserts itself and becomes one with the fire into which she gazes. The fire leaping and tugging at the wood is seen as the rough bear, the tousled curls of the flames its fur. Fire and bear are captive as the girl; she feels herself lost and wandering in the forest of captivity which is also the earth of her energies, the dark heats of desire stirring in her, and afraid, and unafraid; baited and yet keeping her forest-virtue. The further image intrudes of the domestic cat basking before the fire: that is what the girl seems from outside, but in truth she is the harassed and chained bear seeking to escape like the furry fire. And the little poem concludes with the statement of the ultimate union of the girl and the earth, her obstinate spirit-of-life that will not be beaten down however cruelly it is oppressed.

The difficulty comes solely from the compression of image and thought, the way in which bear, fire, girl, cat, forest are all merged. But there is no confusion.

Or take a lighter moment, that of *Mariner Man.* Here the child looks at an old sailor and wonders at the strangeness, the sense of distance of salt horizons that he exhales. The dialogue utters the silent exchange of their looks. Here the key-image is one of curving and rondure—the round earth which the mariner has compassed. This image is carried on into the undulating wrinkles on the old man's face, which are like the curving marks of the tide on the sands, and which are linked and contrasted with the wheels of the train. The train is seen (like a toy-train) going round in circles, returning on itself, and suggests the rounding curves of the arched

146

porpoises in the water. The smoke too curls like the wrinkles and ribbed sea-sand (again a toy-image). And all this movement is going round and round like a merry-go-round:

> The burly, the whirligig wheels of the train,
> As round as the world and as large again.

The fields are full of the round clover, and the train is off to Babylon and Troytown—further images of rondure; for Babylon is its own hanging-gardens, the spirally-ascended ziggurat or world-image, and Troytown is *Troia,* the womb, the rondured maiden-castle—*Caer Troia,* as the Welsh shepherds call their games of turf-mazes, the Towers of Turnings.

Edith Sitwell could scarcely have known all this about Troy, since it has been brought out only by recent scholarship; but with the *felicitas* that is also *curiosa,* the luck of art that is always somewhere the result of hard work, she gets the right word. And indeed Troytown has always been a world-image in her work, derived partly from folk-sources, partly from an intuitive reading of the inner meaning of the literary tradition.

In referring there to folk-sources I was thinking of such phrases as that used in Cornwall, "All of a Troytown," for a state of confusion. Edith herself admitted that she had no knowledge of *Caer Troia* and the like, but said she was enthralled by my remarks, as it showed, in a way (she thought), why the name *Troy House* was attached to her maternal grandmother's family-house in Wales—a house now lost to them—and why the name always had such an effect on her mind. "I am entirely, physically, and in nature, like that side of the family," she added, "although they are practically centaurs, and I cannot get on a horse without trembling." And then, as a final comment, she said, justly, "I always, I think, go back to first principles, and that, I suppose, was what I was doing, unconsciously, in the use of that word."

Mariner Man thus turns out to express the child's sudden awakening to the sense of space, gained in the moment of human contact, and the ironic question of the last two lines:

> But what can that matter to you, my girl?
> (And what can that matter to me?)

utters the sense that it matters infinitely to everyone; for "that" is the Earth, is human experience. But the irony defines the sense of separation that intrudes at this very moment of union, of expanded apprehension—the recoil of fear at the vastness which the adventure of contrast has revealed, and the complex problems of human relationship which the toy-imagery has momentarily controlled but which yet remains to be explored.[1]

In each poem the meaning is also embodied in the rhythm and sound-texture. *Dark Song* has a brooding set of vowels and *-rs,* and its rhythm echoes a nursery-rhyme, yet breaks the cadence till the last moment. *Mariner Man* tumbles with its dactyls in the undulating movement of its image-theme; and mixed with onomatopoeic effects like "snorting and sporting like porpoises" are linking sounds like "the burly, the whirligig ... curl ... girl ... world," the whirling pivoted on the plunge of "over" and "clover."

This kind of analysis could be made of every one of the poems. They bring a new poetic concentration into our language. The difficulty is not one of externally devised complications, but is valid because inherent in the new concept of poetic unity.

Here I was at last making a more precise analysis of what I considered her achievement; and I am pleased that I did at least this much for her. But I should have carried on with the same sort of thing in a much extended form, covering adequately each phase of her work. However, I shall cite here the general comments with which I followed the above:

The next stage is *The Sleeping Beauty,* one of the very loveliest poems in the language, with its emphasis on lyric delight. The image of beauty, the new life which is the old, reawakened and transformed, is not to be easily or prematurely gained; the thorns of the darkness of alienation lie between. But here the beauty to be won is securely defined. Irony gives way to a tragic note of "the lost and terrible innocence."

A poem of childhood, of the lost Eden cut off by awareness of the

[1] Many more points might have been added. The mariner-man suggests the Ancient Mariner with his guilt-quest; the term used for him suggests the days of sail, and so his staring at the train brings out the contrasts of time (the craftworld and the industrial world). The time-aspect is further stressed by the opposition of age and childhood. So the poem defines a sudden sense of the reality of time as well as of space. Similarly in *Jane, Jane,* the creaking is also that of light hardening in the boughs, and suggests the oppression of heavy work on the girl's frame, indeed her alienation from her own body; the possibilities of bird-freedom have been turned into their opposite—the crane suggesting a clumsy lack of motion—and so on.

world's evil and of death, but also a poem of the creative process itself, in which the primal pang and its resolution go as deep as life itself. Hell is also in the unearthly sunset-glow of the Words-worthian Memory: it "has the same bright-coloured clarity . . ." Yet the beauty is there in the innermost thicket, to be won, and the quest goes on. The sense of transience and of young eternities enters a new level. "Ladies, time dies."

In *Bucolic Comedies* and similar poems she had strengthened the panged sympathy for life in its crisis-moments of growth, the grasp of imagery that uttered both the withering loss and the tentative green tendrils. *Elegy on Dead Fashion* completed this trend. Here the contrast between façade and reality, fashion and personality, dress and body, achieves a poignancy that the couplet controls with echoes of neoclassic symmetry. What is sought is the moment of pure humanity, of life in apotheosis; and it is found that death is always there. The human face breaks up into fronds and crystals. That is happiness and horror both. The tartan leaves and the feathered flowers, the lost ghosts and the warmbodied girls and the abstract nymphs: the moment of change, death and life, life and death. The gyre of metamorphosis breaks the set elegance.

After that I went on to *Gold Coast Customs,* the war-poems, and *The Shadow of Cain.*

Perhaps I may pause here to ask what it was that Edith gained from my writings on poetry and from the discussions we had. Continually she herself said that she felt a new birth, that after reaching a sense of complete loss and impotence, she felt herself stirred with a great sense of restored powers and had new per-spectives opened up before her. In part those emotions of hers were delusory. She was too old and too broken with physical sufferings for her to attain the full renewal of her poetic energies which she kept on momentarily feeling. But on the one hand my defence of her poems, and the terms in which I defined poetic process in general, were certainly of much value to her, helping her to complete her own ideas and to feel that the deepgoing understanding and appreciation for which she yearned were not to be withheld from her. And for the extent to which I thus gave her happiness and some serenity of spirit, I feel grateful and honoured.

On the other hand, the stimulus she thus gained did help her to continue her work and to turn it in a direction to which my analyses contributed. If the large-scale renewal of her poetic expression, of which she dreamed, did not come about, she yet wrote certain poems which she would not have otherwise written. I have already indicated some of the ways in which my ideas had their impact on her and appeared inside her poetry. Above all she felt confirmed in her faith in love and in the deep-rooted need for brotherhood in men. The compassion and anguish of the war-poems had issued in the great vision of redemption from alienation and division in *The Shadow of Cain*. But with her failing strengths she felt herself unable to sustain this vision. What she gained from me was the capacity to sustain it and to reach the clear definition of *A Song of the Dust*. In the process, elements of her renewed hope asserted themselves in her other poems of those years; and the question of Time presented itself to her in new ways, behind which lay the thought of Lancelot Whyte and myself. The main fruit of this fresh brooding on Time was *The Road to Thebes*, which she showed me at various stages and which I discussed throughout with her. This is a difficult poem, which plays with contending ideas of time, of life, and of death. Only a long and detailed examination could show how the conflict works out. Here it is enough to say that the poem presents in a shifting skein, a series of changing balances or patterns, the emotional conflict which is resolved in *A Song of the Dust*. And without the movement of thought and emotion that we find in the poems from *Street Acrobat* to *A Song of the Dust*, I feel that the corpus of Edith's work would be much the poorer. That movement, I believe I can claim, would never have come about as it did, without the dialogue which this essay seeks to reveal.[1]

[14]

Why then did I write no more about her? Above all, why did I never publish *The Starfish Road,* on which she set such high hopes?

---

[1] The poems in *The Outcasts* are not negligible, but they add nothing essential. *Praise we Great Men,* it may be noted, uses the Porphyry phrase from *Byzantium into Europe,* adding honey to the forms of compressed fire. *His Blood Colours my Cheek* must have been written much earlier than 1962; I find among my papers one of Edith's drafts for it.

There was no question of any difficulties about getting it into print in 1949–50, as Dennis Dobson was keen to do it. But I lost my nerve; in a sense I lost my interest. The main reason, I think, lies in the political situation and in the struggle I was conducting with my fellow-Marxists. *Marxism and Contemporary Science* was sharply criticised by Emile Burns, and nearly led to my being expelled from the CP. If I were convinced of the truth of a position, I should then, as at any time of life, have stuck to it despite any consequences. But though I had felt sure I was on the right track as I wrote this book, the severe attacks upon it made me feel that I must be convinced I was not mistaking personal wilfulness for intellectual conviction. I had already been for some time in collision with Marxists in leading roles on cultural matters. I disliked and attacked the Zhdanov disquisitions; I had continually set out what were taken as heretical attitudes in the discussions we had every fortnight in a Writers' Group at the Salisbury pub—the attenders numbered anything up to sixty or more, and we had genuine and searching arguments; a fair section of the younger people, I think I may say, supported me. At two meetings held to deal with some points I had made on the inadequacies of Marxist formulations of the time I was attacked by almost everybody of any standing in the cultural sphere of the CP. (The only defender I can recall was Edward Thompson, who had rushed along immediately after a return from Yugoslavia.) At a large meeting called to discuss Sartre, I alone insisted that he had many valuable elements and that the question was to carry on the dialogue with him, not to damn him. I was much trounced for this heresy.[1]

Looking back, I think I can say that on the whole the heresies I then propounded have now become commonplaces of the Marxist world, or are at least now tolerated. Though there were many rash

[1] Paloczi-Horvath records in his book on his experiences after he returned to Hungary in, I think, 1948, that on his arrest the secret-police there interrogated him at length about three English traitors, one of whom was I. The Stalinist secret-police must then have had me down as a special villain, to be liquidated, as they said in Hungary, after the heroic British working-class had taken power. (Oddly, the other two traitors were Bernal, because of his work in the Peace Movement, and Gallagher, because his son had held a commission during the war—a proof that Gallagher had sold out.) I met P.-H. only for a few moments, once, before his return to Hungary.

formulations in *Marxism and Contemporary Culture,* and much that I would rewrite now, its general argument looks in the directions that Marxism has since taken, while the absolutely-assured condemnations it attracted would now be widely considered sectarian and narrow. (Adam Schaff in Poland was the only Marxist anywhere who had a good word for my book; he made a careful and sympathetic analysis of it.) I feel then that I can assert with some confidence that the elements of serious and responsible thinking in my work outweighed what was insecurely cocksure and unbalanced.

Two factors, however, at the time undermined my belief in myself and my readiness to keep on arguing about the matters I had raised. First, there was the rapid growth of the Cold War about that time. More and more I felt loath to do anything that could be taken in any way as helping the anti-socialist enemy. I am aware that there were fallacies in such an attitude, which had analogies with the attitudes taken by many good persons in the Soviet Union at various times under Stalin. They felt that any complaints which "objectively" helped the anti-Soviets were worse than the existence of evils against which they chafed. I did not at the time know anything of such an analogy. And in any event the dilemma was a real one. In a complicated situation, it is easy, and indeed necessary, to ask oneself: How much of the truth do I know? Am I overvaluing aspects which in the total situation are relatively unimportant? Am I mistaking my personal vanity and my intellectual pride for a superior grasp of the truth? And so on. And yet, in the last resort, one has to take one's courage in one's hands, accept one's own deepest judgement of what is happening and what is at stake, and then stand on one's conviction of the truth, unshaken by the entangled problem of consequences. While struggling with this sort of conscience-problem, I could not but feel, however, certain changes of emphasis going on in my mind and heart—my sense of loyalty to the forces of revolutionary change, in whom alone lay the hope of ultimately halting the alienating process, grew stronger, and my concentration on certain intellectual and moral issues grew slacker. I do not mean in any sense a weakening of intellectual and moral interests, but the material to which they turned, the questions they asked, was insensibly changing. One aspect of this change was my shift from historical novels like *Men of Forty-Eight* and *Fire in Smithfield* to contemporary works like *Betrayed Spring*, which sought to draw a largescale picture of England at the moment and to grasp its patterns of change, the immediate issues stirring and affecting the common folk—in *Betrayed Spring*, those in London, Lancashire, Yorkshire, and the Tyne area.

But most subtly important of all, in affecting this shift, was my visit with Ann to the Pushkin Celebrations in the Soviet Union in the summer of 1949. (Shaw and O'Casey were also asked, but said they could not go.) This was the first time I had visited the Soviet Union, and I was deeply affected. In retrospect I see that I had many illusions and was unaware of many reprehensible things that were going on; I accepted much at its face-value of freedom which was in fact repressive and contrary to my principles. And yet when the worst is said, the essential thing to which I responded was really there and did not deceive me: the fact of tremendous changes in people, a very widespread though often naive interest in culture, and a different moral atmosphere, buoyant, ardent, and healthy. Though I would now modify many of the opinions I held at that time about the Soviet Union, and though my response to the elements I have mentioned may indeed have had its own naivety, I believe I was essentially right in the response. The result was in some respects to confuse me; for though I disbelieved many stories which we now know to have been all too true of Stalinist Russia, I disliked several aspects: the whole Zhdanovist line about the arts, the obviously doctrinaire way in which Marxism was taught, the authoritarian stress on leaders. And I did not see how to harmonise these backward or rigid aspects with what I felt of a deep creative flow in people in general. I fell back on theses of the extraordinarily low level of cultural and political development in 1917, which still continued to leave its limiting effects and its distorting marks—and of the cramping and regressive consequences of imperialist encirclement, which necessitated the perpetuation and the strengthening of the State and all its system of force. And so on. Points which were all true enough in their way, but which did not simply explain away what was backward and oppressive.

But, linked with these attitudes and affecting them, was a growing pessimism about my work having any possible effect on the situation in England. Our complete failure with *Arena* and the series of Key Poets had much to do with producing this conviction. The effort to fight on two fronts had merely had the effect of attack or boycott alike from both. The political atmosphere of those years was harsh. Certainly no one would then have published any of my work except the Bodley Head, where Greenwood was in charge, a genuine liberal, aided by Norman Denny. Neither Greenwood nor Denny shared my political views; but they thought that work they considered of value should be printed. (The Bodley Head also printed James Aldridge and Howard Fast, whom no one else would have then touched.) Dobson, it is true, was ready to do my *Starfish Road*; but his firm was a comparatively small one, with its own particular interests.

Still, all these considerations do not wholly explain why I shilly-shallied so much with *The Starfish Road*. My feeling that it would have attracted no notice whatever was correct, I think. But that should not have deterred me from publishing it, if only out of a sense of duty to Edith. I still consider the level of critical taste in England to be abysmally low; but I want to publish this book about Dylan and Edith.

Anyhow, in my conviction that there were no readers for *The Starfish Road*—apart from Edith and Dylan—I lost the impulse to see it in print. At first I did nothing, despite all Edith's pushings. Then I expressed my disillusioned discontent by a revision, which incorporated a few ideas that had come up in *The Sunset Ship*, but which mainly consisted of new sections. I now attempted to deal with German and Russian poetry as well as French and English: analysing George and Rilke, and trying to bring out the conflicts and confusions making the triumph of Nazi ideas possible; and then going on to Russian culture, dealing with Blok, Bryusov and others, Gorky and the Peasant Poets, and then Mayakovsky. These additions, however, did not really help to clarify the book; they merely overweighted it.

Edith, however, was still enthusiastic. She said of what I wrote about Eluard and Tzara that it "is so illuminating it gives one a sort of extra life." She was interested in what I had said of Stefan

George. "I am sure he was a horror." She thought his work threw much light on the Nazis. She asked my permission to copy out a considerable number of passages. She said that she now felt up to such a job. For some time her head had started swimming if she did anything but read; she was being held up in getting on with her film, while the director was howling for her script. I think that it must have been about this time that Dobson for a period stopped publishing; for in my notes I find her continually raising the question of a publisher. She said she would try Macmillans with it, but she thought Squire and MacCarthy would get in the way. "Dunderheads," she called them, and said that she felt sure no work could ever get past them if it found value in poets like Tzara and Eluard, who were French, after all, as well as being terrifyingly new and agile.[1] She wanted my permission to put the book up to Duckworths. However, I never came to the point of letting her speak to them.

In letters and conversation she kept on repeating all she had said of the work. She said that she considered it not only as a literary work but as one that would draw the nations together in better understanding: "a book that one can read endlessly, and always find a new truth, a new illumination." She had already known something of the work of Eluard and Tzara, but it was only now, she said, that she realised in fullness what they had achieved, and found it of the utmost importance. The new section on Russia she found interesting, but said that in her view the great Russian expression was in prose. There was no Russian poet she could take to her heart unreservedly as she had now taken Eluard and Tzara. "They are the real, real thing. Instinctive born poetry, as well as worked poetry, and how magnificently you write about them. (As you write about everyone, with immediate understanding as well as long, long thought.) Reading you on the subject of these two poets, and reading your translations of them, make me come alive." That, she insisted, was the true function of

[1] She was hardly being fair to Desmond MacCarthy. I had come to be fairly friendly with him at this time (through PEN), and once he said, "Perhaps you know about a book by someone rather left. I forget his name. I read it for Macmillan and I thought: I don't agree with much he says, but it's interesting and deserves to be in print. So I recommended it." I asked him if he was thinking of *Illusion and Reality* by Christopher Caudwell, and he said, "Yes, that's who it was. I've several times remembered the book. I thought it was quite original."

a book: the degree to which it penetrated into the life-process and enriched the life of the reader.

She said that tears came into her eyes when she read anew what I wrote of her. Some of the passages in the book were taken out of the *Life and Letters* essay, and she knew them well, but in the context of the book they took on a new life and only then revealed their meaning. She was once more pleased at what I wrote about Eliot—and in a different way at what I wrote about Dylan.

But now for a few years I put all thought of *The Starfish Road* out of my mind. I completed *The Sunset Ship,* making it a long analysis of poetry from Thomson to Wordsworth and Coleridge; I also wrote a work on the Spasmodics, a detailed examination of what happened between the deaths of Keats and Shelley, and the rise of Browning and Tennyson. Neither work I tried to publish, and I did not even show the whole of the second one to Edith. I felt that in these works I was writing for my own interest and satisfaction, to clarify my mind on various problems of poetic development. I wrote *The Spasmodics* at a difficult time for me. Ann had been found to suffer from cancer, and was in the Tunbridge Wells hospital; the Korean war was on. I was living alone in our forester's-cottage surrounded by great oaks and beeches, with the Medway on the other side of some scrub—with squirrels in the roof, wild bees in the eaves, and (one day) a grass-snake across the threshold; a giant beech at the back overhanging the pool into which the stream flowed steeply down the hillside.

In 1954–55 she more than once suggested that I should write an essay on Dylan, collect other essays or accounts from persons who had really known him well, and publish the result as a book. She offered to contribute and to place the book. I tentatively agreed, but did nothing. For one thing, I felt sickened by the way that so many persons who had had a drink or two with Dylan in the pubs round the BBC were rushing into print or on to the air about him—an emotion which I put into the poem here given at the end of my Dylan essay. More deeply, I shrank from the project, I think, for the same reasons as I had failed to carry on with *The Starfish Road.* Then Edith gave up trying to push me.

However, in 1956 my conscience smote me; and I asked myself

why I had never published *The Starfish Road*. I read over the manuscript, and felt that many of the formulations were too simple and immature. So I set to work again, taking only the essential poets and attempting a fuller account of them. The main points were unchanged, but I hoped to present them more adequately. I wrote a first chapter on some aspects of Keats, taking them as an example of the highest level of poetic consciousness achieved by the Romantics; then went on to Baudelaire and Rimbaud, omitting minor figures like Laforgue and Corbière. I was uncertain whether for my purposes to include Mallarmé. However, I never got beyond Rimbaud. Edith welcomed my return to the theme so dear to her heart. She was suffering from eye-trouble (as a child she had had Egyptian ophthalmia) as well as acute sinus; some four months late in her work and agonisedly wanting to get back to poetry, from which she had been more or less separated for three years. But she eagerly read the new manuscript. She begged me to extend what I had said of Lautréamont and once more made her point about the untranslatability of Baudelaire, whose poems were "entirely within the language." (She repeated that she felt that was true also of de Nerval, but now added Verlaine, or at least certain poems of his.)

But I had at the last moment added a chapter on Ebenezer Jones, whom I had studied when writing *The Spasmodics*. I thought that he, who had so important an effect on the young Rossetti, would serve admirably to bring out the breakdown of the essential poetic impulse in England in the 1840s, the failure to carry on from Byron, Keats and Shelley to whatever would have corresponded here to the Baudelairean advance into the hell of the city of alienation. I was using Jones as a type of failure, but Edith seemed to consider that I was elevating him to the level of Baudelaire and Rimbaud. Perhaps, in my sympathy for his baffled effort to break through into new dimensions of thought and feeling, I wrote more warmly of him than I should have done; but I think my point was clear enough. Edith, however, would have none of him. Because he was a Chartist (though in fact he wrote only two poems that could in any sense be called directly political), she assumed I was introducing him because of his political ideas and civic virtues; and she roundly trounced him as jejune and platitudinous.

I pointed out to her that I was only saying at more length what Rossetti, the last man to be seduced by civic virtues, had said in his tribute to Jones; and that Rossetti maintained his high opinion of Jones, for he stimulated the reprint of his poems, to no effect, in the 1870s. But nothing could mitigate her contempt of Jones; and this outburst of hers depressed me, so that I abandoned the revision of the book.

Only once before had she resisted any suggestion or formulation of mine; and that previous instance was a trivial one. I had said that I would like to give her a copy of *Song of the Earth,* a translation from the Greek of my friend Tefcros Anthias— though I mentioned that the translation was not good, so that the book must be read with a sympathetic eye which could see through to the genuine poetry underneath. But the title of the poem, and my comment, irritated her. She vehemently declared that only vile poetasters wrote poems with a title like *Song of the Earth,* and that she was surrounded by such nuisances, who threw Songs of the Earth at her almost daily. I dropped the matter; for I felt sure that with such a prejudiced start she would never read the imperfect translation with any insight into the original. A pity, for I am sure that Anthias was a person who would have delighted her: a poet who, having begun as a singer of traditional chants at Cypriot fairs, still composed his poems always as songs, with their own spontaneous melody, though his intellectual reach had grown adequate to the great themes of our world.

[15]

There then is the story of our relationship. In a way it is the story of a friendship which, after at the outset developing a great heat and ardour, gradually ran down. But by that I do not mean that we were ever anything but very close in our sympathies. In 1949, writing from the USA, she said, "How much we shall have to say. Our friendship is to me, one of the most important things in my life, coming, too, at a moment when it would be most important to my mind and the development of my mind and the character of my work, on which it has begun, already, to have a great influence." And she kept up that attitude to the end.

When Ann died in early 1954, she wrote to me from Hollywood: "I have only just got your letter. I am *heartbroken* at this terrible news, and still can hardly believe it. Why should this dreadful thing have happened to two of the kindest, best, most gentle people in the world. It is most terrible to me to think of you under the desperate weight of this most desperate grief. I loved Ann very much. I think she was nearer being a saint than almost anyone I have ever known—saintly without censoriousness, good without weakness, sweet without weakness. Everyone who knew her will miss her desperately. She was the same age as Dylan, was she not? One feels sick with grief. If *only* there was one thing one could say that would be of any help to you. I send you—and her—my love, my deepest sympathy, all my thoughts. How thankful I am that you had Mr and Mrs Swingler."

And in June 1957 she wrote to me of my *Elegy* on Ann (written in early 1954, but now printed by myself on a hand-press): "The beautiful conversation with Ann is most deeply moving. It is *exactly* what everyone to whom you and she are dear, would most wish you to have written. Across the gap of loneliness, of grief, one sees that dear, ever-to-be-remembered face. I think I never saw any face with such a light of goodness on it, and of peace." She herself was suffering from being cut off from her poetry, and was hoping for a period of quiet in which she might give herself up to it.

In 1954 we saw little, if anything, of one another. She was part of the time in America. I was abroad most of the year: in Italy, Holland, and then in the Soviet Union (three months). Perhaps after this break our relations were never quite so close again. In 1957 her eye troubles grew worse, and she complained much of her heavy struggles with her work—throwing in as well, as one of her jokes, an endless battle with the University of Texas. She still hoped for *The Starfish Road,* but I had dropped it. In 1959 she declared that the last two years had almost crushed her, but "that does not alter my old affections." The last letter I had in her hand came in March 1960, from Italy. She blamed the Italian post for losing her letters. She was reading my version of Petronius, though she was in much pain and unable to sit up in bed.

Next month I sent her a couple of galley-proofs from the second volume of my autobiography, *The Roaring Twenties*, in which I described my discovery of her poems in Sydney and their impact on me. Her secretary wrote back to me, on her instructions, that she was very ill and unable to read anything, so that it would be best not to send her any books.

After that I waited to hear from her again. I had never at any time gone to see her except at her invitation, and I did not feel like forcing myself on her now, when she was ill and clearly near her end. At the same time I wanted to do what I could to help her in any way and to show my sympathy. But I did not know how to do so. I wrote one or two short notes later and received polite replies from her secretary. In 1964 I met Lancelot Whyte in the London Library, and he said that he had called on Edith at the London flat which she now had, and had been sadly struck by her failing condition. He advised me to visit her. However, I found it hard to bring myself to a visit which was not an invitation from Edith. I put off going, and did not go.

When I heard the news of her death, I at once felt a bad conscience about *The Starfish Road*; and thinking back, I found it almost impossible to understand why I had not published the book when Dobson was keen to have it. I recognised my profound scepticism that it would have any readers; but that did not exonerate me from my responsibility to Edith to get it into print. Now I regretted deeply that I had succumbed to pessimism and failure of nerve. It seemed to me, and still seems, that I badly let Edith down and made a bitter mistake in not seeing that to fight for the cause of poetry, as I understood it, was the most important thing I could have done in 1949–50 and the following years.

EDITH SITWELL IN LONDON

(*I showed this poem to Edith; and she said she liked it and would be happy to see it in print. So I print it here.*)

In Trafalgar Square, the heart of the maze of fetishes,
the mask of the snake sodden with black blood,
the ragged knife of stone and the idol blotcht with nail-heads:

Along the Embankment the naked women wailing
with rivermud bubbling in the wounds of their faces
and the sacred harlots sprawled in the streets of Westminster:

Who does not see these things is blind with the single sight
that reflects dead surfaces only. The midnight worships
spiked in the mangrove-swamps migrate at a crueller magic,

Commodity-fetishism; and Europe with all its history
sunk to a radio-whine of pretences and abstract skills,
leaves Africa human, itself a mere market of deathdolls.

The faces on London streets are stranger to me than masks of the
    Congo.
The terror is there, and the menace, but flabby with daydream
    evasion.
The terror is there, but blurred and evaded, shapeless.

The masterful planes intersecting—the power over space.
The ripening rhythms of dance—the power over time.
These are all gone. Are all gone. But the terror remains.

The Thing remains. The Thing with power over all.
We are lost in the maze of the fetishes, things of the Thing.
And he who can't see it has had all his eyes picked away
by the vultures of money in deserts of lonely sleep.

★

When the façade leans out, cricks, cracks with a puff of dust,
we see the hidden faces that crawl beneath our wallpapers
and melt with medusa-chills on the clammy pillow of tears.

Then is the moment to walk through the wall of granite.
The doorway is suddenly there. The light of the future
come beating up from behind the high red ramparts of longing.

The poet catches in a single palm
the lice brusht out of the fur of the sliddering devil
and the lichens of crystal blown from the worlds far ahead.

The exposed present is the cross of love
and the wings of transfiguration, amoeba-division
and a body of light that leaps from the furthest horizon.

And something else, that unites and divides, in judgement;
in action, divides and unites.

★

You hold in your open hand
the forest of ancient sleep
with a moon in every pool
and fernsides grottoed deep.

In a frock of sprigged muslin
a naiad informs each shadow,
and a dance-ring burns silver
turning in each meadow.

There in the spiralling silence
the smith in his cave of smoke
beats iron for all men
and knots for the stormy oak.

This moment is your pulse
when the façade falls down
and the deathless girl of the kiss
is every girl in town.

When poetry comes true
and England at last arises
the song then meets at each turn of the streets
its own wildwood surprises.

The mirror of transformations
cracks in its jealous flame
as men and women each moment
beat it at its game.

New dares, new tests and trials
confront the poet then—
without a bethlehem strawcrown
among his fellowmen.

For he who watched the murder
must sham that he's not there
or that he's out of his legal wits
with straw in his penniless hair.

Meanwhile you hold in your hand
the jagging lights of hell,
the thicket of ancient sleep,
and the dream, the saving spell.

Aragon, Eluard, Tzara

I SPENT THE YEARS 1930–41 wholly away from London and the literary world (as I have told in *Fanfrolico and After*). So I did not take part in any of the conferences, congresses, or discussions held by the antifascist intellectuals of the 1930s. I met Aragon for the first time soon after the war had ended, when he came to London to give a lecture at the French Institute. The lecture, in which he talked about his poetry of the war-years, deeply moved me; and a day or so later he gave a talk on French writers and the Resistance to a couple of dozen party-intellectuals. His remarkable charm worked strongly on us all. He was still young enough to wear his daredevil debonair aura as a sort of pertly-tilted halo; and with his reputation as a poet-fighter he exercised an irresistible spell. Boyish, gasconading, gaily sincere, he talked easily (in English) and told his tale as clearly and forcibly as if he were addressing a maquis-group and priming them with the information necessary for an operation to be carried out within the hour. He told us not only of the Resistance but also of the postwar organisation of intellectuals in *étoiles,* a system based directly on the underground formations of the war. He gave us the feeling of an enormous moral and poetic liberation, which raised the whole concept of *nation* to a new level, purging it of all its old associations of guilt and division, and opening up new roads to a secure brotherhood. The only actual words of his that I can recall, however, were of a lighter kind— uttered in reply to Beatrix Lehmann's question about the role of actors in the Resistance, where some had functioned honourably, some not so well. "We didn't judge them too harshly," he said with his young smile. "After all, actors are not usually very intelligent people." A comment that hardly satisfied Beatrix with her anguished intellectuality.

The meeting must have lasted a couple of hours. Aragon's spell was so strong that when he left he was still surrounded by several of the audience, who couldn't bear to see him go or who still had something to ask. At least half a dozen jumped on to the bus after him. Indeed, I jumped on myself. But at once felt foolish and jumped off again.

I met him personally not long after, when Ann and I were in Paris. Nancy Cunard, that indefatigable and ardent worker in all lost causes, arranged a meeting between us and Tzara and the Aragons. At the café running off at right angles from the Deux Magots in the Boulevard St Germaine. We spent a pleasant evening, sipping wine and listening to Aragon talk. His English was better in conversation than my French, so much of the talking was in English—though Tzara denied knowledge of that language and his side of the discussion was in French. Aragon with his easy wit and swashbuckling charm seemed to me to incarnate all that I loved of Paris; and though I saw him as the communist poet-hero, I also saw him as the Paysan de Paris, elegantly ironic, passionately serious, adventurously gay. Somehow in his presence the desperate work of the Resistance and the whole inferno of the Occupation seemed to turn almost into a piece of surrealist legerdemain, a spontaneous and necessary conjuration from the witty unconscious with its inexhaustible improvisation of dream-motives. A condition in which poets were immortal—though the other side came up at the end of the evening when we had risen and were going down the Boulevard past the Flore. Elsa shuddered, "I hate that place. I can't forget." She didn't say what she couldn't forget, but she made it evident that dark memories of underground work were linked for her with the café.

She hadn't had much to say before that except in a common-sensical way. Her strong handsome face, with its weight of chestnut hair, had a quality of merged repose and impatience. As the heroine of *Les Yeux d'Elsa,* she was invested for me with all the ardours and subtleties that I had found in the poems, which sought so variously to evoke the poetic overtones of the French past, to embody them all in her, to see and reveal her as

France, as the Revolution, and simply as the Poet's Beloved. I felt at the same time that she was a little bored by the evening; but perhaps the aspect of listening for something behind her, all around her, in the air and deep in earth, was an inheritance from the dangerous years—or perhaps it expressed something brooding in her nature, a sort of dark sensitivity to the whispers and tremors of the world. A guarded concentration of forces. I felt rather the same element of strength and of beauty gathered in upon itself, when, some years later, I stood by Lili Brik in Moscow. The sisterhood of the two was plain, but Lili seemed more vulnerable, in some way I could not estimate. But perhaps the difference between the two women could be measured in terms of their differing lovers, Aragon and Mayakovsky. Now it was only as we left the café and walked down the Boulevard that Elsa seemed to grow more tender, more gently aware of the here-and-now.[1]

Tzara also did not say much, but then he was not the sort of person to assert himself against Aragon's eloquence. I mean, when the eloquence was being used in the vein of that evening. I recall however having some words aside with him on the question of Yugoslav poetry, the development of the traditional forms to express the spirit and the actions of the Resistance. He felt there the possibilities of something great and new. I said yes, but in a way it was more interesting to watch how things shaped in Czechoslavakia as socialism took root. For after all there was a society with a fairly solid industrial basis, the only such country being thus changed. We should find more to learn from it. Tzara demurred, being more concerned with actual than hypothetical developments—though I could not make out how he expected Yugoslav poetry to carry on. No doubt he was overestimating the energies of the spirit released in Yugoslavia, as I was overestimating the depth of transformations in Czechoslovakia. In

[1] I have the feeling that the great value of Elsa to Aragon the writer is that, deeply aware of Mayakovsky, she has from time to time, or perhaps all the time, pointed out "the tasks of history," thus helping to canalise an exuberance that could have burst out in too many directions. (Early, in *Anicet,* Aragon wrote, "The game consists of reaching its limits in all directions before dying. May everything be occasion for extending myself," and in 1960 in *Les Poètes* he repeated, "Shame to him who finds his limit, to whom his limit suffices." And Eluard wrote, "With my friend Aragon men know how to express themselves/in their limits/and beyond their limits/in their boundaries/and beyond their boundaries.")

those years it still seemed possible that the great antifascist upsurge of the peoples of Europe, Britain included, would keep on successfully asserting itself in new forms and sweeping away the reactionaries who wanted to reimpose the old prewar systems of division, with an end of the new conceptions and formations of brotherhood. A hope soon to be rudely checked.

Aragon above all had the conviction of the need and certainty of a continuous forward movement, a profound belief in the people, in the French people. And he expressed this conviction with all the authority that his experiences in the underground movement had given him. This calm certitude of his was however linked, as reaction began to regather its shattered forces, with an anxious fear, an impulse to hit out which could get out of control and provoke further the very discord it most wanted to avoid. "Aragon is all nerves, fineness, dryness," once said Claude Roy. "He's got a way of smiling on top of everything that softens all the sharp edges and angles with a great charm. He knows very well he owns that charm, and he uses it, sometimes abuses it. Yes, he goes everywhere with tremendous distrust and a clutter of conspiracies in his pockets, denouncing left and right. And so, till in the end facts prove him right—prove that men aren't all angels—one is liable to feel on edge and be tempted to send him to the devil with all those indignations of his, those rages, that nest of hissing serpents he brandishes under our noses. But the next minute he is all sweetness. He's calm, gay, unconstrained, pleasant—with a suspicion of insolence." And he added, "One wonders when he works, when he writes—and he writes a lot, he's an immense worker, between two issues of a paper he's editing, on the corner of a table, a café-bar, though he's not a café-frequenter, at home. Nothing escapes him, nothing is without its song. He's devilishly generous, and he's got so much mistrust and caution only because generous people are so often duped. He certainly terrorises his friends, imposes on them, violent, quick, sometimes unjust, and often literary. I forgot to mention: he's brave."

He was one of those people who seem to have no inhibitions and to live always in the very centre of his personality. With his fame as an underground-fighter drawn round him as a sort of conspiratorial romantic cloak—enjoying his role though without the least element of posing or of consciously leaning on his fame— he naturally infected me with a kind of hero-worship. Whether or not I would have modified my feeling of his blithe athletic singleness of purpose if I had known him better, I cannot say. I never came to know him personally as I came to know Eluard and Tzara. I met him only at his offices of *Ce Soir* or at the Maison des Intellectuals, the fine house near the top of the Champs des Elysées which he and other writers of the Resistance had managed to get hold of in the confused days at the end of the war. Such meetings were with his public self, eagerly assured and finely poised. Not that I mean by the phrase "public self" that there was anything forced and artificial about this radiant personality of his. I mean only that in the full daily round, in which tiredness and moments of unbalance cannot but occur, no one is able to maintain such a stable pattern of responses. However, I have the feeling, for what it is worth, that, within the range of emotions mentioned by Claude Roy, Aragon was a person whose public self was far more harmoniously merged with his private self than is generally the case.

I recall one episode at the Maison which brought out his strong admiration of the French workers. Three or four workers, I think from Marseilles, were there to take part in the discussion; and after a while Aragon took me aside. "Listen to them. Listen to their phrases and their idiom, their way of presenting an argument, their pronunciation. Language isn't a class-matter with us as it is in England. They're expressing themselves better than we writers can. Dress a French worker in good clothes and you could take him into any drawing-room and no one would tell him by his accent." This seemed to me an extreme exaggeration, though it may have held an element of truth. However, the infectious enthusiasm with which Aragon put his case convinced me for the moment. Certainly the workers in question were more than holding their own.

[2]

As Aragon in particular and French Resistance poetry in general had a powerful effect on me at this time and determined many of my lines of approach to postwar cultural issues, I would like to sketch here what happened among the poets in France. What I later tried to do with *Arena,* and ultimately the whole focus in which *The Starfish Road* was conceived, was the result of my reactions to Aragon and other French poets whom I shall mention, and then to Tzara and Eluard. Not that I saw the latter two poets as apart from the others; I saw them as carrying to the highest point certain aims and ideals held in common, one way or another, by all the poets.

Aragon had been working on *Ce Soir.* When it was suppressed in August 1939, he was drafted into the army as an auxiliary doctor. Put into a labour regiment on account of his politics, he succeeded, in his desire for a more active fighting role, in getting transferred to a light motorised division, which in May 1940 went into vanguard action across the Belgian frontier. In the retreat his detachment fought its way back from behind the German lines. In *Lilac and Roses* he defined the *drôle-de-guerre* and the reality of betrayal behind it, the roses of a lying attitude reddened with the blood of the real battle and becoming the emblems of a nation in the pangs of rebirth:

> Transforming month when flowerbeds unclose
> unclouded May and June stabbed to the heart
> I'll not forget the lilac and the rose
> nor those whom Spring has folded far apart . . .

He uses a lyrical idiom that seems to turn back to various romantic forms of the past in order to evoke the false hopes, the sense of nostalgic regret and loss, then inverts it with savage touches and effects of unrealised menace, so that when the romantic note returns, it has a different, an anguished emotion of something that lies in the distance and must be reclaimed in the blood and sweat of conscious struggle.

> Bouquets of Flanders lilac that first day
> sweet shadowcheeks death painted with the dew
> and tender roses bouquets of dismay
> tinged with far fires the roses of Anjou.

These effects were typical of much of his war-poems, though the range of emotions which those poems roused by the subtle manipulation of echoes and overtones was very much wider than any single example can show. Thus, in *Complaint for the Newtype Gutter-organ,* which I give in full, he draws on popular song and folk-imagery to express the hell of defeat and disillusionment and the way the national forces are being driven down to bedrock in the people; the lie is ended.

Those whom the barrage harried back
return as noonday does its worst
halfdotty dropping in the track
        return as noonday does its worst
        the loaded women bent to ground
        the men who look as if accurst
the loaded women bent to ground
while children for lost playthings cry
and with their big eyes stare around
        the children for lost playthings cry
        and cannot grasp the world they see
        their illdefended line of sky
they cannot grasp the world they see
the hotchkiss in the crossroad dust
the ash of the big grocery
        the hotchkiss in the crossroad dust
        the soldiers speak with voices low
        a colonel in a yard nonplussed
the soldiers speak with voices low
counting the dead and wounded there
along the schoolroom in a row
        counting the dead and wounded there
        what messages from sweethearts follow
        my darling my remorseful care
what messages from sweethearts follow
each fellow with a photo sleeps
the sky at last survives the swallow
        each fellow with a photo sleeps
        on canvas stretchers huddled in
        soon earth lies over them in heaps
on canvas stretchers huddled in
the lads are carried off outspread

with belly red and greying skin
      the lads are carried off outspread
      but who knows what's the use at all
      O leave then sergeant they'll be dead
but who knows what's the use at all
if Saint-Omer they reach once more
who then will answer to their call
      if Saint-Omer they reach once more
      the enemy they'll find, outwitted
      his tanks have cut us from the shore
the enemy they'll find, outwitted
I hear he's taken Abbeville
and may our sins be all remitted
      I hear he's taken Abbeville
      or so the artillery chaps have said
      watching civilians hurry still
for so the artillery chaps have said
like painted ghosts all grim and pale
eyes here and somewhere else the head
      like painted ghosts all grim and pale
      a passer laughed with wild mad sound
      to see them and to hear their tale
a passer laughed with wild mad sound
he was as black as mines in mien
as black as all the life we've found
      he was as black as mines in mien
      this giant slouching home again
      to Méricourt or Sallaumines
this giant slouching home again
shouted Hellsbells get homewards you
despite the shells despite the rain
      shouted Hellsbells get homewards you
      better to croak at home by far
      a bullet in your guts or two
better to croak at home by far
than scatter off to foreign parts
better die living where you are
      than scatter off to foreign parts
      O we'll come back O we'll come back
      with bellies light and heavy hearts

O we'll come back O we'll come back
without a weapon hope or tear
we'd go but not along this track
        without a weapon hope or tear
        those who from safety watch the farce
        have chivvied us with policemen here
those who from safety watch the farce
sent us where bombers come in waves
and we have said They shall not pass
        sent us where bombers come in waves
        and we return in ragged ranks
        no need for us to dig our graves
and we return in ragged ranks
with wives and children still quite game
no need at all to mention thanks
        with wives and children still quite game
        highway Saint-Christophers our band
        who've walked along the road of flame
highway Saint-Christophers our band
giants dark-patterned going forth
with nothing but a staff in hand
        giants dark-patterned going forth
        against the whitening sky of wrath.

Evacuated from Dunkirk, Aragon reached Plymouth, but chose
to return to France at once via Brest. He then fought on along
the lower Seine. Captured, he escaped and was twice decorated
with the Croix de Guerre and once with the Médaille Militaire.
Demobilised at the end of July, he succeeded in finding Elsa and
they spent a few weeks in a rose-castle of Limousin, then went
on for four months to Carcassone. *Unoccupied Zone* recorded this
moment of lull, escape and remorse, fear and revived purpose.
(The first word *fading* is in English.)

        Fading of grief forgetfulness
        the broken heart cries less and less
        with ashes now the ember greys
        like a sweet wine summer I've drunk
        all August-long in dreaming sunk
        in a rose castle of Corrèze

What sudden sobbing then arose
heavy in the gardenclose
a dull reproach in sighing air
O do not wake me up too soon
only *bel canto* a moment's tune
demobilises this despair

For a moment something stirred
out in the wheat I thought I heard
the noise of arms confused with fears
that brought regret back wild and deep
not rosemary nor pink now keep
within their heart the scent of tears

I've lost but how I cannot tell
the black secret of my hell
in turn the shadow flaked and broke
I sought to hold unendingly
this pang without a memory
when the September dawn awoke

In your arms my love I lay
someone outside across the day
sang an old song of France unseen
at last I recognised my pain
and like a bare foot the refrain
troubled the quiet's pool of green

Now began what Pierre Seghers, a young poet, called the Conspiracy of the Poets. Aragon, Elsa, and Seghers met at the little hill-village of Les Angles, then moved to Nice. Seghers, called up in September 1939, had founded the first publication of soldier-poets, and on the fall of France began *Poésie 40,* with its first issue at Les Angles. Aragon contributed poems from *Crève-Coeur.* From now on *Poésie* had the hard task of acting as the legal voice of the Resistance without giving its function away to Germans or collaborators. However the latter steadily attacked it in such magazines as *Nouvelle Revue Française,* and it had to close down shortly before the Liberation, Seghers, going underground.

For a while the Aragons were living at Nice under an assumed name, and Claude Roy remarked of those days, "He used to do all shopping. When he came home with the polenta and tomatoes, which was all there was to eat, he'd pull crumpled bits of paper from his pocket, and those were the verses of Broceliande. He didn't give a damn for policemen, strangers, men in the street; and the whole community rather liked the nice M. Meyzargues—and I ought to add that he too likes people a lot." *Nice Weather* depicts the demoralised condition of the bourgeois remnant who had given up the struggle in which they never shared—though it also jauntily evokes the excitement of masquerading among the masks of fear, delusion, disintegration:

Devilish weather having its own bad way
at Nice but thinks it's at the Châtelet
the Promenade des Anglais it fills today
      with traps for the unwary
A most odd set of freaks you there behold
folk lined with gold who shiver in the cold
and naked folk who seek a king enrolled
      with any tart and fairy

Birdheads who change about at every gale
ready for anything Hearts trumps For sale
Play black Get to a nunnery or fail
      upon the stage instead
Everything said sounds like an echo here
wan-green as kidneybeans the waves appear
and the Nigresco as the rainbursts veer
      looms plaster-pale ahead

Its devilish will the weather never knows
March in a handkerchief blows his snotty nose
blue as a thousand-franc note the heaven shows
      then down the rainclouds spill
A brand new shadow follows you as you go
what have you done to lose it What a blow
the price you took for it was far too low
      poor Peter Schlemihl

You try to borrow another anywhere
Exiled from walls and earth and the common share
wandering symbol of Forty-one you fare
    upon the broower's dole
Devilish weather putting his watch in hock
his wife's out but no jealous fancies flock
he says the wolf at the door provides no shock
    the wolf's a friendly soul

Devilish weather coupons or else no fun
hats look like bonbons now on everyone
with hambone and not flowers in hand we run
    the password laugh-and-burst
Devilish weather those you thought your friends
turn enemies before the handshake ends
wrong's now good-form and black with whiteness blends
    the best is quite the worst

The secret organisation went on side by side with open activities like *Poésie*. In June 1941 the Aragons travelled to Paris to establish contacts there. Arrested by a border patrol, they bluffed their way through. On the return-journey they met Léon and Jeanne Moussinac at Castel Nouvel. Léon had been jailed as a communist by the French government, but had managed to get out and was writing poems. Now in the autumnal cold the Aragons arrived. "La Santé, the Exodus of June, the Camp of Gurs, the Proceedings of Perigueux": Aragon summed up Léon's story. "Of the calvary that led the poet of Gurs to Perigueux there will remain only a singular springtide of fourteen-syllable verses, that wonderful marchtune: *Don't fear today that I will stray when I am on the march.* I heard in a hotel-room the first of the poems read by the ticket-of-leave man. I took them away. It seemed there was nothing one could do with them but show them to friends, but I had the idea of providing Moussinac with a new personality." Elsa, who had thought of the names of *Poésie* and *Fontaine,* devised the pseudonym for Léon: Jacques d'Ayme.

Aragon explained: "The name would tell the censors nothing, but it's a pleasant thought. Hidden friends recalled through it the almost-happy days of old, Léon Moussinac singing in the vein of the shepherds of Quercy, who sent out of the valleys on to the slopes and uplands the responses of that ancient song, that nostalgic and lost song, of Jeanne d'Ayme in the Langue d'Oc, which in their mouths has still the taste of chestnuts. So Léon became Jacques, and in the papers of the Free Zone men spoke of the new poet with the troubadour's name: the poet of Quercy who spoke out as did nobody else of his land after it ceased to be the land of troubadours."

The Aragons next contacted Taslitzky, an artist working at the Aubusson Tapestries, and suggested the use of verse-slogans for legends. Lines of Aragon, Eluard, Apollinaire were duly used. At Cahors a group with a press in a cave printed *Éditions des Francs Tireurs Partisans Français du Lot*. After another visit to Seghers, the Aragons went on to Sadoul at Toulouse, and through him met Jean Cassou, who shortly afterwards was arrested. Aragon moved to the Lyon area to organise writers there. The Vichy Jeune-France was used for underground work. One of its leaders, Claude Roy, became a staunch supporter of the Resistance. The first manifesto, composed by Aragon, circulated at meetings in Avignon and Villeneuve. By October 1941 the Aragons were back in Nice, where they hastily changed lodgings and for a while escaped notice. Then, when an engineer in the group based on the Musée de l'Homme in Paris was shot by the Germans, Aragon wrote his poem *X . . . Français*. After that he had to work entirely under pseudonyms or in clandestine sheets.

In Paris, Paulhan had introduced Claude Morgan to Decour in a café, La Frégate, on the Seine quayside. Decour, communist and devoted student of the German romantics, had issued an appeal for a national front among writers with a paper as its organ. The first intention had been to use *L'Université Libre,* edited by Decour and Politzer; but now it was decided to produce a new underground magazine, *Les Lettres Françaises.* Then came the murder at Chateaubriant of twenty-seven political prisoners whom Vichy had handed over to the Germans as hostages. Aragon wrote *Les Martyrs.* The Gestapo grew more aware of the threat of the writers. When in 1942 the first issue of *Les Lettres Françaises* appeared, Decour, Politzer and the physicist Salomon were arrested by Vichy and transferred to the Germans. In May they were shot. "A greatness that I cannot describe emanated from these men," said an eyewitness. Loys Masson wrote:

> All the doves of the world are not worth Politzer's hands,
> to staunch Peri's hands all the bees would not avail . . . [1]

Among poets murdered by the Germans were Saint-Pol Roux, Desnos, Max Jacob.

Aragon had two books printed in Switzerland; met Matisse, on whose work he wrote a fine essay; and discussed action with various writers. Tzara, who had moved down into the Midi after the occupation, came over from Sanary and joined in. He was writing the poems which Editions de Minuit published as *Une Route Seul Soleil*—i.e. URSS, the Way that is the Only Light-of-Life (as he pointed out to me later with a pleasant pride in the cipher). Seghers was meanwhile acting as a rallying-point. Many of the Resistance writers passed through Villeneuve and paused there: Sadoul, whom the Gestapo were hunting as he went about with a briefcase full of pamphlets and who wrote for Seghers as Claude Jacquier; Francis Ponge; André Rousseau and André Frenaud among the first. Also Duach, who came in 1941 to ask for material to go into the first clandestine magazine, *La Pensée*, and who was soon to die before a firing squad. Paul Eluard, who had sent *Poésie et Verité*. At Paris, Philippe Dumaine saw about the distribution of the forbidden works.

In July 1942 the Aragons again called on Seghers and carried out organisational work from near Villeneuve. Claude Morgan was editing *Les Lettres Françaises* at Paris for the reorganised Committee of Writers, which included Eluard, Sartre, Vercors. At the height of the danger Eluard had joined the Communist Party. During the summer the Aragons and Seghers visited the Drôme and prepared to go underground. They put two German refugee friends in an abandoned chalet at Comps, in the hills, near Dieulefit, where many intellectuals had gathered. After that they went to Lyon for a conference and returned to Nice via Villeneuve. Then came the allied landings in North Africa.

---

[1] These lines, which Edith read in my translations, especially moved her.

Vichy France was occupied. But by the time the Italians reached Nice, the Aragons had gone off to Comps. There Aragon edited a collection of Decour's studies of German Literature for *Éditions de Minuit*.

On the first day of 1943 the Aragons again went to Lyon to help the formation of the National Writers' Committee for the Southern Zone. Aragon made this committee the basis for a general grouping of the professions. Co-ordinating committees of the arts and sciences, *Étoiles,* were set up in hundreds of areas, and Aragon edited a monthly review. Before the Liberation nineteen issues had appeared. By then two hundred newspapers, with a circulation of about 200,000 weekly, were being put out. From Lyon the southern writers maintained contact with Paris. Seghers made liaison visits, and at Paris Eluard kept in touch with the hidden printing-works. With Lescure he had edited and published *L'Honneur des Poètes,* and throughout he worked with Claude Morgan. By July, as Lyon was now unsafe, the Aragons moved to the village of St Donat. All the time Louis was writing poems, stories, appeals; and Elsa was working at story and novel, as well as getting into contact with Russian prisoners escaped into the hills.

In the autumn of 1943 the Writers decided to hold a full national conference in Paris, to prepare for the uprising. The Aragons made a second trip to Paris. The Gestapo searched their train, and by sheer accident Elsa was saved from having her incriminatory bag searched. As the searchers were coming to her, they were called from the carriage to attend to something else and forgot to come back. At the conference were Eluard, Morgan, Paulhan, Vercors, and many others.

Back in the south, at St Donat, the Aragons in July 1944 took part in collecting parachuted arms. In a few hours the Germans plundered and burned the village, raping fifty-seven women between the ages of thirteen and fifty-eight. The Aragons got away into the hill-vineyards. But the end was near. They acquired a car and took part in the command of the Drôme maquis. After news came of the landing in Normandy, they edited the combat-newspaper of the area.

It is understandable then that I saw concentrated in Aragon the whole new force of defiant love and poetic transformation: poetry with the last barrier between it and the world of action broken down: poetry resuming the magical processes, the power over change, the ability to embody all the violences of reality, which Rimbaud had wanted, but overcoming the final check which had made those powers and glories seem to Rimbaud a snare and a delusion. It seemed that he had made possible the achievement of poetry as action. Not as a substitute for action; not as something adulterated and made impure by an effort to subserve the needs of history and thereby taking its directives from the outside. But as a force, which while busy with a world of practical purposes, remained integrally poetry, operating by its own laws, needs, purposes. Here indeed seemed revolutionary poetry which was able to preserve its integrity because in all its involvement with circumstance it was never satisfied by any criterion save that of true human unity, the concrete universal.

Well, though I still admire *Crève-Coeur* and *Les Yeux d'Elsa* and the occasional poems struck fierily out on the anvil of the Resistance, I do not now see them quite all that. I would content myself by saying that they represent one particular facet of the struggle for a true poetry-action. (In the following years I turned more and more to the work of Eluard and Tzara.) I still think Aragon spoke nobly when he defended his composition of love-poems in the midst of bloody struggle. "I hope a day may come when, looking back on our night, people will see a flame yet shining in it, and what flame can I burnish but that which is me?" And again: "What matters the thing that comes of it, if in the hour of greatest hate I have shown for a moment to this broken country the resplendent face of love?" Proud words, which ring true.

He did in his own way succeed in making the poems gather together all that France meant to him of love and honour, of beauty and strength, of great achievement and endless promise. He did link his personal expression, precisely because of the depth with which he made it personal, with the energies of his people:

> even a prisoner can strike up a song
> a song as pure as water from the spring
> white as the white bread baked in olden time
> above its cradle freely hovering
> so clear so high the shepherds watch it climb.

Echoes of Villon, La Fontaine, the Troubadors, Chrétien de Troyes, Lamartine, Hugo. They also are France, as Claude Roy observed.

Yet this very line of approach showed that Aragon was not simply and solely a poet as Eluard and Tzara was. Even as far back as *Le Paysan de Paris,* he had differentiated himself from his fellow-surrealists by his greater objectivity, his restless eye for the real world as well as for the free associations and dream-transformations that it stimulated. In the Thirties he had largely turned to the novel. And there was another factor. The implication with action had its pure moments, especially during the war, but the balance wasn't so simply maintained as it seemed to me in 1945–46. With such an impetuous character the equal union of poetry-action could not but tend to work out as poetry serving action. In so far as a conscious drive took over from the deep impulse of love that had issued in *Crève-Coeur* and *Les Yeux,* the stress could not but be on the needs of the situation politically considered. And so the pure union of love weakened before the power-drive, the overwhelming demand for success in a good cause which justified the use of poetry as a means. And this element of unbalance linked with the stormy mixture of gay frank friendliness and suspicious angers; the power-drive got into the political tactics of literature and in turn affected the poet, who edited *Ce Soir* for years, as well as carrying on multiple political activities and becoming a member of the Central Committee of the French CP.

I make this analysis with some misgivings, as it concerns a part of Aragon which I never personally encountered; but the point seems necessary to make, if one is to explain the extent to which Aragon became an explicit politician, and the various conflicts (for instance with Sartre) that helped to break down the united front which was Aragon's deepest hope and dream. In a poem like

The Bittern's Cry, written about 1948, he could write over forty lines of rather heavy denunciation of Sartre and the Existentialists; after a light-hearted section on "seasons lovely seasons":

> . . . my country's seasons ceaselessly at change
> what's it all mean unless I'm one with all
> who scrawls my darling's name on every wall
> my country's seasons

The denunciation begins:

> In serious garb offensive to the season
> who are these deaf folk with a weakened reason
> these heart-sore women in their corset-mystery
> these housedoor lectures who their misery blazon
> these hell-kids and these chaps who lap up poison
> who thump their hearts and stamp the earth of history . . .
>
> They write a braille unknown to any blind
> they use queer speech conveniently designed
> three or four words achieve a queer sea-mutter
> scarcely returned from their long daze they find
> the Absurd's the asphalt their bare feet least mind
> and the Bizarre's their eye their sweet the Bitter . . .

Thus he often obstructed his own plans for the union of all true Frenchmen; and though he could inspire great devotion, I could name at least one leading Resistance writer-fighter who came to the point of being unable to stay in the same room with him.

In his attitude at this time to poetry he stressed the circumstances of a poem, reviving Goethe's dictum in new terms. Poetry was a form of knowledge; the poet sought to diminish "poetic mystery." But this position was not rationalist. It held that in writing or understanding poetry we must seek to circumscribe the primary unknowable that is the song; we begin from the pure unknown and struggle to subdue it to consciousness. Thus we serve both mankind and poetry, whose destinies merge; we give poetry its place in society, which is of light and not of darkness. We might perhaps call this viewpoint a surrealism mastered by marxism; the free impulse from the depths, from darkness, dream, and unconsciousness is accepted as the inescapable starting-point for the creative act, but the act itself is directed, not towards greater darkness and dream, but towards the transformation of the unknown into the known—not a reduction of it. Thus, Aragon was able to show how a poem of Mallarmé's reproduces the Victorian bric-a-brac of its setting, yet at the same time originates from a point in the unknown, and in its total definition reveals a dialectical fusion of unknown and known which brings about a new quality of consciousness. At the same time the struggle to transform poetic mystery into an activity of the consciousness does not occur at an abstract point of time and space. By its circumstance it belongs to history, and the struggle to transform darkness into light is also the struggle to transform unfreedom into freedom, division into union, subjection into brotherhood, alienation into wholeness. So Aragon's line of approach seemed to me to move logically into the positions I had set out in *The Starfish Road,* and helped me to clarify my views and to feel confidence in them.

I liked too his stress on Joy, his acclamation of Matisse in *Happiness is a New Idea,* which came to him in 1941 "in the double night of defeat and Nice,"—a "special remedy for all the sorrows of France."

Yet, though I felt that I learned much from him and was satisfied to do so, I never was able to carry on any dialogue with him as I was able to do with Eluard and Tzara. I recall once trying to draw him into a discussion of the ideas in *The Starfish Road* on one of the balconies of the Maison, with the traffic hooting in the distance through the rich trees of the Elysian Fields. He said amiably, "It sounds all very interesting, but you don't need my advice. Just write it all down." Eminently sensible advice, but not what I wanted. If it had been Eluard, his hands would have trembled, he would have been speechless for a few moments in an excessive uprush of images, and then he would have gone on talking nervously and rhapsodically, saying nothing perhaps that was formally to the point, but bringing out all the more richly how the active dream which was poetry went to the heart of the revolutionary transformation of life in a stubborn patience of love. If it had been Tzara, he would have raised his brows and looked mythologically owlish-wise, he would have bit his lip a moment, leaned forward, and then said something like, "Yes, there are such laws governing the movement of poetry, and we must stress what links us all, Baudelaire and Peter Borel, for instance, to Apollinaire and whoever wrote a true poem at five o'clock this morning. But we must also ask how far at this moment we can think of picking up the threads from the torn fabrics of 1939 and 1940, and how far we must make a new start, and what this new start is. To bring poetry into key with the spiritual life of our times, to make it an active part of that life—I confess it grows ever more difficult. We are confronting a process of actualisation which as always has the effect of paralysing and crushing the observer—the participant—and yet if poetry is to survive it must reverse this effect. The dead man must rise up. The violence with which the world assails us must be transformed into the spiritual power by which respond . . ." For that was the sort of way in which Eluard and Tzara did in fact reply to my questions, my demands, my appeals.

In passing I may mention that we each did make an attempt to get the other's work published in translation. I read each volume of *Les Communistes* as it appeared, and, since there was no hope of any ordinary commercial publisher handling it in England, I did what I could to get Lawrence and Wishart to undertake the work—quite a substantial proposition. For a while it seemed that the series would be done; then it was decided to publish instead the much inferior and more politically orthodox trilogy of André Stil (of which however only the first volume appeared in English). Aragon for his part did his best to get my *Barriers are Down* and then *Men of Forty-Eight* done by Hier et Aujourdhui. However *Barriers* (set around A.D. 450), which I wrote in 1941 before being called up and which dealt with Western Europe in total disarray and breakdown (between Huns and revolting peasants), was read by Dennis Saurat, who grew enthusiastic and pressed it on the notice of a literary Professor of Paris. The latter acted as a tout for a publisher, a newly-founded house, and arranged for this house to publish a translation. Professor P. and his comely suspicious-eyed wife struck me as unreliably careerist, cynically and not very competently manoeuvring for a position somewhere between the existentialists and the tentatively-reviving collaborators; and Q., the publisher, as equally unreliable, posing as a millionaire on somebody's blackmarket gains. He told me that he was keen on the novel and was determined to plunge me right in mid-swim of the literary current of Paris. Even if he had been in a position to do so, I would have resisted and refused the plunge; but I felt increasingly dubious about his intellectual or commercial pretensions. However out of curiosity I accepted an invitation to afternoon-tea at the vast flat into which he had moved on the Avenue Foch. He and his plump gilded wife kept apologising for not having yet finished the furnishings; and occasional pieces of Empire furniture and very modern contraptions lay about the huge glittering rooms, watched distantly by third-rate specimens of sculpture. I remember the finely-stockinged wife pouting darkly or rattling off something Parisian I couldn't follow as the trolley with the afternoon-tea things took an interminable time to come from the kitchen, propelled by a grumbling peasant-woman who was explained as a family-heirloom.

Q. went on postponing completion of translation, and then of publication; nor was I successful in getting the 20,000 francs named in the contract as due on its signature. First there came news that the man working on the translation had died *"subitement d'une embolie. C'est une grande perte, car c'etait un homme d'une très belle culture. Il n'etait âgé que de 35 ans."* As Q. didn't like to bother the family by asking for the copy of *Barriers,* would I send another? I sent it. Nine months later another translator had been found and half the book was done. The delay was partly blamed on the fact that the firm closed for the whole of August. Fourteen months later, Q. was asking urgently for another copy of *Barriers*. I sent it. Still nothing happened. Then, when I called on Q. at his office during one of my visits to Paris, he explained humbly and furtively that he was wholly dependent on a bank for his finances and had to submit to them the text of each book he intended to publish. He had submitted the translation of *Barriers,* and the bankers hadn't liked it. So he couldn't publish. I pointed out that I had a contract in which he undertook without qualifications to do the book. He grimaced and made various gestures of despair. Yes, but what could he do since the bankers didn't like my novel?

So *Barriers,* taken from Aragon to give to Q., did not appear. Meanwhile Aragon was trying to get *Men of Forty-Eight* done by Hier et Aujourdhui. I forget all the details; but after the book was accepted, it fell a victim to economising cuts and various chess-moves by parties with different interests in the firm. At the last moment Aragon told me that he had to sacrifice the book in order to protect some larger plans of his; and that those who wanted only a certain amount of funds to be allocated to translations from English had pointed to the very large work, *Handbook of Marxism*—"by, I think, Emile Burns, is that it?" said Aragon.[1] Finally I may add to complete the story that he pushed the firm into agreeing to do *Betrayed Spring* in 1955; a contract was signed; I had a considerable correspondence with the translator—and nothing happened.

But, in parting here with Aragon, I should like to emphasise afresh that undefeated youthful side of him, and the gay pathos he has been able to evoke by the conflict in his body and spirit between that persistent youth and the facts of age and defeat. I cited above some lines from *The Bittern's Cry.* Here are some others, in which his true lyric self speaks:

Mark a moment this mad girl with upended shoe
with all the streams of the world in her shining airs
with all the birds in the hat of straw she wears
and in her handbag the dreams of her twenty years too

Mark a moment this mess of tulle and anemones
this dream as dusty as a cinderman with bent back
it's yesterday's leaf left on the almanac
the withered refrain of a song with autumnal wheeze

Mark a moment this smile and flutter of the heart
something is needed if you're to trust what you see
and not the mirrors' consummate cruelty
this wilted reflection which plays an abjuring part

[1] I was to some extent recalling this comment as a sort of private joke when I dedicated *Betrayed Spring* to Emile Burns and Aragon, but the dedication was also seriously meant. Though Emile and I were often antagonists, I came to like him personally and one side of my mind had a sympathy for his positions. The stimulus of what I felt as the positive side of his struggle with me, plus the stimulus and challenge I felt from Aragon's work, especially *Les Communistes,* issued in this novel.

It's my life and I had better admit the truth
it's my life this song out of tune and I see it at last
on a fine evening the future is called the past
it's then that you turn and look back and see your youth

If with volcanoes dead the heaven lacks splendour
the day is not so clear or the night so tender
till the last moment my heart you hear its call
it is my life and there's only that after all

what chance or what adventure do you desire
what glory all yours what theft of luck to spend
grist to the mill that's all you are at the end
body to torture ashes to the fire

That child has not had time to open eyes
a truck wiped out the other who liked to sing
not azure or phrases but hardship outfaces the thing
cut to your measure and free from all dabbling skies

Truly I don't see here what holds you racked
or gives you the right to cry at night what you feel
your fate's quite like you and trots along at your heel
the mad are but those who think they're others in fact

It's enough already to have for a moment the will
the power in your feeble way to shake off the load
history's enormous wheel in the rutted road
so it falls back against your shoulder heavier still

For henceforth nothing can be done that matters
but you've affected it with your slight strength
old wounded beast you can kneel down at length
while hope holds others happily in its fetters

Nothing decreases his energy. In a recent note to me (early 1966) he says, "You have heard perhaps that Elsa and I are publishing what one calls here rather queerly our *Crossed Works,* it means thirty-two books—sixteen Elsa's, sixteen mine—novels and short stories of all our life, and I am re-writing (not in the usual sense, but plainly writing anew) certain of my novels (entirely *Les*

Voyageurs de l'Impériale and *Les Communistes*), we are writing prefaces for all the books, rather long prefaces, and for us important, we got the job to collect ourselves the illustrations of the books . . . but this is only the main object of the year (we began a year and half ago). And as you can see, I am still politically active, I am making a film about Elsa's life, I write a long novel for which I still have no time, I promised a big book on Henri Matisse to Gallimard (who publish a poem of mine next week), and this is only a part of what I have to do . . ." At the same time he was hoping to squeeze-in a spring-month of holiday in Italy.

[4]

Before I go on to Eluard and Tzara, I should like to mention a few others of the Resistance poets whom I came to know a little. First, Pierre Seghers, then young, keen, capable, volatile, absorbed in the problem of finding ways and means of keeping the Resistance spirit alive among the poets and of providing them with vehicles of publication. I did get a novel of mine translated into French in these years, done by Seghers. This was *Hullo Stranger,* a more or less documentary account of women going into war-industry (here aircraft engineering, Handley Page), which I had written while still in the army. (A slight work, though my dear friend Marietta Shaginyan in Moscow, always unexpected in her judgements, thought it one of my best works because of its conclusion: Courage is to be aware of others. Which I had worked towards as a reply to *Huit Clos'* moral that awareness of others is hell.) The main value of the publication was that it gave me money to put down for a Picasso lithograph, the one that I think is the finest of them all, of two figures on a beach in strong sunlight. I had happened to go in with Isak Grunberg, an Austrian journalist, a kindly fellow with many contacts in the artworld, for a chat with Kahnweiler, and could not resist the lithograph, of which advance-proofs had just come in.

At the *vernissage* of my novel at a bookshop (where also Nancy Cunard was signing copies of her translations of the book of poems on France she had collected near the end of the war in England) I was told stories of the way that the British Council had refused to co-operate and had done its best to sabotage the small event. In those years I seem to have been a special bugbear of the British Council. A little later in Prague, at some cultural gathering, the representative of the Council, on hearing my name, halted his movement towards me and executed a remarkable backward-slide which made me realise that the cliché of novelists about someone recoiling did after all have its basis in fact.

Seghers was full of schemes and devices. A little poem of his, *Song of him who kept changing names,* while expressing the dodging-around of the many underground-poets and the unity of their purpose, also brings out unintentionally the way in which he as zealous organiser and publisher reflected momentarily the identity of the others whom he loved and wanted to preserve:

> Truth's here at play
> venom of chance
> the weeks all dance
> to *you* and *me*
>
> Today I write
> Peter I'm called
> yesterday Paul
> Louis tonight
>
> Pass each passes
> Léon my name
> Robert I claim
> password of choice
>
> on crossword days
> months on the margin
> I spread myself large
> the identical voice
>
> warm under its lures
> white in the wind
> sings for assurance
> *I live I endure*

Then there was Jean Marcenac, smallish but full of fire, dark and brilliant-eyed, who had escaped from a German concentration-camp and worked as liaison-man for Aragon's Committee in the south. Once he was sent with important manuscripts to a town at some distance, and instead of promptly returning he stayed on for two months to fight with the local maquis. Aragon reprimanded him sharply for leaving his post-of-duty, but at the same time strongly sympathised with him. The restless reckless element in Jean wanted a total poetry at a blow, the whole of life packed in a gesture, an image, a rhythm, dangerously realised. Once he said, "It's the I-don't-seek-I-find of Picasso; and I myself add: And I bow down sometimes before my god-send." His verses sought to express his sense of overflowing life, of the moment become miraculous because of its suddenly obvious perfection and completeness:

> Around us lay a very lovely city
> our love and the river had the selfsame water
> nothing invented now remained in us
> the curtain rose on the supreme performance
>
> Nourished on pure heaven the bird was preening
> in the fine garden of the glance
>
> It needed now to keep alive
> only the density of its song
>
> and it needed for its song
> all the density of life

Léon Moussinac in these years was tall and thin, meagre as if burnt out with a fierce suffering which he denied. He was suffering from heart-trouble, for he told me at Wroclaw that he disliked flying by air, which put a strain on his heart. He had applied for a transit-visa on these grounds to the Americans, who refused to give it to him. In his different and humble way he said something rather like what Marcenac said: the fulfilment was here and now, or it was nowhere and never. If we realise the imperfect and broken action, the stormtosst and defeated aspiration, in their full implications, we realise them as part of something that cannot be broken or defeated, and we become truly human and achieve poetry. Not because the action or the aspiration is merely subsumed in something bigger than itself, but because the wider relations are drawn back into the self and become a vital ingredient of it, a passionate and joyous element of its own realisation in the here-and-now, the organic wholeness of the moment. (In a sense, we see, all these poets were making a reply to what was narrow, solipsistic, *huit clos,* in the existentialist position; but they were not doing so polemically—they were simply expressing what they felt deepest in their experience.)

> The winds of purple rising now
>   have torn death's wings away.
> Archers and angels of our thoughts
>   all stand disarmed today.

The old established controls and disciplines had fallen away as each man stood alone, hopeless, reborn, in the shattering defeat of France. The old kind of dream was ineffectual and deaf. Now in a world of sheer violence a man was thrown back on the deepest resources of his spirit. He had nothing else to rely upon. But if he was secure in the new desperate depth of spirit that he had plumbed, at the spring of renewal hidden in his own body-and-spirit, then he had found in his absolute loneliness and in his new terrifying freedom the key to union with all his fellows—with all who were undergoing the same experience. The secret of the future lay in this intense and sustained moment, or it lay nowhere.

> Happy the man whom faith has knotted
>   to his flame-raft fast.
> Less from his triumph than his drama
>   earth will live at last.

Always Moussinac's poetry came back to this point:

> Hark, I've at heart far more than all the roses
> whose blood and velvet Ronsard left effete.
> The winds are up, blaspheming at the gates.
> Clouds of my darkened days, sweep by above.
> Better than victory in my spirit waits . . .

To announce to me the hour and plan
no one from heaven will descend.
For the essential I attend
the song of the enduring man . . .

Amid the mess of worlds and stars
his hands of crime and purity
with blows of knowledge and beauty
victories and disasters
man in singing re-makes his unity

I was deeply affected by the way in which these poets, whether
the grave and calm Moussinac or the gaily passionate Marcenac,
had found a renewal of hope and faith out of the breakdown of a
world which in the last resort was one of hypocrisy and oppression. Though the circumstances seemed to leave no room for
hope, the very fact that the old prisonwalls had collapsed
heartened them all with a conviction that now life would be built
up afresh, this time on pure and truly-human foundations. Love
had taken on new colours, new contours, new certainties. Not
only love in its more general aspects—love of man, love of
motherland, love of nature—but also love in its most personal
sense, love of woman, love of a particular woman who was
bound to the poet by the peculiar luck and disaster of the
apocalyptic moment. Here Aragon had gone first to the heart of
the matter with his keen dramatic sense; but Eluard too, essentially a poet of personal love, could not but find his powers
sharpened and enriched by such a situation. For Tzara it meant a
deepening of his sense of the springs of renewal in men.

I must mention also a small solid Breton, Guillevic, who composed in a style compounded of the concision of proverbs and
the laconic brevity of a sort of lyrical instantaneousness. The
butterfly pulsations of a short flight from flower to flower.
Perhaps folksong had had a part in shaping his style; for I have
been with him in café-bars where he burst easily and unself-
consciously into song. (This capacity he shared with Hamish
Henderson, who once stayed a while with us at Wellington Road,
and who was liable at any moment to illustrate his remarks by

raising his voice in folksong, in the street, in bus or tube, without the least sense of doing anything unusual.)

Once Ann and I were sitting at the Deux Magots and Guillevic ambled across the open space in front of the seats, came up with his customary poker-face, accepted a drink, and then silently handed me a copy of a small book, *L'homme qui se ferme.* "That's me," he remarked. "Apposite. I've just been fired. Not that it matters."

I knew he had some sort of job in a government office. "Why?"

"Simply a matter of principle. Not that it matters."

I waited, but he made no more comment. He watched the people going by and accepted another drink. I found that he was hard-up. "Have you got any plans?"

He seemed surprised at such a suggestion. "No. Why? But it doesn't matter. Something will turn up."

Next evening he was singing folksongs in a café near the lower end of the Boulevard St Germaine. Nothing was solved. Nothing mattered. Except of course the songs.

> My daughter, the sea,
> already you've guessed it,
> isn't a present
> that someone can give you
>
> My daughter, the wave
> is another world
> where the foot is buried
> and nothing answers
>
> The horizon, my daughter,
> is a great lord
> that will take you in
> when you have opened it
>
> My daughter, the bramble,
> you've noted already,
> offers no friendship
> that won't be a struggle

My daughter, the dance,
how may I teach you?
it's there in your eyes
and you will follow it

and hope, my daughter,
more strong than the sea
more strong than the bramble
the wave and the dance

Eluard enjoyed these poems by Guillevic, and drew my attention especially to one entitled *Life is Expanding*. Not long after the meeting with him at the Deux Magots, I wrote some verses on him in the Luxemburg Gardens, which I cite as holding my response to his personality and poetry in those days. The last two stanzas use images from his own poems.

Guillevic like a Breton headland
ignores enormous waves
that rave and rumble vaguely about
his absentminded feet

round as a ball of granite rolling
along the Paris street
a block requiring spectacles
but otherwise complete

in melancholic gravity
he meditates his parables
in strict concision and derision
wondering where he'll eat

and if as night links arms he tries
a song of love or bread
he sings in the café till thrown out
and takes his song to bed

He lost his job and took a knock
We had the luck to meet
"Simply a matter of principle . . ."
he mopped his brow in the heat

The rage of government offices
had closed above his head
but calm and maddening as a rock
he stood by what he said

in aphoristic indifference
there by the Deux Magots
he sipped vin rouge, stared back at the clock
and watched his chances go

As long as I've a song a song
of loving to repeat
I'll grit my teeth and whistle along
and not admit defeat

they can't call up the fire-brigade
against a flagrant flower
or sock a circle in the jaw
and I'm beyond their power

Why worry? I understand the law
and see the issue plain
as long as I can close my eyes
and open them again

Among the prose-writers whom I knew a little at this time were Vercors, neat and glowingly handsome, with his confidently capable wife; Claude Aveline (whose detective stories Ann translated); Claude Morgan, dashing and keen-edged; Roger Vaillant, with his air of intellectual assurance; Georges Ribemont-Dessaignes, with a fragile and shy air of indestructibly buoyant, merry, and indignant anarchism. And among the poets I should not forget Jean Cassou, with a quick glancing mind and solid body, who in prison had composed sonnets which he lacked materials to write down. So he memorised them all. After he was freed, he encountered a group of the mercenaries they called Mongoles, and was badly beaten up. The sonnets, dealing with the crushing loneliness of the dark cell, express the deepening division of the self in its struggle with otherness; the poet enacts in his solitary space the lot of all men in his world, in a pure drama of anguish, and yet at the same time moves towards the integration of himself in resistance, so that his shadow-conflict reaches out also into the day of liberation—not simply of France from the Germans and the traitors, but of mankind from the alienating forces which have existed in France as in Germany.

> Come, at chagrin's blind turn, his face we'll meet
> deep in night's plane where crystal shadows are.
> Only his likeness have we known so far
> now he himself draws near on thieflike feet.
> What were we but a double silence there,
> a shadow-pair with hands of twined deceit?
> Our hands, reclothed in sudden truth, complete,
> bless now the dread advancing messenger.
> It's late, and darkens. Keep yet far from me
> the stifling dark, this life of deathly malice!
> The rest be but a thread of dusk, a pause,
> skyline of blood within the bitter chalice
> that smiling angel from our thirst withdraws,
> we'll bring the angel down and drink the sea . . .

Once, noting in *Humanité* that Cassou was to speak in a hall in Saint-Denis, at 7.30 p.m., we thought it would be a pleasant idea to surprise him by turning up. It was or must have been in 1948, for the theme was the Revolutions of 1848. Forgetting for the moment how unpunctual French meetings could be, we turned up at 7.30, to the immense surprise of the doorkeeper, and found ourselves the only persons present. By about nine o'clock the hall was half-full, and by half-past it was full, and Cassou arrived to lecture. Afterwards I spoke to him, and was drawn into celebrations with the mayor and pilgrimages over various parts of St Denis, I never quite made out why. Then, about three a.m. we arrived back in Paris 5e with him in a taxi.

Nancy Cunard too must not be forgotten, keeping up a vast network of correspondence with all Spanish poets in exile; discussing with Kay Boyle the endless problems of a foreigner living in France, black markets and the maddening trivial villainies of bureaucracy; much absorbed in odd friendships, such as with a gendarme who was troubled at the antidemocratic violences in which he had to take part, and whom she was consoling and counselling. Elio Vittorini volubly and cheerfully arrived in Paris to recuperate from illness. Giacometti, lean, intent, emaciated, saying nothing, whose clothes seemed to keep on getting baggier as he shrank with his concentration on skeletal forms of movement—so much so that when I saw him again at the Tate in 1965 I was surprised to find him much shorter than he had sprouted in my memory. Many times he sat at the same table in the Flore as Tzara and myself, but I cannot recall a single word passing his grim lips; he seemed lost in the spectacle of surrounding voices and movements, yet totally detached, with eyes compassionate, calculating, defensive, ironic. And for days in the spring of 1949, writers from all over the world, Howard Fast formidably efficient, Mike Gold genially a street-urchin, Du Bois introduced to me by Fast as "our greatest Negro," Simonov and Fadeyev taciturnly saturnine (whom I heard Fast berating at the huge rally for having no idea what America was really like), Pablo Neruda suddenly appearing on the dais out of his long clandestine flight from South America to embrace Picasso. And so on.

Two more memories, though set this time in Poland, on the mountain-slopes of the Tatras, at Zakapane. After Wroclaw. Somebody arranged for a group of mountaineers to come along and do their songs and dances. The electric light system in the hall was in a bad way, and the lights kept going on and off. When the mountaineers with their axes had finished, and there was more confusion over the lights, several French writers got together and started singing folksongs, songs of the partisans. Somehow, in the dim and distracted hall, the songs came over with an authentic effect. I felt deeply stirred, as if I had stumbled, by some accident of time and place, on a band of maquis encamped in the ravaged hills; as if I had mysteriously sounded the simple depth of patriotism in Aragon's war-poetry and knew as I had never done before how truly it rang.

The other memory is of Roger Vaillant. I had seen him a few times at Wroclaw, but he disappeared after the congress ended and no one knew where he was. One afternoon, over at one side of Zakapane, where there was an overhead car swinging up further into the mountains, we met Roger coming down the slopes from the rugged and frozen heights. He had with him the girl who had struck me as the most handsome, the most vivid, of all the women at the congress. A Brazilian with subtle olivine skin, finely and fully built, who in my memory ripples all over with delicate silver lights—an effect from a dress she wore one evening. Coming down the mountains she was more serviceably dressed, and her face had a warmer glow under its olivine bronzes. They had gone up into the mountains and wandered about—ten days or more, I think, though my memory may again have here romanticised the episode. We went into the refreshment hut nearby and drank cognac; and the raw heat, all the stronger in its impact because of the cold from which we had come, seemed a sort of singing tribute as it coursed through the veins—a tribute to Roger's debonair note of triumphant well-being. A young writer, master of the rarefied air of mountain-heights and lover of the loveliest of Brazilian girls. And the singing of the cognac-heat in the blood was one with the singing of the maquis on some desolate hill of French darkness. All these men whom I admired, whether young or old, Vaillant, Aragon, Moussinac, Marcenac, Eluard, Tzara, seemed to me to live in a richer and fuller dimension of space and time than anyone I knew in England—to have gone through trials and tests that penetrated deeper into the spirit, and to have known triumphs, exalted or serene, that made them, more simply, happily, and maturely, human beings in the vast scope of that term.

[5]

I thus accepted unquestioningly at this time what Aragon said of Moussinac. Words that I applied to all the poets.

> I recognise in these verses that insensate effort to maintain human dignity, that appeal from the depths of the abyss of fallen man, that refusal to accept the destiny of the defeated. I recognise in these verses deep as mirrors that appetite of greatness which is never more keen and imperious than when the very sky is nothing but mud in the quenched eyes of man. I recognise in these verses not only my friend Léon Moussinac who seeks his way across filth and darkness, and the stars at last rediscovered, but also other men who were, like

myself, in his likeness during those terrible years. I recognise in these verses the man of France who advances through the grim thickets of the flameless hell where he now finds himself, he knows not how, precipitated. I recognise in these verses an extraordinary thing: that trust which men, without taking counsel together, then placed in poetry, and more particularly in forms of poetry which they had previously seemed to despair of, forms of poetry which were for them bonds with other singers, with the silenced songs of the centuries, with the echo left in their hearts by French cadences. And this could happen as well with lays as worn as seashells, carried on since the middle ages in so many mouths, with those airs come from spinning-wheels and fountains, as with sophisticated poetry . . . And so this could happen as well with *Au Claire de la Lune* as with Mallarmé . . .

I still believe that he was speaking truly of what happened in those years and was carried on for a while into the years of peace; but what he, and we others, hoped to be a stable gain, was bound up with a passing phase of struggle—even if it also held a prophecy of what will someday come about in a period of more comprehensive and yet more deeply upheaving storms of change. Some poets were able to respond to the great moment while it lasted, with glimpses small or large of what it portended. But there were two of whom it may be said that their whole previous existence seemed as if a preparation for that moment, who were able to give it the expression it deserved, and to continue with the poetic definition of its meanings after the firm basis broke and fell away. Eluard and Tzara.

I never met Nusch, a fabulous creature now indistinguishable from the poetry that Eluard lavished upon her; but the words of Madeleine Riffault give her for me a momentarily separate existence: "Nusch who carried through the barrages messages as dangerous as grenades." At one time Paul, doing organisational work between the two zones, fled from the Gestapo into the mountains of Lozère and stayed for two months in the Saint-Albin lunatic asylum, deeply stirred by the miseries of the mad folk whose lot he was sharing. Louis Parrot told of meeting him there: "I see once more the vast plateau of snow that the whirl-winds icily combed through. The lofty creviced house. The windows behind which haggard faces watched. The little grave-yard like those in *romans noirs*. He talked in the snow and the cold, and caught the train to the little town nearby where he had to correct proofs. It was at Saint-Fleur he was editing the *Bibliothèque Française*." He said also, "I met him again at Clermont-Ferrand, where he had found several friends, after meeting a host of others from Antibes and Villeneuve, and worked out the main lines of what they could do fruitfully to-gether." He added, "Never had his belief in the victorious issue of the Resistance weakened."

In my notes I have lost the name of whoever it was that thus described Eluard's work in Paris: "I see him pale, pale, pale, Rue du Dragon, waiting for the cyclist from an underground printing-works, who never came. But in the end he made of all things a disconcerting and detailed enchantment, whether they were dangerous or merely boring, envelopes to be stuck down, leaflets to be folded up. One forgot altogether, living with him that poets could be murdered, so often are murdered." His *Critique of Poetry*:

> Fire awakens all the forest
> the trunks and hearts the hands and leaves
> happiness in a single posy
> confused light melting luscious
> it's a whole forestful of friends
> who gather now at the green fountains

> Garcia Lorca has been done to death

> House of a single word
> and of lips joined for living
> a quite small child without a tear
> within his pupil of lost water
> light of the future
> drop by drop it's filling man
> up to his triumphant eyelids

> Saint-Pol Roux has been done to death
> his daughter has been tortured

Towns frozen with identical angles
where I dream of fruits in flower
of the whole sky and earth
like virgin girls discovered
in a game that knows no ending
faded stones unechoing walls
I avoid you with a smile

Decour has been done to death

"He couldn't change his residence without taking his universe along. In his refuge-lodgings he took all that he needed for living—his wife Nusch of course, no money, no papers but false ones, no address, but walls hung with Picassos, Miros, Max Ernsts, Légers, and the first editions which he had so pleasant a way of caressing, with his fingertips."

Yes, he was the poet of touch. So much of his sensibility seemed concentrated in his fingers; and yet they suffered from a trembling affliction in their fine movements. Controlled and questing movements, like someone newly-blind rediscovering the world, discovering it with a new sense of the subtle direction of contours and of plastic depth. His fingers trembled as he poured out wine, but he never spilled a drop. His large body—it wasn't really so large, but it suggested sensuous warmth and expansion, as Aragon suggested the spring of movement and Tzara the concentration of thought—his body sent its perpetually quivering delicacy of response out into those fingers. If I had been a surrealist painter, I'd have painted him with fingers of seaweed floating and undulating in minute tremors answering the least current in the flow of his environment. This quivering tendril-responsiveness of his hands corresponded to the way in which his poetry dissolved and recombined the world around him in terms of a dynamic process.

The naked countryside
where I shall live for long
possesses tender grasslands
in which your warmth is snug

springs in which your breasts
draw down the light of day
roadways where your mouth
laughs at another mouth
woodlands where the birds
halfopen up your eyelids
beneath the sky reflected
upon your cloudless brow

my only universe
my light my promised wife
in nature's rhythm your flesh
will nakedly endure

In Eluard's idiom nature is not a symbol or image of the
beloved, the beloved is not a symbol or image of nature. The
union has gone far beyond such a level. And through it a vital
relation of man and nature has been re-established, recognising
alienation but overcoming it in the ceaseless adventure of experience. More, this relation, based as it is in the union of man and
woman, is one of love. Man is not only reunited with nature; he
is also merged with it in terms of a love that takes him right into
the heart of the meaning of process. There is no abstraction of
purpose, but everything has purpose within the unitary process
that embraces both man and nature. The demarcation of human
and natural is affirmed only to be broken down, broken down to
be affirmed. Woman is the intermediary; and because of her
greater power of participation in process, both passively and
actively, because of her "generosity of blood," she heals the
wound of alienation. Through her existence in all things, she
ends the emotion of *absence,* on which the paradoxes of poetry
from the Trobadors or Hafiz to Mallarmé had been based. The
element of estrangement and violence in the Rimbaudian derangement of the senses is eliminated by this comprehension of
the transformative process of life and art. The senses are separate
and are one, and are part of the flow and change, the formative
movement, of nature. Focused in touch, in Eluard's trembling
fingers, they achieved this new unity of man in woman and
woman in man, in the perpetual flow of love.

This love, dynamically centred on the love of man and woman, is also love of all men—a universal love saved from all abstraction or emptiness by its origin and endless renewal in the senses. Eluard incarnated this love, as no one I have known or can imagine. He was a man indeed of such transparent honesty, kindliness, gentleness, that he inspired affection in all who knew him. Even his anger was always an aspect of his love, as in the little poem cited above, *Critique of Poetry*. Once I mentioned an English writer who had said he'd rather see the atomic bomb used than meet a Communist world-triumph. Eluard was so affected that he rose and could not keep still, he moved anxiously about the room with the horror chilling him, his hand touching familiar things. "Why, rather than have the bomb used I'd prefer to see class-society last for ever." Yet the thought of class-society thus lasting would have meant the end of every dream and hope he had for men.

He reacted with this instant and complete pang to all cruelty. It would have been easy in one way for him to have enclosed himself in his capacities for enjoyment and have been simply the poet of the endless shifting balances and patterns of engrossed love. He was all that; but his sense of responsibility towards love and happiness made him feel with every fibre of his being that he must struggle for the fulfilment of all men in love. With his infinite gentleness he was also the poet who edited *L'Honneur des Poètes* at the risk of his life, with the following preface:

> Whitman animated by his people, Hugo calling to arms, Rimbaud aspiring through the Commune, Mayakovsky exalted exalting: it is towards Action that the poets with the vast vision are sooner or later drawn. As their power over words is complete, their poetry cannot be weakened by what is more or less a rough-and-tumble with the outer world. Struggle can only renew their forces. It is time to repeat, to proclaim, that poets are men like others, as the best of them never fail to maintain that all men are or could be poets in their degree.
>
> Before the danger that men run today, poets have come to us from all points of the French horizon. Once yet again poetry, set on defiance, co-ordinates afresh, rediscovers a direction suited to its hidden violence, cries out, accuses, hopes.

Here we see the surrealist formulas of poetry as rightly a universally shared activity, and of its spontaneous uprush, applied in a new sense. The editorial in *La Révolution Surréaliste* of December 1924, signed by Eluard, Vitrac and another, had stated, "Solitude of writing, you will no longer be known in vain, your victims caught up in the gears of violent stars will come back to life in themselves." Now the solitude was mated with action, and the transformatory violence of the poetic image implicated more than a subjective explosion. The inner and the outer worlds had met in a fuller dialectics than Breton ever dreamed of.

When I knew him, as I have said, Nusch was dead, exhausted by the anxieties and hardships of the war-years, and he was living alone. He was suffering deeply from his solitude, his memories; and for once the power of poetry and love was failing to turn absence into presence:

> I was knitted with hands together
> doubled with two hands in my own
> I was knitted with two eyes
> which used my eyes to gain their sight
> but here today I feel my bones
> crack beneath the absolute cold . . .

He defined his condition in *From the Horizon of One Man to the Horizon of All Men*. "After utter abandonment, when there was left in his depths but the vision of his dead wife, he was shaken by a great revolt." In conversation he made fun of his condition, conjuring up fantasies of a man islanded in an oceanic tumult of women, who tried to storm the house but were beaten off by a dauntless concierge; of a man lost in a world wholly without women, wandering in eerie streets where even the shop-window dummies refused to notice him, in a world slowly drying out through lack of the female principle. But also a world full of miracles, where the impossible was sure to happen. Out of loss came a deeper sense of all that union was. The only answer to the death of Nusch was to root his love securely in the realised fellowship of all men renewing life in labour and in the struggle to end the class-world:

the gulf of her womb sets mankind free
Living is sharing solitude I hate
the strands of death still hold me back
and truly no one now I clasp as once I did
bread was a sign of all felicity
good bread which makes our kisses warmer yet
One shelter is possible the whole wide world
to live for me today is to unknot the riddles
and quite deny the blind despair of birth
in pure loss always star without a glint
to live to lose oneself that one may rediscover men
Then let the river's pallor wipe the gutter out
and let the marvellous eyes see everything in place
misery effaced and all the glances in order
an order swelling with seed in flower and tree
a quickened structure shoring up the universe
The child renewed from man to man and laughing

But to record Eluard's conversation is impossible. Perhaps if one had tried to write it down with the echoes still lively in one's ears, one might have managed to catch some of the rich hurrying tones evanescent in their gay and sad glints of fancy, of self-mockery and tenderness—something like his own poems discursively broken up into ever more fragmentary images, yet combining into consistent perspectives; momentary effects, with a zigzag precision; a fidelity of impulse and sudden perceptions, small and sliding, but given ultimate breadth and harmony by his personality. If I try to recall his conversation, it turns by the cheat and the truth of memory into his poems. "And, by the mediation of the senses, gradually solidarity was reborn. A man for friend, a woman for friend, and the world begins again, and shapeless matter again takes on a body. A straight line linked and passed through the breasts. Once more men are together, and the unhappy one started to smile afresh upon them, with a smile perhaps a little less pleasant than before, but a juster smile, a better smile. He began to imagine again what his brothers could be if they broke down their solitude. He heard the groundswell of the song rising up from the compacted crowd. He was no longer ashamed." His hand, trembling and sure, reaches out again to fill my glass:

> In the scale of delicate touch
> in my sombre embrace at will
> can this body teach me living
> when I have lost the one I love

He was interested in our plans, especially those for *Arena*. Once he grew so excited in the midst of discussion that without consulting me he sprang up and went to the telephone. I found that he had arranged for me to call on Louis Casanova, then in charge of cultural matters for the French Party. Eluard had a high opinion of his views, his sense of tactics; but though I was interested enough in meeting him, I did not see how he could be of any help in the matter of *Arena*; conditions were so different in England that the problems of a left literary magazine were quite unlike those of *Europe, La Pensée,* and so on. Isak Grunberg was there with us, and I asked him to come along for the meeting, which had been arranged for the next day. The address was a building that must have been the Party HQ, for it was guarded and organised so as to be capable of resisting attack—though I did not ask if this was a hangover from the last days of the war, or if there were still possibilities of some kind of fascist violence.

We had a long meeting with Casanova; I can hardly call it a discussion. I merely gave an outline of our project of a magazine, and said that Eluard's enthusiasm had hurried him into making the appointment—which I welcomed, though I rather felt I was present on false pretences. Casanova, however, brushed away my semi-apologies. He seemed to think it was natural for him to dispense advice on the matter, and he gave a leisurely and brilliant account of what he considered the right relation between intellectuals and the Party, and the necessary respect for all that was genuinely avantgarde and drove ahead into the unknown of life, the aspects of experience that eluded or resisted the existent forms of consciousness, the new possibilities of exploration and spiritual adventure that ought to emerge as the old divisions of labour broke down. I had time to reflect, as he broke off to answer the phone, how different his words were from the dictatorial discourses of Zhdanov. Much of what he said I read later in *Le Parti Communiste, les Intellectuals, et la Nation*; but in conversation he put the matters more informally, with more supple resources of argument. "And indeed it happens that giants of thought carry their vision so far ahead that the things they discern are hardly perceptible to others, who all the same desire to follow them. Communist know this. They hold to the principle of fighting at the head of the masses and of sacrificing nothing of the future's values. They will never reproach anyone for having his eyes fixed on the heights and for determining his movement in terms of the future's needs." All he said showed much tact and understanding, and helped me to understand the best aspects of the French Party's treatment of artists and intellectuals, such as Picasso and Léger. Though I knew also that the formulations and the methods of polemics could be extremely rigid, sectarian, intolerant, and sometimes unscrupulous, solely concerned to prove other people wrong and making no effort to find common points for give-and-take in a valuable development. (I saw a little more of Casanova later, for instance at Wroclaw, and felt that he was an impulsive and shy person underneath.)

Eluard was liable to make abrupt arrangements like this with Casanova. Another time he decided that he must without delay give me a copy of the book on Picasso at Antibes, which he had done with Jaime Sabartes, photos by Sima. But he had no copy at hand. So he jumped up and arranged for me to collect one at an art-gallery, at an odd time—about 9 p.m., the only time for some reason when anyone would be there next day. It happened to be inconvenient for us, but, in view of his kindness, I didn't like to say so. We went to the gallery, and had to wait for some time amid paintings by Paul Delvaux, while the assistant poked about for the book. Delvaux' large and luxurious nudes reclined in vague nooks of melancholy or meandered through corridors of shadow aimlessly looking for lovers, mirrors, lost stockings, or mislaid virginities.

When, married again, he visited England in 1952 I spent a day with him at Roland Penrose's house in Hampstead, going through my translations of his poems; and at a lunch which the Authors' World Peace Appeal gave him, he asked Ann and me to spend the summer holidays with him—a month or so at some seaside place, I forget the name. We gladly accepted—but not long after we were invited to go with a group on a six weeks' trip to Rumania. I wrote, putting off the project for the holiday, and went instead to Rumania. The trip was of much interest, but now, in a fuller perspective, it seems a very trivial matter next to the chance of spending a month or more with such a poet as Eluard. I find it impossible to think how I could have made the decision to go to Rumania rather than to the Earthly Paradise of sea and sand and light mixed with Éluard's poetry. He died in November 1952, of angina pectoris, and at once I felt what an irreparable error I had made. Now I feel it a thousandfold more.

Here I would like to end with his poem *Poetry has practical truth for goal*, written "to my exigent friends":

If I tell you that the sun within a wood
is like a womb that yields itself abed
you believe me you approve all my desires

If I tell you the crystal of a day of rain
chimes always in the idleness of love
you believe me you prolong the time of loving

If I tell you that on the branches of my bed
a bird that never cries yes has built its nest
you believe me you partake of my unrest

If I tell you there turns in chasm of a spring
the key of a stream halfopening the green
you believe me even more you understand

But if I sing my whole road with no twists
and my whole country like an endless road
you believe me no longer you go into the desert

For you travel without a goal unknowing that men
are driven by need of union hope and struggle
to grasp the world explain it and transform it

With a single step of my heart I'll draw you in
I own no force I have lived and still I live
but I am bewildered at speaking to enchant you

when I'd rather liberate you to unite you
as much with the seaweed and the rush of dawn
as with our brothers constructing their own light.

[6]

Finally now, Tzara. The meeting that Nancy Cunard had arranged
led to a close relationship. At that time he was staying at a hotel,
10 Rue de Condé, near the Odéon. At his suggestion we stayed
there too for a couple of weeks in 1947, and I had a specially good
chance to see a lot of him and to discuss his poetry. I have managed to find a letter of his, dated 30 December that year and
written from the hotel:

> Que je vous souhaite d'abord, aussi qu'à votre femme, une heureuse
> nouvelle année, meilleure que celle que nous venons de passer et
> qui a vu tant d'espoirs et d'inquiétudes à la fois se projeter sur un
> avenir difficile. Mais, il faut se dire que le progrès s'accomplit à
> petits pas, en attendant qu'un saut nous amène vers une realité
> meilleure.
>
> J'espère que bientôt vous pourrez venir à Paris, ce qui me ferait
> un grand plaisir. Je suis toujours à l'hotel, en attendant le 15 fevr.
> date à laquelle j'ai la promesse d'avoir mon appartement. Mais il y a
> déjà eu tant de promesses, que je ne sais plus que penser. Mlle G. est
> à Tchécoslovaquie où elle joue actuellement au théâtre; elle espère
> venir ici au printemps. Je vous ai fait envoyer un petit livre: "Le
> Surréalisme et l'après-guerre" qui vient de paraître et j'espère que
> vous le recevrez bientôt.

And he went on to say he had shown some of my versions of his
work to Cicely Macworth, and to suggest I should discuss a few
points with her. He had been struggling for some time to get
back his flat in the Rue de Lille, which a collaborator had taken
over. Mlle G. was a buxom blonde Czech actress, with a certain
hardness spoiling her noble proportions. She always seemed
calm and biddable, if a trifle detached, when with Tzara. But she

certainly had a temper and a temperament. One day Ann and I were lunching at the restaurant at the corner of the Rue du Dragon, a little up from the Flore on the opposite side, and we found ourselves seated next to Mlle G. and two other Czechs at another table. The trio were deep in some angry discussion, which went on for more than twenty minutes. The dispute was carried out in very loud voices, and Mlle G. seemed highly indignant, expressing herself with decision and flashing-eyed vehemence, with strong gestures that should have stood her in good stead on the stage; but as it all went on in Czech, we had no idea what it was about. Finally, over coffee, the argument came to a dead stop rather than to any agreed conclusion, if we could judge by stubbed-out cigarettes and yet-smouldering eyes. Then Mlle G. looked round for the first time, and saw us. She did not seem very pleased, but nodded politely, made a few subdued remarks to her companions, and went out. Perhaps they were only discussing the state of the theatre in Prague; but the episode left us with the feeling that Mlle G. could be a difficult character if crossed.[1]

Tzara had perhaps a liking for large women. He was himself a small man. At the time of the Peace Congress in Paris in the spring of 1949, I had written to say we were coming over with Randall Swingler and his wife Geraldine; and Tzara replied that he wasn't feeling well and had to leave Paris. I had the conviction that he was making excuses and that he didn't want to be involved in the proceedings; I knew that while he liked discussion and argument on a more direct and personal level, he shunned large gatherings. There was no sign of him during the congress; but, a couple of days later, we were walking late one night down the Boulevard St Germain to the Hotel de la Place de l'Odéon

---

[1] The Czech was followed in Tzara's affections by a Swede: with many emotional ups-and-downs. But I know little of the inner reality of the situation. Tzara, however, as far as I could see, was not the man to find a harmonious love-relationship such as Aragon and Eluard, each in his different way, did find. Nor to make a woman the still, secure centre of a furiously wayward life, as Dylan did. Perhaps he was both too secure in himself and at the same time too little secure, unable to make the same sort of surrender as those others. At the heart of life, he remained also detached from it, and I feel it was characteristic of him that he got great satisfaction out of walking in the streets *behind* women, enjoying their presence in the complex scene, but not wanting to confront them eye-to-eye.

where we usually stayed in Paris, and one of us noted a very large woman engaged in what appeared to be smothering operations, leant over someone at one of the tables on the pavement in an otherwise deserted café. I glanced across and saw the hidden man disengage himself sufficiently to show his face round one side of the woman, and to my surprise recognised Tzara. At the same moment he recognised me. I had halted irresolutely, uncertain whether or not to walk on, but Tzara with considerable agility shook the woman off, stood up, and, with unimpaired dignity, came smiling across to us. I introduced him to the Swinglers. He said that he was pleased to have encountered us, having only returned to Paris a few hours earlier. He ignored the woman, and after a brief exchange we walked on. I didn't like to look back, and am not sure if Tzara rejoined the woman.

This, however, was not, I think, a characteristic episode. On all other occasions when I saw him, he behaved with impeccable correctness. We often had rendezvous with him at cafés, mostly the Flore; for lunches he used to take us to a *bouillon* not far from the Odéon station, where a bulky glistening woman sat at the front amid the soup-fumes; and now and then we were asked to his flat, which after many setbacks he did succeed in regaining. A letter of 23 August 1948 from Le Château, Villarvolard, Gruyère, announced the news.

Mon cher ami,

Votre lettre m'a fait un grand plaisir, celui partout de vous voir en pleine activité. Inutile de vous dire à quel point je me sens honoré de la place que vous m'accordez dans votre livre, surtout quand ce livre est de vous! Je l'attends avec impatience et ce qu'en dit Edith Sitwell me fait qu'ajouter à mon desir de le voir paraître. Quand pensez-vous qu'il sortira?

Je suis ici depuis le début du mois, dans un petit village très calme ou je songe surtout à refaire ma santé qui a été un peu ébranlée ces derniers temps. C'est la raison pour laquelle, malheureusement, je n'irai pas en Pologne cet été. Mais j'espère fortement, à votre retour, vous recontrer à Paris. Je vais déjà beaucoup mieux et vers le 15 Sept. je serai à Paris et peut-être même avant, dans le cas où je n'irai pas dans le Midi de la France.

Enfin, j'ai pu récupérer mon appartement; ma nouvelle adresse est: *5 Rue de Lille* (7e).

Ici j'ai terminé mon Introduction à la nouvelle édition de Rimbaud qui doit paraître avant la fin de l'année. Je vous l'enverrai. Bien des amitiés à votre femme et cordialement à vous, Tristan Tzara.

It was one day at the *bouillon* that he suddenly began talking in English and admitted that he knew it quite well. I think it was the same day that I mentioned I had performed the unusual feat of reciting a poem in a dream—and what was unique for me, a poem in French. He was very interested and asked if I could remember any of the lines. I told him that when I woke up I felt sure I had the whole work in my head, but in a few moments only a part of two lines survived. What were they?

> . . . et le tonnerre qui mugisse
> dans sa caverne préhistorique . . .

As I spoke them I found that they limped badly; and Tzara completed my demoralisation by observing dryly, "*Tonnerre* is masculine, not feminine."

Small and neat, he looked more and more Rumanian as he aged. Or perhaps I felt this Rumanian aspect of him more acutely after visits to his homeland in 1952 and 1953, when I often thought for a moment that I saw him coming down the street. And yet those other Rumanians were not really like him. They lacked the intense intellectual awareness of his face, the acute responsiveness to every nuance of what was going on around him, the satiric half-smile that was liable to intrude and tighten the curved lines at the sides of his mouth. Only in that flickering glint of amused and penetrating awareness could one recognise anything of the resolute slim devil-may-care comely lad of the Zürich photos of Dada-days. Despite the obvious capacity for a shattering mockery, which at times he let loose on some figure of the literary or artistic worlds whom he considered to be phoney or pretentious, I always found him kindly, patient, helpful; and it was clear that he was always ready to aid or encourage young poets of genuine talent. Though he could speak sharply and brilliantly when the occasion demanded, I never felt the least straining for effect. At least in the years I knew him, he was quiet and retiring, and was not a character who at once detached himself from any setting and dominated things, as in their varying ways Aragon, Edith, Dylan, even Eluard did. But when one had come round to noting his presence, his quality of intellectual force more and more asserted itself. I felt humble in his presence, but he never gave me the least cause for that feeling. As I came to know him, I realised that he was peculiarly responsive to a genuine interest in his work and that in the last resort the humility was all on his side. He was intensely grateful for anything he considered a good turn, and this emotion was not a passing spasm. It entered deeply into him and carried on, providing a stable basis of friendship. Like all artists with a profound and stubborn purpose, set against all compromises with a corrupted world, he was harassed with uncertainty and anxiety; and perhaps for this reason, once he felt that one was wholeheartedly committed on his side of things, he threw down all defences and was simply happy, grateful, warmhearted, in his companionship. Thus, in his own way, he achieved the unguarded simplicity that appeared in Eluard from quite another point of the spiritual compass.

Though in the complicated working-out of the relations between surrealism and politics in the 1920s and 1930s there had been rifts and divergent positions, I am glad to say that Tzara, Eluard, and Aragon in these years seemed to me happily united, going their own ways but aware of a deep fraternal bond.[1] Around 1949 Tzara said once, "Aragon is growing ever more mellow and delightful. And oddly he's become quite clairvoyant. When one goes in to see him, before one's got time to open one's mouth he looks up and answers the remark one hasn't made. He knows why one's come." And indeed that was what happened when I did next go to see Aragon at *Ce Soir*; but as my visit was connected with some matter of the Peace Movement, perhaps one didn't need an excessive power of clairvoyance to guess why I had come.

Edith once drew a comparison of Eluard and Tzara: the first, a

---

[1] Eluard wrote in *Poèmes pour tous,* "Of all the poets I have known, Aragon was the one who was most right, right against monsters—and right against me. He has shown me the right road." He spoke warmly of Aragon to me.

poet who built his own personal world, a sort of nest or sensuous cavern, in his poems, though always without severing his contact with the real world of his fellows and its problems—the second, turned always into the world of bitter and often desperate change, mortally entangled with it, yet at the same time grasping the otherworld of poetry, the immediate satisfaction and the paradisiac core. A pair who worked by diametrically opposed methods for the same end, the freedom and fullness of life.

From his early days Tzara steadily fought out his poetic positions. From Dada in Zürich till his latest poetry he was engaged in a strenuous struggle to understand the place of the poet in the modern world and to find a valid ground on which to base his activity. No other poet of the twentieth century has carried on so consistent, so deepgoing, so passionate a quest; and for this reason I believe that Tzara has a place all his own in the literary history of the first half of that century. He smashed up everything; he recreated a universe without departing from the strict and angry laws of his destroying period. Therein lies his claim to greatness. In poetry he showed, in his own way, the wide-ranging furies and raptures of destruction and creation which Picasso has shown in art. If one estimates the progress from the Dada manifestos and *La première aventure céleste de Monsieur Antipyrine* (1916) up to *De Mémoire d'Homme* (1950), one sees the creation of a secure earth of poetry (which involves a new sense of brotherhood and of meaning in history) without the least loss of the integrity of defiance and resistance to the world's evil that he began with.

> I advance slowly
> I have known pointless departures
> and arrivals nowhere
> arrivals in the void new points of departure
> springs jetted out and I was nowhere
> the roads went rolling avalanches
> hopes snared for an evening's pleasures
> illusory reposes
> lying of years
> time began to run more fast
> than foxes under the moon . . .

the advent of love
pride and uprightness
high and yet higher despair high victory
over fog and night
let night come henceforth what does it matter
for it will skirt the bed of our ardours
like ice on the stumps of broken trees
love will chase off the grievous reason
let the rain come and blind the gardens
the flowers will ring in the ears of children
joy

That anyway was the interpretation I made of his poetry, his life. A wild but considered effort to break down all structures compromised by the part they have played in the world of bourgeois alienation; then, on the cleared ground, the deliberate chaos, the slow acceptance of the unpolluted elements, the slow building-up of a new world out of tested and purified fragments, the ceaseless fight to expel the corruptions that seek to rush in and reassert their grip; the discovery of allies, of causes, which can be accepted without retreat and surrender; the final linking of the lonely poet's struggle with the struggle for the classless society in which alienation can in time be overcome. In its general lines this thesis of mine was accepted by Tzara. As stated in *The Starfish Road,* it was wholeheartedly welcomed by Edith as the definitive statement of the essential poetic experience in our world, and of the necessary lines for the development and resolution of that experience.[1] Though I had arrived at similar conclusions from my study of Baudelaire, Lautréamont, Rimbaud, Apollinaire, of Blake and Edith, I felt in Tzara's work an immense reassurance and fortification of my positions—as if here was indeed the pure and complete example of my thesis, the classically simple and complex working-out. (Though I had previously had some idea

[1] As I have said, Edith arrived at Tzara in any thorough or intimate sense through *The Starfish Road* and its analysis. She was extremely interested in my contacts with the French poets and read the considerable amount of translations I made, especially of Eluard, Aragon, Tzara. In a letter of 1950 I find her writing, "I am glad you and Ann enjoyed being in Paris, and found the poets." She was pleased when I pointed out that at a certain stage in both her own poetry and that of Tzara the imagery and idea of Fire became centrally important. Tzara was keenly interested in *Arena* and gave its first number a section of his *Le Surréalisme et l'Après-Guerre.*

of Tzara as a Dadaist and as a serious poet, it was not till I met him, read his works thoroughly in the order of their creation, and discussed them with him, that I realised anything like his full importance.)

As well as discussing the general bearings of his work, I also went through a few poems or passages (e.g. of his play, *La Fuite*) in some detail. And I can say, as I said of Edith's *Façade*, that despite the way in which he seeks in his own fashion the Rimbaudian derangement and invokes the Dadaist and the surrealist systems of chance, there is also a poetic reason for everything in his poems. In the last resort all the systems of chance-impact, irrationality, dream-association, and so on, express (in true poets like Tzara or Eluard) a new order of purpose, rationality, consciousness. Automatism becomes the method of a new organising power; the most reckless free-association reveals a significant human truth. The absurdity that Dada set out was on the one hand the unrealised imbecilities, contradictions, lies, illusions, of the bourgeois world revealed in a more naked form, raised to a higher level of concentration—for this reason it was also, at the same time, a satirical critique of those imbecilities, contradictions, and so on. Further, to the extent that it was a critique, it expressed, in however embryonic a form, the dynamic order of truth that must take the place of an outworn system in which the corruptions and falsities had become dominant. For a critique implies a criterion, which implies, if it is to have any creative value, a worldview.

This was the sort of thing that came out of our discussions. Tzara stressed the destructive side of Dada; in his view, unless it was understood at every point and at every moment as a total repudiation of all bourgeois systems, it was hopelessly falsified. True, he admitted, in so far as genuine poets or artists were involved, they could not help adding elements of their own creative organisation; and so Dada, in its serious exponents, was already orientated towards a new art and poetry. But for the Dadaist phase, he held, this underlying element was not to be stressed—otherwise the polemical and centrally destructive impulse would be slurred over and the way opened to a compromise with the world. Only when the revolt was carried to its bitter end—and it must be a bitter end—could the stress change and the question of evolving a new creativeness come to the fore. For Tzara the decisive moment arrived in 1917 with the return of Platen to Zürich from Moscow, bringing news of the Revolution. The Dadaist opposition to the war—its central impulse and reason-for-existence—took on a new colouration. Ball turned from abstract poetry to politics and then to a life of voluntary poverty. Serner and Tzara hailed the Russian Revolution as their ally, concerned at this time primarily with its role in the struggle to end the war. In it, and in it alone they saw a force capable of ending war altogether. Henceforth the ruling question was the relationship of the poetic revolution and the political one.

But the working-out of this question was a prolonged and complicated matter, involving moments of approach, contact, collision, swinging-apart, antagonism, renewed approach, and so on. The oversimplified rationalism of political parties seeking to grasp the way-forward into a classless society had to find a common point with the overstressed irrationality of poetic groups seeking to grasp a new organic wholeness. After Dada the next step had to come with surrealism, which set as its aim the liberation of creativeness, thus using what Tzara called directed thought, but taking as its object all the forms of consciousness for which no easy rational explanation was (yet) possible or which seemed to run counter to the assumptions on which rationality was based. Hence a new dialectic between conscious and un-conscious, between creative organisation and the denied body of life, was set up. Between the limited consciousness of directed thought and the vast mass of impulses, needs, sensations, aspira-tions, desires, from which the crucified body and impoverished mind had been alienated.

Tzara had given a great deal of thought to all that was impli-cated in this dialectical struggle of directed and non-directed thinking—or as he also called it, manifest poetry or poetry-means-of-expression and potential poetry or poetry-activity-of-the-spirit. The two aspects had to be present if poetry was to mature and move beyond a primitive level of revolt and effervescence. But woe to the poet who tried to make his work a means-of-expression unless he had totally given himself up to the struggle with life, the struggle to grasp always the potential poetry seething around him. After reading Tzara's poetry and talking with him, I have often felt an intolerable and yet exalting sense of this potential poetry in our world. The self totally unguarded and vulnerable, crushed under the burden of ubiquitous alienation; and yet for this very reason lying open to all the shattering impacts from the new. And this new? Something that ranged from the immediate sensations of walking down a Paris street (in, say, 1949), surrounded with all the manifestations of that moment in time and space, from the advertisement-hoardings and the shopwindows to the industrial noises and the patterns of lighting—to the immense possibilities of which one was vaguely yet powerfully aware in all the fields of thought and expression, art, science, poetry, technology, and, beyond that, the possibilities in the social and economic fields of union, happiness, peace and plenty. And again the distorting, dividing, alienating forces everywhere at work, zigzagging across the face of the world and one's own face. All this momentarily summed up in the interval between two sounds, the lines of force in two converging or separating figures, the clanging and disposition of changing lights, an itch in one's palm, or a bell of hidden laughter. Above all, in certain patterns inexorable and unstable, imposing a harsh derangement of the senses and yet dissolving on the edge of impossible harmonies. Motorcar headlights snared in a shop-window and high heels tapping behind me, the grain of a street-tree's sooted bark and the rotted fringe of the shield round a pissoir. All fused in a single pattern of pure chance and terrible significance.

Tzara's poetry expresses all that, the broken world and the tantalising dream-promise of escape, the reality of the only struggle that can make us whole. And quietly, angrily, doggedly, it was all there in his personality. Total defeat; complete hope. Not Aragon's bravado, nor Eluard's victory-by-surrender. He was too unceasingly aware of the omnipresent and immeasurable violence of the life that surrounds us today. For this reason his moments of affirmation are reached with a terrific force:

> Let earth come upon earth
> and the seed of its kingdom be multiplied

For such moments do not express a random imposition of order on a flux out of control; they emerge at nodal points of a terrifyingly sustained conflict, which they resolve.

Here is the plainly affirming poem in his book done during the war: *Up Sunlight's Single Road* (USSR).

> knives stand upright
> our lives lack breath
> crows share out and fare well
> our farewells are cancelled
> the year of stone falls with a crack on our plight
>
> how much smoke I have seen untwist
> from springs suddenly crossed
> the chain of mists
> broken on the hovel
> and liberty lost
>
> I walk upon moss
> with an ear grown deaf
> a night has come over me
> round as a chestnut
> beyond all the hushes
>
> it spoke of a man afar
> acted the part of a dream
> cast scraps of sun
> to the poor folk we are
> richer than mountains
>
> and I have followed the star
> divined the delight
> words with a heart of mint
> what is this space
> which breaks within me in light

The poet, in this philosophy, is a man who meets the violences of the world in the open. "Knives stand upright." He meets them without defences—except his poetry. At all costs he must let the new, the unformed, the future, stream through his mind and senses, so that he can hold and form it all, making the future safe for men—himself then pressing forward into another unknown dimension. Tzara gave his definitive expression of his view of the poet in *On the Starfish Road,* dedicated to Lorca. He told me that he wrote the poem on the Basque coast, where he was staying when the news of Lorca's death reached him. There had been a terrific storm during the night, and when he walked out along the beach, brooding on the news, he found himself stepping on and over a vast number of starfish that had been thrown up by the waves. The storm, the starfish-road, the news of the murdered poet, the light across the waters, all merge in the imagery of the poem.

In his regained flat he had a number of his treasured art-objects, paintings and carvings from Africa or the Pacific. The first time I visited him there, he showed them all one by one, with tender hands. Touching a Picasso, one of the first of his pictures with collage, he said, "A great invention. Something which alone would deserve immortality." He did not have the same attitude to Picasso as Eluard, who saw in the artist the rich force of metamorphosis touching and entangling every aspect of modern life. Once I met him in the street just as he was coming back from a visit to Picasso in the South of France. He took me into the nearest bar for a drink and shook his head. "I've just spent several days with him," he said, "and I've never known a man in all my life so unsure of himself, so lost and anxious." And he launched into a eulogy of Matisse as an artist securely and concretely based in the warmth of the living world, which he loved. And yet Tzara as a poet was much nearer to Picasso as an artist than Eluard was, while Eluard one would expect to feel closer to Matisse with his sensuousness, his varied response to embraceable women.

Tzara had a wide and deep knowledge of almost all aspects of art. Once I discussed Romanesque art with him and was overwhelmed with his thorough learning, his subtle appreciation, his acquaintance with the works not through books but from the actual sites. When I saw him first after Wroclaw, I showed him the photo of one of the Baba statues I had seen at the back of the Radzovill Palace (country-house of the Union of Writers) in Poland. I knew little of such statues then, though I saw many the next year in the Ukraine. He at once gave me a long lecture about them, historical, archaeological, artistic. In 1963 I sent him a copy of my *Short History of Culture*. In his reply he remarked: "En attendant, je me permets de vous signaler—mais vous devez déjà le savoir—que quelques erreurs se sont glissées dans les légendes de certaines illustrations. Le cliché 7 représent une échasse de cérémonie des Iles Marquises. Le cliché 6 me semble representer une statuette des Iles Leti (Asie du Sud-ouest). Le cliché 22 représente selon moi une sculpture du Cyclades. Ou je me trompe?" No doubt he was right about nos 6 and 7, given as from West New Guinea and Easter Island; I had chosen them, with several more of the illustrations, to reduce costs, from other publications of Studio Books, who still had the blocks. His complaint about no 22 was the result of a misprint "Parian marble-harper" instead of "Parian-marble harper." But the ease with which he noted mistakes over Pacific art was derived from his fine scholarship and his strong feeling for it.

Perhaps I may divagate here into a few words on another Rumanian who played an important role in shaping modern art: Brancusi. I spent an afternoon, with Grunberg, at his studio, a rambling shedlike place filled with his works and their shadows in the Impasse Ronsin, off the rue de Vangirard amid shabby shops. He seemed distantly grateful to have someone to whom he could show his works, wandering round silently and starting off the mechanism that made his Seal revolve. There was also a young couple there, lovers, rapt in themselves even more than Brancusi was. So he kept his attention for us, as if our reactions meant something to him. Which surprised me. After we had gone round, there was a confused interminable conversation, in which he set out his philosophy and his very peculiar historical system. But I was more interested in watching his face and gestures than in following the odd mishmash of his conceptions—the sort of thing one finds at times in a highly intelligent worker who has read very little but has formulated a vast superstructure of philosophical fantasy on top of the little he knows, a system logical in itself but madly inadequate in its material, expending much energy in propounding or solving questions that have long ago disappeared into the limbo, and ending in a vast inane.

But here the fabricator was a peasant, and the constructions were almost wholly of fantasy. I had mentioned that I was a Communist but admired his work greatly; and that stirred him up, for he was fiercely anticommunist. He wanted to show me the error of my ways and how all the forces of history, rightly interpreted, were against me. As an admirer of his work, I deserved to be put on the right track. But it wasn't his semi-illiterate fantasy of history that held my attention so much as his strong old face, at once wise and crafty, a peasant face in its impressive force, with a slightly crazed note in its ancient wisdoms. The beautiful subtle simplicities of the statues with their organic curves: the life-process caught at a moment of pure balance, with everything eliminated but the clear symmetries on which all that was most stable and characteristic in the form, the living form, depended. Later when I visited Rumania and saw much of its countryside, I realised how Brancusi came straight out of the immemorial folk-structures in wood, with their fine balances and noble simplifications—though he had added the sense of organic form, curved down to bare essentials and yet showing itself at the moment of fullest expansion in its functional reason-for-existence. Especially his endless columns rising to the skylights showed the kinship. And I thought of the other Rumanian, Tzara, in which the same capacity to strip life to its naked root had a diametrically opposite effect: revealing always the moment of most extreme instability, of breakdown under outer attack and inner uncertainty or division, with symmetry (stability) reasserted only at the very last heartbeat, on the giddy verge of chaos. And I felt that there must be something vital in Rumania itself, with its French culture developed among the intellectuals and its mixture of Slav and other lineages among the peasantry, which produced two such men to play their part in illuminating and stimulating the French spheres of art and poetry at a crucial moment of change. And through France the whole modern world.[1]

[1] I heard the story that Tzara had once said he was *trist en tsara* (sad in the country), liked the sound, and took it as his name; but I did not ask him if this was true. He rather liked mystification about himself. A close friend Tilly Visser tells me that she thought his grandfather, though Jewish, was a landowner, his father a doctor, and that Tristan had enjoyed going about in the countryside with his grandfather. (There is a photo of the three of them, 1912, in R. Lacôte's selection of his poems.)

Tzara always enjoyed the conflict of ideas. Long after the provocative explosions of Dadaism and early Surrealism had ended, he liked the public exposition of what he stood for. In a card from Tunis on 21 November 1951 he wrote

Mon cher Jack Lindsay, Je suis en Tunisie actuellement où je fais une tournée de conférence. J'y ai trouvé le soleil et le printemps. Je vous remercie de votre lettre et j'espère vous voir à Paris, ce printemps. Bien des souvenirs à Ann et de tout coeur à vous. Tristan Tzara.

He liked *une tournée de conférence,* and it must have been bitter for him to feel unable to keep up in argument and avantgarde conflict as he would have liked to do. The last time I saw him was in Paris in 1959. I had gone over with my niece Cressida to spend a few days looking at works by David and his school, Gros, Géricault, for my book *The Death of the Hero.* The only person I tried to see was Tzara. I dropped him a card and he asked us along to tea. I found him looking older, though full of interests as always. He was working at cryptograms in Villon; and was so excited over some discoveries that I did not mention the work which I knew had been recently done on the subject, though I decided to get hold of it and send it over to him on my return to England. He asked Cressida what was going on among the younger poets here, and listened attentively, nodding his head. But I felt that he was suffering from strain. He remarked about Paris, "A heartless place, always after the latest sensation. Nothing lasts." He seemed weary and I felt that he no longer found it at all easy to hold his own in the only way that satisfied him. He thought the political situation stagnant and depressing. He pressed us to stay a few days more so that we could at least dine with him; but I said that we had to go.

Watching his tired and stressed face, I tried to see in it the face of the young Tzara of Zürich in 1917, gay, vividly handsome with

Whether or not the above facts are "correct," I cite them as the sort of impression Tzara gave his friends. He turned aside any query as to his ancestry by saying, "I was born a Rumanian." Probably he was refusing to be involved in the sectarian issues of a country with so many national minorities as Rumania, and simply considered his essential cultural roots to be Rumanian. He was not naturalised as French till after the second world-war; his scientist son is Christophe Tzara.

intellectual zest and confident aggression. And I thought of how far he had come to reach this quiet nook of afternoon chat, withdrawn from the noises of Paris. The zest was still there, but the lines on his face were of wisdom. How much did the frustration I scented in his spirit come merely from an aging body? how much from deeper sources of disquiet? I felt in him, as I had felt throughout the years of our friendship, a patient power, a steadfast endurance. But I had not known him in his years of more agitated struggle; and I wondered if I had all along been idealising his character, blind to aspects that would have complicated things if I had been less of a spectator, more actively involved in the situation in France. It seemed to me that the conflict, such as it was, between the skilful showman, the tactician, the avantgarde expert, and the true poet concerned only with the wholeness of the poetic image, had been resolved. The poet of *De Mémoire d'Homme* was simply a great poet, and yet that poem would never have been achieved without the battles precipitated by the showman, the tactician, the avantgarde expert. It struck me that one of the points of interest in poets like Aragon, Eluard, Tzara, different as they were in themselves, lay in the way in which they dragged poetry into the dust of all sorts of public conflicts and manifestations, yet in the long run begot a purer poetry. The public exploits brought about all sorts of power-struggles as well as throwing bricks at the bourgeoisie; and therein lay a source of contamination and confusion, tainting men of lesser creative energies. Tzara has been vastly ambitious, and perhaps some of the weariness I sensed in him came from the inevitable failures and rejections that attend any ambitious career in a long working-out. Eluard had been saved by his devotion to the beloved; Aragon, in the last resort, by his devotion to Communism; Tzara, by his love of poetry for its own sake, for its intractible destiny. Perhaps what I had felt at this moment in him was the final defeat of the ambitious tactician, the final triumph of the unpredictable poet. In a weariness of frustration, in an infinite peace of acceptance. I was grateful to have known him. I am grateful.

I heard shortly after some rumours that he had left the Communist Party. Aragon, however, tells me that he never made any break. "He didn't retake his card, I don't know exactly when it was, it seems to me around 1960, perhaps later. But he never ceased to be a Communist at heart, and always voted for the Party."

My last letter from him was dated 1 April 1963, and came from the Rue de Lille.

Mon cher ami, Il y a longtemps que je veux vous écrire. Tout d'abord pour vous remercier de l'envoi de "Franfrolico" et de la "Courte histoire de la Culture" qui m'ont, tous deux, vivement interessé. Mais je tenais à vous dire aussi que la dédicace de "Masks & Faces," dont vous m'avez envoyé des épreuves, m'a fait un grand plaisir.

Je sors à peine d'une clinique où j'ai été soigné d'une maladie malencontreuse. C'est vous dire que je vais déjà beaucoup mieux, bien que je doive encore suivre un long et embêtant traitement. Peu à peu je commence à reprendre mes occupations habituelles. Je me propose de parler à l'editeur Bordas de votre "Courte histoire de la Culture." Je vous dirai ce qu'il en pense. [Then he made the comments on some of the illustration-texts cited above.]

Il y a bien longtemps que vous n'êtes pas venu à Paris. Si vous y passez un jour, prévenez-moi, cela me ferait une grande joie de vous revoir, Très amicalement votre Tzara.

Soon after that he died.

ON THE STARFISH ROAD

To Federico Garcia Lorca

what wind blows on the solitude of the world
making me call to mind the ones I've loved
frail desolations blown drawn-in by death
beyond the clumsy chases of hunting time
the storm took pleasure as its end came nearer
in the sand already rounding its hard haunch
but pockets of fire upon the mountains
emptied out with sure claps their light of prey
as wan and brief as any friend gone out
and no appeal to the horizon has time to succour
his form that's graspable only as it vanishes

and so from one lightning to another
the animal always stretches his grievous rump
across the enemy centuries
through certain fields of pomp and other fields of greed
and in its fracture memory's outline clears
like wood that creaks in token of a presence
and disparate necessity

and there are fruits as well
and I am not forgetting wheats
and sweat that made them sprout goes mounting to the throat
we know however well the price of sorrow
wings of oblivion and the endless drillings
level with life
the words that can't succeed in holding fast the facts
scarcely to make them worth a laugh

the horse of night has galloped out of trees to sea
and joined the reins of a myriad charitable obscurities
he has dragged along the hedges
where the breasts of men held back the assault
with all the murmurs caught against his flanks
amid the enormous roars which overtook each other
while in full flight from the sheer power of water
measureless they came in succession while quite small murmurs
refused to fall engulfed and swam on top

in the invincible solitude where the tunnels passed
the forests the droves of towns the harnessed seas
a single man with the breath of several countries
merged into one cascade and gliding over a smooth blade
of unknown fire which sometimes finds at night an entry
as doom of those whom sleep has brought together
in their profound remembrance

but don't let's speak of those who have bound themselves
to fragile boughs and nature's nasty humours
those very ones who submit to the boisterous blows
hold out the neck and on their bodies' carpet
when birds aren't pecking at the grains of sun
clatter the stiff boots of the conquerors

they have departed from my memory
the birds seek other springtime jobs
which to their minds are sinecures
held by infatuations in charming flocks
the wind close at their heels
O let the desert be set to their account

off to the devil with nice cautions
diversions poppycock and company
the cold is scraping
and fear mounts up
the tree is drying out
and man is cracking
the shutters bang
and fear mounts up
no word is tender half enough
to bring back home the child of roads
who has lost his way inside the head
of someone at the season's edge
he looks up at the vault
he looks down at the void
watertight bulkheads
smoke in the throat
the roof's worn out
but still the famous animal flying-buttressed
in muscular awareness and twisted under the spasm
of lightning's giddying flight from rock to rock
runs wild with the appetite of joy
morning remoulds his world
in the measure of his slavery
looters of seas
you stoop beneath the weight of waiting
and then rise up and every time you hail the sea that's drunken at your
    feet
upon the starfish road
deposited by columns of incertitude
you stoop and rise again
salutes braced-up in bands
and yet across the heap you're forced to walk
even while coasting round the finest still you're forced to walk
you stoop

along the starfish road
and at the other end my brothers cry with pain
we ought to take them all intact
for they're the hands of sea
held out to men who own nothing
a glorious road along the road of starfish
alcachofas alcachofas my beautiful Madrid
with eyes of tin with fruitful voice
open to all the winds
waves of iron waves of fire
it's all a question of the splendours of the sea
and we must take them each intact
those too with arms bentback or broken
along the starfish road
where leads this road it leads to pain
men fall when it's their will to stand upright
men sing because they've tasted deep as death
and yet you must go walking
walking on above
the starfish road by columns of uncertainty
though you are tangled in the voice of the lianas
alcachofas alcachofas my beautiful Madrid with sunken fires
open to all the winds
and over long years invoking for me nettles
it's the head of a king's son of a harlot's son
a head it is a wave that swirls in foam
it's yet upon the starfish road
that all the hands are open
they do not speak of beauty or of splendour
nothing beyond reflections of minutest heavens
and the imperceptible twinklings of the eyes around
the broken waves
looters of seas
but it's Madrid that's open to all winds
and stamps the word inside my head
alcachofas alcachofas
cornices of stiffened cries

open infinite heart
and make the road of starfish penetrate
deep into life as countless as the sand

and the seas' joy
and make it hold the sun
within the breast where shines tomorrow's man
man of today upon the starfish road
has set the vanguard sign of life
the life we ought to live
the flight the bird has freely chosen right to death
with eyes fixed clear upon the world's sole certainty
whose streaming light planes almost at the level of the ground

(1936)

Last Words

THERE THEN is the picture of these poets as well as I can paint it. I began this book as an act of piety, to recall their faces, their minds, which had been dear to me; I felt that perhaps I had something to record of them that no one else would quite put down on paper. I am thinking of Dylan and Edith, with Aragon, Eluard, Tzara coming in as a natural addition—needed if I were to evoke at all effectively the spirit of those days and what we felt as their vast potentiality. In trying to recall the poets, I found I had to think also of their poetry and seek to grasp the ultimately-indissoluble unity of personality and poetry. The creative struggle appears from one angle as an inquiry into the nature of poetry itself—of poetry as exalted life, life caught in the elusive quick of its transformations. And so I feel that I would like to end with a brief sketch of what I feel to be the worldview shared in varying degrees by all my poets here.

Dylan, Edith, Aragon, Eluard, Tzara: their works were extremely varied and each poet differed deeply from the others. Yet I think that deep down was a shared and fundamental element. It involves both a general concept of poetry and a particular view as to the way in which poetry must operate in our world if it is to preserve its integrity, the fullness of its purpose. I do not need to attempt any restatement of what I consider to be this concept of poetry and the ways it must struggle with our world if it is not to succumb to its arch-enemy, the alienating process. If I have not given some idea of my attitude in such matters in the essays on Edith and Tzara, I cannot hope to do so in a few final words. But, after having done my best to show the particular character of each poet, I want here to stress the shared element, the faith in poetry as an essential integrating force and in the consequent need for an all-out struggle against the divisive and distorting forces of our

233

world. The concept of poetry as revolutionary activity seeking both to celebrate and glorify life, and to change life at the root. There is no contradiction in the simultaneous acceptance and rejection which this outlook implies. For life is not a static thing, a sum total of separable elements or oddments. The choice is not between simply accepting all that exists as a given unalterable sum, rejecting it all, or giving the signature of one's approval to one set of selected factors. Life is a process, a violent unity of conflicting opposites, and the poet's loyalty is to *the formative process* itself, which involves the future as much as the past and the present. For the future is always present as the unseizable directive factor precipitating the next stage—whether one is thinking of the whole world or of one's own body-spirit. In this sense all true poetry is prophetic, since it grasps past-present-future in a single image of dynamic movement, where direction is determined by the totality of the process. That is why poetry, if it be true poetry, expresses in its own vital unity the wholeness of the individual, even in a situation where that individual and his society are rent by the most terrible of alienating pressures.

Though each of my five poets would phrase this sort of position in his or her own way, I can claim that they all hold to it. When, however, I look out at the world beyond my window as I write here, I feel how uncontemporary we all are. (Aragon and I are alone living of those in the story; but the poetry of the others lives on, and so I write in the present tense.) The fragmentation against which my poets have all protested and fought seems to have won the day (and the night) as far as all that is fashionable in art, music, and literature is concerned. They may well seem old-fashioned in their stress on the struggle for human wholeness and in their belief that it was attainable—not in the sense of a static goal where struggle ended, but as a dynamic factor deepmost in the creative spirit. In our smugly disintegrated culture such positions may well stir the superior smiles of those who know perfectly well how pointless is life, how cribbed, cabined, and confined in absurdity, how condemned to treadmills of the viciously-circular self with its traumatic compulsions. But bad as things are, I feel that they are continually trembling on the edge of a genuine upheaval, of the sort of which my poets become the

234

triumphant mouthpiece. In the darkest night of society and the spirit, if one believes in poetry, one also believes in the possibility and inevitability of renewal, in the revolt of the young, in the miraculous gift of sight for the nation of the blind, in the return of the consuming hunger for wholeness. And this is not in the least a blind faith. Rather it is a defensible belief that when contradictions seem about to rend all things apart, they are also on the point of stirring a new consciousness, a sense of all that goes beyond them.

My five poets, it seems to me, embody both the break with tradition and the recreation of it. Apart from Dylan, they go back to 1900 or the other side of that year. In their experience they had thus absorbed the pre-1914 world of full bourgeois flowering, the exposure of that world in the 1914–18 war, the dramatic rupture of the Russian Revolution, the period of phoney-recovery and of reasserted masks in the 1920s, the largescale breakdown at the end of that decade and in the 1930s, with the advent of Hitler, the huge menace of Fascism, and the final cleavages of the Spanish Civil War, then the complex war of 1939–45 with its culmination both in a great antifascist development among the peoples and in the infernal retort of Hiroshima. And after that the repetition of all that was most phoney, lying, and unstable in the 1920s, in the new riveted masks of the post-war period, under unceasing shadow of world-end.

Further, all this means living as well through the periods of Futurism, Dadaism, Cubism, Surrealism, with their entangled mixtures of true and illusory revolt, true and illusory integration. Dylan, the most limited in range of the five poets I treat, was still able, by reason of his provincial Welsh origins in the 1920s and early 1930s, to irrupt with a full romantic appetite, a Rimbaudian all-or-nothing throw of the dice, upon the literary scene of London where almost nothing of the tradition I sketch was surviving except in the neglected work of Edith and the desiccated versions of Eliot. (I should add the work of Yeats; but that work, with its roots in William Morris and Ireland, introduces so many new questions that I cannot do more than name it here—pointing out that though its influence often added a saving grace to superficial and talented writers like Auden, it could not transform them into poets truly aware of their world as were Edith and Dylan.)

The historical experience in poets like Edith, Eluard, Tzara, which I have indicated above, gave them genuine roots in the past of Rimbaud, Mallarmé, Apollinaire—this latter, at least in the early years, not of the past at all. And at the same time it carried them on, over two world-wars and the Russian Revolution, into the period of the atomic bomb, when world-end ceased to be a fancy or a symbol. Compassing such a period, a poet had to rise to the full possibilities or be crushed beneath them. These poets rose to the occasion. And so I feel that what they had to say, and the way they have said it, is of crucial importance to those who have grown up in the postwar years, in the terrible world of the atomic bomb with its enormous increase in alienation, an increase that grows in tempo all the while—and with its material advances that are used to cover up the worsening instability of all the bases on which men depend.

Everyone knows in their bones, even if they do not understand the reasons, that pretences grow ever more hollow. Everyone knows that the Welfare State, the American Way of Life, or whatever one calls it, cannot last and is steadily piling up some awful nemesis. Everyone knows that the judgement day is nearing, a world-end pushbutton war or a furious chaos that defies imagination. And so almost everyone wants to rush on without thought in the goodtime racket, the profitable rat-race, the accumulation of gadgets and domineering things, or else to rationalise absurdity and disaster in artforms that draw on reality only enough to deaden and acclimatise people to a purposeless world with rats in the foundations. Yet many sections of the younger people, here as elsewhere, feel that the situation is hopelessly wrong, even if, comprehensibly, they do not know what to do about it; and it is in the hope of a few of them happening to pick up this book and finding in it something of use, that I have overcome my scepticism and forced myself to finish it.

There is one further point I should like to make, briefly, on the difference between such movements as Dadaism and Surrealism (in its vital period), and the diluted repetitions that occur at a later phase. What is called Modernism in the arts and literature today is almost wholly a form of tame academicism, often linked with big business or big advertising. It is thus in effect the diametric opposite of the adventurous movements on which it superficially bases itself. Poets like Baudelaire, Rimbaud, Tzara, discovered the bourgeois world as the actualisation of hell; and their work was meant to shock people into the same discovery, with all the revolt it implied. But in the tame or imitative phase, the verse or the art derived at second or fiftieth hand from such creative explorations aims instead at conditioning men to accept hell as the sole natural habitat of the species, an unchangeable state of *angst*, absurdity, or disintegration. The whole point of Dada lay in shocking people into an awareness of the total dead-end represented by bourgeois culture and its war-corollaries. The moment any particular form or tactic of expression ceased to have this effect, it was dropped and another was sought. The very idea of building an artform out of anti-art was something that betrayed the whole aim of the movement. Yet this is what the later gimmicking pickers-up of the motives of anti-art have set out to do.

Marcel Duchamp, certainly the most potent single influence behind modernist methods and ideas in art today, has put the point more strongly than I could. "This Neo-Dada," he says, "which they call New Realism, Pop Art, Assemblage, etc., is an easy way-out, and lives on what Dada did. When I discovered ready-mades I thought to discourage aesthetics. In Neo-Dada they have taken my ready-mades and found aesthetic beauty in them. I threw the bottle-rack and the urinal in their faces as a challenge and now they admire them for their aesthetic beauty." After the first phases of Surrealism came the debasement and sell-out by those artists who quickly found connections with big business and advertising. Nowadays, forms like Optical Art, which derive from the longpast experiments of men like Duchamp, find their immediate and moneymaking basis in the world of advertising, commercial design, interior decoration, textiles. An so on indefinitely.

This is the sort of degeneration that Tzara several times pointed out to me. His way—of struggling to develop *a truly organic art on the ground cleared by anti-art*—was the exact opposite of the pretences that anti-art can be aestheticised. Of course a vein of this sort of genuine art runs through the work of many practitioners in the modernist sphere, especially the older ones who have had contact with the original sources of revolt; and the last thing I am proposing is a return to the positions demolished by men like Tzara and Duchamp. But unless a serious effort is made to distinguish the struggle to create art out of the new chaos of alienations and the meek cashing-in on the now-academicised levels of Modernism, there can be no critical values.

Here is the deepest problem in our culture. For whereas the real struggle is one that seeks always to attack and defeat alienation at the point of its strongest grip, the fashionable academicised modernisms and abstractions seek to intensify alienation, to define it as the condition of man, and to rob creative expression of all genuine impact. The latter way is the easy way-out, as Duchamp said, and it is inevitable that most practitioners will turn to it, since it brings money, fame, status, as did the naturalist academicism of the Victorian age. I offer this book in the hope that it may do a little, in the literary sphere, to clarify the problem.

Index

Index

Adam, 54, 61, 78, 109
Adams, T., 131
Anthias, T., 158
Apollinaire, G., 77, 217, 236
Aragon, Louis, 57, 60, 102, 120, 128, 130, 167–86, 199, 200, 203, 212, 215, 217, 220, 226, 233–4, 236; see also Triolet
Arena, 60, 65–6, 81, 87, 106, 111, 128–31, 154, 217
Auden, W. H., 35, 61, 119, 122, 138–9, 235
Authors' World Peace Appeal, 37–8, 76–7, 209
Aveline, C., 197

Barker, G., 130–1
Barras, M., 112
Baudelaire, C., 61, 77, 79, 120–1, 143–4, 157
BBC, 4, 156
Beaching, J., 130–1
Beethoven, L. van, 108, 132
Blake, W., 58, 64, 67, 81, 113, 131, 217
Bodley Head, 154
Boehme, J., 63
Bottomley, G., 117, 130
Boyle, K., 198
Brancusi, C., 223–4
Brinnin, M., 34–5, 40–1, 44
British Ally, 127
British Council, 191
Bryher, 98
Bruno, G., 54

Cameron, N., 130
Campbell, R., 100–1, 135
Camus, A., 128
Carlyle, T., 80
Carpenter, M., 51–3, 130
Casanova, L., 208–9
Cassou, J., 178–9, 197–8
Caudwell, C., 130, 155
Chelsea, 3–4, 6–7, 21
Clark, Sir K., 98, 117
Coleridge, S. T., 137–8, 156
Comfort, A., 76
Connolly, C., 105, 120, 134
Coppard, A. E., 76
Corbière, 157
Cunard, N., 168, 190–1, 198, 211

Dada, 57, 66, 69, 121, 214, 216, 218–9, 235–6
Dali, S., 119, 237
Davenport, J., 36, 38
Delvaux, P., 209
Denwood, J., 130
Devas, A., 24
Dickens, C., 23, 44, 80
Dickinson, E., 86
Dobson, D., 111–2, 118, 120, 151
Dostoevski, F. M., 132
Drda, J., 128
Ducamp, M., 237–8

Eliot, T. S., 66–7, 107, 112, 117–9, 123, 127, 138–9

Eluard, Paul, 44, 57, 60–1, 66, 73, 113, 128, 155, 169, 171–2, 179, 180, 182–3, 190, 196, 201–12, 215, 217, 220, 222, 226, 233
Evans, S., 52

Fadeyev, A., 127, 199
Fast, H., 154, 199
Films, 4, 7, 11, 15, 28, 30, 32–4, 38, 46, 97–8, 159
Fitzgibbon, C., 21, 25, 30
Flaubert, G., 134

Gascoygne, 98
Giacometti, A., 199
Goethe, J. W. von, 63, 184
Gorer, G., 74, 98
Graves, R., 67
Gray, T., 122
Grigson, G., 67, 100, 106
Grindea, M., 109–10
Grunberg, I., 190, 208, 223
Guillevic, 194–7

Hamnett, N., 51
Hegel, G. W. F., 81, 115
Herring, R., 98
Hurry, L., 52

John, A., 29, 30
Johnson, P. H., 30, 39
Johnson, S., 122, 132
Jones, E., 157–8
Joyce, J., 21

Kafka, F., 132
Keats, J., 120, 144, 156
Key Poets, 130–1, 154
Kierkegaard, S. A., 131–2

Laforgue, 157
Laughlin, J., 112–3, 118, 122
Lautréamont, 108, 140, 217
Lawrence, D. H. L., 22, 26

Lenin, V., 78
Life and Letters, 54, 61–2, 78, 137–9, 156
Lindsay, Ann, 53, 61, 75, 88, 102, 107, 110, 113, 126, 137, 153, 156, 159, 197, 209
Lindsay, Cressida, 86, 125
Lindsay, Jack: works by: Anatomy of History, 84–5; Autobiographies, 125, 131, 160, 167; Barriers are Down, 186–8; Byzantium into Europe, 99, 134–5, 150; Daphnis and Chloe 102; Death of the Hero, 225; Dickens, 104, 110, 126, 132–4; Discovery of Britain, 85; Loving Mad Tom, 67, 106–7; Men of Forty-eight, 70, 108–10, 135, 153, 186, 188; Meredith, 136–7; Other novels, 99, 106, 135–6, 153, 188, 190; Short History of Culture, 223, 227; Song of a Falling World, 134; Spasmodics, 156–7; Starfish Road, 66, 75–9, 82, 92, 105, 108, 111–3, 118–9, 121–3, 126, 128, 137–43, 150, 154–7, 160, 185, 217; Three Letters to Tikhonov, 75; Music, 110–1, 124
Lindsay, Meta, 86
Lindsay, Norman, 25, 124–5
Lindsay, Philip, 3–7, 20, 22–3, 29
Lorca, F. G., 35, 202, 224, 227
Lowry, M., 128, 131

MacCarthy, D., 104, 132, 155
MacDiarmid, H., 51, 128
MacOwan, M., 4
Macworth, C., 211
Mallarmé, S., 66, 140–3, 157, 185, 201, 204, 236
Marcenac, J., 192, 200
Marx and Marxism, 79, 83, 99, 104, 112, 114, 116, 129–30

Masson, L., 180
Matisse, H., 185, 222
Mayakovsky, V., 169, 205
Meanjin, viii, 125
Miles, B., 111
Mitchison, N., 76
Morgan, C., 179–81, 197
Morris, W., 235
Morton, A. L., 29
Moussinac, L., 178–9, 192–4, 200–1

Neruda, P., 130, 199
Nerval, G. de, 157
New Directions, 112–3
Nicholson, H., 54–5, 110
Nietzsche, F. W., 44, 54–5, 124–5, 131–2

Oken, L., 63
Our Time, 53–4, 65, 70, 78, 102

Paloczi-Horvath, G., 151
Parrot, L., 201–2
Pasternak, B., 128
Patchen, K., 93
Peace Movements, 33, 76–7, 127
Penrose, R., 209
Picasso, P., 190, 192, 199, 203, 209, 216, 222
Platen, 219
Plato, 131
Polemic, 106
Pollitt, H., 126
Potts, P., 35
Pound, E., 117
Priestley, J. B., 133–4

Quincey, T. de, 108

Ribemont-Dessaignes, G., 197
Rickword, Edgell, 29, 61, 65
Riffault, M., 201

Rimbaud, A., 57, 66, 77, 79, 121, 144, 157, 204–5, 217, 236
Robeson, P., 73–4
Ross, J. M., 32
Rossetti, C., 86
Rossetti, D. G., 158
Roy, Claude, 170, 177, 179, 183

Sartre, J.-P., 151, 180, 183
Schaff, A., 152
Searle, H., 46, 92, 98
Seghers, P., 176, 179–81, 190–1
Shaginyan, M., 190
Simonov, K., 199
Sitwell, Edith, 25–7, 51–163, 215, 231, 235–6; Ancestors, 109, 136; Christening, 52; Cliques, 124; Compassion, 73, 89–91, 107–8; Disasters, 92–7; Durrant's Hotel, 63; Germs, 109–10; Greek, 86; Greek Myth, 62–3; Catholicism, 82–4, 94–5; Hollywood, 97–8, 159; Honours, 79, 111; Hunger Marches, 80; Montegufoni, 84, 100, 159; Nuisances, 91, 106–7; Osbert, 62, 66, 68, 79, 88–91, 93, 98, 107, 111, 126, 138; Parents, 62, 68–70, 90, 136; Peace Movement, 76–7; Politics, 65–6, 72, 74–6, 78; Racialism, 72–4; Renishaw, 68, 87, 89, 97, 100, 109, 111, 126, 136; Rootham, H., 73, 89; Sacheverell, 71, 84, 98, 111, 120; Sesame Club, 54, 63–8, 71–2, 88, 93–7, 99, 100, 104; Sufferings, 87–92, 123–4, 157, 159; Thomas, Dylan, 22, 25–7, 35, 51, 66, 96, 106, 117, 119, 144, 156, 159; Tzara, 77, 121, 155, 215–6; U.S.A., 62, 72–5, 77, 88, 101, 107, 109, 118, 122, 137, 139, 158–9; Wit, 67–8,

243

Sitwell, Edith—*continued*
71–2; see also J. Lindsay, Ann
Lindsay, Tchelitchew.

Works by: *Bucolic Comedies,*
146, 149; *Chain Gang,* 111;
Coat of Fire, 62, 102; *Colonel
Fantock,* 109; *Dark Song,* 146,
148; *Elegy on Dead Fashions,* 149;
Façade, 51, 69, 70, 72, 114, 137,
144–6; *Gold Coast Customs,*
78–80, 90, 92–3, 114–5, 126,
149; *I Live under a Black Sun,*
78; *Madwoman in the Park,* 63;
Mariner Man, 146–8; *Outcasts,*
150; *Poet's Notebook,* 107; *Road
to Thebes,* 91, 150; *Shadow of
Cain,* 53–6, 58–9, 78, 81, 112,
115, 123, 127–8, 149–50;
Shakespeare Notebook, 144;
Sleeping Beauty, 109, 114, 148;
Song of the Dust, 75–6, 150;
Stone-Breakers, 111; *Street Acro-
bat,* 81, 106, 150; *Taken Care of,*
68–9; *Young Girl,* 60
Skoumal, A., 36
Slater, M., 65, 76
Smart, C., 139, 140
Smith, S. G., 96, 130
Sommerfield, J., 29
Soviet Union, 73, 75–6, 127,
152–3, 159, 180, 221
Spender, S., 35, 61, 93, 98, 100–1,
104–5, 117, 119
Squire, J. C., 57, 155
Swift, J., 78
Swinburne, A. C., 137–8
Swingler, R., 29, 98, 118, 159,
212–3

Tazlitsky, B., 179
Tchelitchew, V., 60–2, 73, 86,
112
Thomas, Dylan, 3 ff, 212, 215,
233, 235–6; Caitlin, 6–13,

15–20, 24, 40, 43–4, 47, 96;
Corruption, 6–9, 15–8, 44;
Drink, 16, 20–1, 23–4; Fear of
death, 14, 39, 42–3; Homo-
sexuality, 25; Marxism, 31;
Miming, 25; Money, 13–6;
Nietzsche, 44; Peace Move-
ment, 33, 77; Persia, 38;
Physical condition, 21–2, 39;
Politics, 27–35, 46; Prague, 29,
36–7, 45; Psychiatrist, 21;
Reading, 22–3; Readings, 7, 11,
22; Religion, 41; Reputation,
22; Rubber, 23; Taylor, A. J. P.,
18; Trease, 28; Trick, Bert,
30–1; U.S.A., 15, 26–7, 44;
Women, 10–2, 25, 40; see also
Philip Lindsay, Films, Edith
Sitwell. Poems by: *Ballad of the
Long-Legged Bait,* 7, 11, 13;
Ceremony After a Fire Raid, 35;
In the White Giant's Thigh, 36;
Into her Lying-down Head, 7, 22;
Our Eunuch Dreams, 28; *Refusal
to Mourn,* 30; *These were the Men,*
32–5, 40, 42; *Under Milk Wood,*
30, 43
Thomson, J., 140, 156
Thompson, E., 151
Times Literary Supplement, 98–9,
136
Triolet, E., 168–9, 175–6, 178–9,
180–1, 189–90
Turner, C. T., 139
Tuwim, J., 130
Tzara, Tristan, 57, 60–1, 66–9, 77,
92, 108, 113, 121, 128, 155,
168–9, 171–2, 180, 182–4, 190,
199, 200–1, 203, 211–31, 233,
237–8

Unity Theatre, 51–2, 58

Vaillant, R., 197, 199, 200
Vercors, 180

Verlaine, P., 157
Visser, T., 224
Vitrac, 206
Vittorini, E., 130, 199

Waley, A., 98, 117, 123
Watson, G., 98
Weil, E., 53, 90–1
West, A., 65, 109, 112, 128

Whitman, W., 81, 205
Whyte, L. L., 61, 98, 107, 125, 160
Wilson, A., 104, 130
Wroclaw, 127, 192, 199, 209, 222

Yeats, W. B., 78, 235

Zhdanov, A. A., 128, 151